# JEWISH–CHRISTIAN
# DIALOGUE

# Jewish-Christian DIALOGUE

## A Jewish Justification

David Novak

*New York   Oxford*
OXFORD UNIVERSITY PRESS
1989

## Oxford University Press

Oxford   New York   Toronto
Delhi   Bombay   Calcutta   Madras   Karachi
Petaling Jaya   Singapore   Hong Kong   Tokyo
Nairobi   Dar es Salaam   Cape Town
Melbourne   Auckland

and associated companies in
Berlin   Ibadan

Published by Oxford University Press, Inc.,
200 Madison Avenue, New York, New York 10016

Oxford is a registered trademark of Oxford University Press

Library of Congress Cataloging-in-Publication Data
Novak, David, 1941–
Jewish–Christian dialogue : a Jewish justification / David Novak.
p.   cm.
Includes index.
ISBN 0-19-505084-3
1. Judaism—Relations—Christianity—History.   2. Christianity
and other religions—Judaism—History.   3. Judaism—History of
doctrines.   4. Philosophy, Jewish.   I. Title.
BM535.N64 1989
296.3'872–dc19                        88-28702

2 4 6 8 9 7 5 3 1

Printed in the United States of America
on acid-free paper

*To my mother and to the memory of my father*

# *Preface*

No matter how abstract a theory about any type of human relationship becomes, the theorist must regularly return to the experiences that elicited his or her concern for it. Without that regular
return, the theory loses contact with its own human content. In
prefacing this presentation of my own theory of Jewish–Christian
dialogue, I return to the first experience in which my concern for
it began. I was eight years old.

Because my parents were proud Jews, even though totally non-
observant, they enrolled me that year in the school of their local
synagogue. There I began the study of Hebrew and the Bible in
English. Both subjects captivated me far more than my parents
realized then or were prepared for later. The summer after that
first year in the synagogue school, we took a train trip, whose
actual destination I forget. Train travel in the 1940s was a different world altogether from the plane travel of the 1980s. It was a
more leisurely human activity: there was room to walk around
and to engage fellow passengers in conversation. The sight of the
landscape was still close at hand. And, in that less fearful time, a
curious child was much less reticent to approach strange adults
and talk with them. This was not my first train trip, and I quickly
left our passenger coach car and made my way into the lounge
car, looking for someone new and interesting to talk to. There I
saw him. His name is long forgotten, but his face has never left
me. He was an old man, in his seventies, with a full head of white
bushy hair and wearing rimless glasses. I knew at once he was not
a Jew. He smiled at me and asked me my name and where I came

from. He then asked me what I liked to read. I told him the truth: "The Bible, sir." "The Bible! And who is your favorite person in the whole Bible, David?" He probably expected me to say my namesake, King David, but instead I said, "Abraham." "And why Abraham?" he asked. "Because he is our father—the first Jew," I quickly answered. And so we began talking about Abraham, and I sensed that he too was Abraham's son, that we both saw ourselves coming from father Abraham, "the knight of faith," in Kierkegaard's magnificent name for him, which I was to learn years later. For riding in that lounge car with the old man, surrounded by people unconcerned with the trip that does not end at any of the train's stops, passing through more than Midwestern corn fields, I discovered that our trip was not at all in truth that of our fellow passengers. Our trip, like father Abraham's, was to that unknown destination. Then and there, we were equals; each of us accepted the other exactly as he was. There was none of the type of make-believe one usually thinks of with regard to the very young or the very old.

That is all that happened. My parents, wondering where I was for so long, came to fetch me, and we said goodbye. My parents and I were fast approaching the destination of this train trip. It was only in the few words of polite introduction between my parents and him that I heard that he was a retired Methodist minister. That is all that happened, but that was enough.

The lasting impression of that memorable experience did not cause me to romanticize the Christians I was to meet later in life, however. In the subsequent years, I have met many Christians indifferent to my Judaism, some who tried to coax me out of it—mostly crudely, once quite subtly—and a few who clearly hated me for it. Nevertheless, that experience did enable me to recognize and talk with those Christians who have been prepared to let me be a Jew, as I have been prepared to let them be Christians. I testify that such mutuality is not only possible but real. I have known some such Christians.

Recently, I have found such Christians in my colleagues at the Center on Religion and Society in New York, whose work has involved a significant part of my time over and above my vocation as a rabbi and teacher of Torah to Jews. The work of the Center has enabled me to see in our own democratic society the force of the common border between Judaism and Christianity for which

I argue in this book. This work, then, has been an invaluable stimulus in formulating this Jewish reflection on the Jewish–Christian relationship as a present reality leading into the future. I especially recognize Richard John Neuhaus (the director of the Center), Paul Stallsworth, Peter Berger, George Weigel, and Stanley Hauerwas for being the type of Christians my childhood experience prepared me to appreciate.

In a book covering such a complex area of human experience as the relationship between Judaism and Christianity, a principle of selection must be stipulated at the very outset; one can only "teach and leave untaught," as the Talmud puts it. Because this book deals with the relationship betwen *rabbinic* Judaism and *gentile* Christianity, it will not deal with the whole historical question of the Jewish origins of Christianity, a question about which a huge literature has emerged in the past century especially. And because this book is a philosophically formulated theological *argument* for Jewish–Christian dialogue, it will not deal with the large number of recent works that are basically designed simply to introduce Jews and Christians to each other in one way or another. Finally, along these same lines, this book will not deal with the long and painful history of Christian anti-Jewishness. For although I am certainly aware of it, I clearly do not regard it as an insuperable barrier to Jewish–Christian dialogue here and now.

During the course of writing this book, I have had the pleasure and privilege of consulting with various scholars whose counsel has, I hope, contributed to its scholarly and theological value. I mention, in particular, David Berger, Seymour Feldman, Lewis Ford, Germain Grisez, Steven Katz, George Lindbeck, Parviz Morewedge, Chaim Waxman, and Michael Wyschogrod. I am also grateful to the Anti-Defamation League of B'nai B'rith, particularly Rabbi Leon Klenicki, the director of the Department of Interfaith Affairs, who invited me to address the convocation in Rome in April 1985 celebrating the twentieth anniversary of the statement on the Jews, *Nostre Aetate,* of Vatican Council II. They have graciously permitted me to use here portions of that address, which they published in their journal, *Face-to-Face.*

Moreover, I am deeply grateful to three distinguished scholars who carefully read the first draft of the entire manuscript and made numerous suggestions for its improvement, most of which I followed. They are Louis Dupré of Yale University (my teacher at

Georgetown University), Jakob J. Petuchowski of the Hebrew Union College–Jewish Institute of Religion in Cincinnati, and William Kluback of the City University of New York.

Finally, I thank Cynthia Read, my editor at Oxford University Press in New York. She originally invited me to write this book after reading a short article of mine, "Jewish Views of Christianity," in *New Catholic World.* Her confidence in my ability and her careful editing of the manuscript have meant much to me and, I hope, to my readers as well.

One last prefatory note. This book is in many ways a sequel to my more detailed study of Jewish–Gentile relations in the classical Jewish sources, *The Image of the Non-Jew in Judaism: An Historical and Constructive Study of the Noahide Laws* (New York and Toronto: Edwin Mellen Press, 1983). Readers with more specific scholarly interests in these classical Jewish sources will find more extensive discussion and documentation of many points in this book by checking the references to that study in the notes. I thank Dr. Herbert Richardson, editor of the Edwin Mellen Press, for his kind permission to rework some sections of that book in this one.

*Far Rockaway, N.Y.*                                                    D. N.
*December 1987*

# Contents

# JEWISH–CHRISTIAN
# DIALOGUE

# Introduction

## Jewish Opposition to Dialogue

Any attempt by a traditionalist Jewish theologian (here defined as one who accepts the full authority of traditional Jewish law—Halakhah—as God's permanent mandate for the Jews) to justify Jewish–Christian dialogue today must first face the fact that many—probably most—of his or her fellow Jewish traditionalists are opposed to this dialogue. Therefore, such a justification must immediately identify this current traditionalist opposition and argue against it. Only then can it proceed to the positive theological task it has projected for itself.

The opposition to dialogue takes three main forms. I shall attempt to show that all three forms of opposition misunderstand the pervasive context of modern secularism in which all interreligious relationships must now be seen, certainly in the West (that is, Europe and the Americas).

The first form of opposition is the one that is most oblivious to the uniquely secular character of the modern world. It simply assumes that the relationship between Judaism and Christianity now is the same as it was in the Middle Ages. Of course, even then, when no value was seen in this relationship, it was still recognized that there was a degree of necessity for Jews to work out some religiously sanctioned modus vivendi with the Christians among whom they had to live in Europe. All the traditional sources examined in this book acknowledge at least that much. None of them actually prevented Jews from living among Christians and thereby sharing with them an elementary political and economic order. However, in the past, the Jewish–Christian relationship was almost always limited to that level, for all these traditional sources were formulated in a medieval context in which Judaism had to ensure its survival in a religious world that was in almost every way Christian (or Muslim). The question was largely one of survival, both physical and cultural. How does a minority community survive within a larger society and culture of an alien religion, one at best unsympathetic and at worst hostile?

Most of the traditionalist arguments opposed to the positive value of Jewish–Christian relations, those that only grudgingly recognize their limited necessity and reject their value, are made as though the old medieval context of these relations still existed. They ignore the fact that a radical change in history has taken place. They are not nearly as perceptive as Rabbi Menahem Meiri in the fourteenth century, who, as we shall see, insisted that his contemporary Christians (and Muslims) were in another category altogether from the ancient idolators mentioned in Scripture and the Talmud and, therefore, that a different Jewish view of them had to be formed. Contemporary opponents of dialogue, in the sense of a valuable, intelligent interreligious relationship, assume that all Christians still relate to Jews with the old confidence (or arrogance) that society and culture belong to them. Their only motive for seeking out Jews is assumed to be either to force them or to seduce them out of their particular isolation into submission to Christianity of some kind or another. Jews who cooperate in this venture are taken to be either crypto-assimilationists or obsequious fools.[1]

The most traditionalist advocates of this negative approach are not asserting an anti-Christian position per se as much as they are asserting their overall rejection of the non-Jewish world per se, Christian or not. In their communities (sometimes called "black hat" by other Jews because of their insistence, like that of other pietist groups in America, on wearing plain eighteenth-century garb to distinguish themselves from all others), contact between Jews and *any* non-Jews is to be kept to the absolute minimum that economic and political necessity requires. No value at all is seen in Jews being engaged with non-Jews in any joint venture, either practical or intellectual. This attitude is epitomized by opposition to secular education for any reason other than to avoid prosecution by the government in the case of primary and secondary schooling, or for reasons of economic survival in the case of post-secondary schooling (always of a technical, nonhumanistic character only).

The second form of opposition, unlike the first, is anti-Christian per se. It seems to assume, basing itself primarily on the contemporary experience of the Holocaust, that hatred and murder of Jews is something particularly Christian. Those who assert this position claim that the Nazi program for the extermination of the Jews is the direct historical consequence of Christian contempt for the Jews. They thus hold that all Christians—whether actual perpetrators of atrocities against Jews or not—are considered to be eo ipso incorrigible anti-Semites. Dialogue with such incorrigible enemies can hardly be regarded as anything other than group masochism.[2] It would take another book, much larger and much more learned than this one, to rationally analyze and judge the basic truth or falsehood of this assertion. It should be noted, nevertheless, that at least as many Christians were anti-Nazi as pro-Nazi, and, for some, this included intervening on behalf of the Jews. Moreover, their antinazism, when expressed as specifically *Christian* antinazism, was based on more theologically cogent Christian reasoning than that of those Christian Nazis who used Christian teaching as a pretext for a doctrine that is prima facie far more pagan than Christian.[3] The Protestant Karl Barth and the Catholic Jacques Maritain, to cite two examples of prominent Christian anti-Nazis, argued a more cogent Christian theology than their counterparts among the *Deutsche Christen*.[4] The latter, by any orthodox Christian criterion, were outright heretics. That is not to say that the existence of Judaism and the Jewish people is not and has not always been a tremendous theological problem for Christianity. However, it can and should be argued that modern secularism, with its explicit denial of any normative transcendence, is a far more immediate condition making for the emergence of Nazi nihilism than is traditional Christian ambivalence about the Jews.[5] Nazism is a distinctly modern phenomenon, not a simple extension of even medieval Christian anti-Judaism. To assume otherwise is to ignore the intervening prevalence of modern secularism.

This second approach also seems to be at a total loss to explain the most modern manifestation of anti-Judaism, that of communism. For communism, unlike nazism, does not use (and thereby distort) any Christian doctrines and symbols, even as pretexts. Its secularist origins are unmistakable. In fact, this distinctly contemporary Jewish opposition to Christianity, supposedly coming out of a direct reaction to the Holocaust, seems to imply a favorable judgment of secularism rather than a critical view of its radical removal of normative transcendence from the modern world, a removal that created the spiritual vacuum that the paganisms (and anti-Jewish hate) of *both* nazism and communism rushed in to fill. It seems to say that Jews can relate to any non-Jews *except* Christians. (It is also mute on the subject of Muslim anti-Judaism.) I suspect that many of the nontraditionalist Jews who have adopted this Holocaust-centered anti-Christian stance are attracted to it, consciously or unconsciously, because it is a species of the rejection of the moral authority of religion per se.

The third form of traditionalist Jewish opposition to dialogue is the mildest of the three. It has been most cogently argued by the influential halakhist and theologian Rabbi Joseph B. Soloveitchik. Appearing as it did in 1964, when the deliberations of Vatican Council II were to add such a fresh impetus to Jewish–Christian dialogue in general and Jewish–Catholic dialogue in particular, Soloveitchik's influence among many of the more acculturated traditionalist Jews precluded the participation in the dialogue of a large segment of the Jewish community who would have been most disposed toward it and who would have had the best credentials for it in terms of religious commitment and knowledge.

Unlike those who hold the first kind of antidialogue position, who see no value in relations between Jews and non-Jews, Soloveitchik accepts some value in such relations albeit with hesitation. And unlike the second group, he does not reject Christianity as the inevitable source of hatred of the Jews. Thus he writes:

> We cooperate with the members of other faith communities in all fields of constructive human endeavor, but, simultaneously with our integration into the general social framework, we engage in a movement of recoil and retrace our steps. In a word, we belong to the human society and, at the same time, we feel as strangers and outsiders.[6]

Soloveitchik's argument seems to be based on the following two premises: (1) there is a fundamental gap between what he calls "the metaphysically constituted society" (that is, a singular religious community) and the world at large; and (2) only when the metaphysically constituted societies of the Jews and the Christians (or any other religious community, presumably) are consciously kept out of the discussion may Jews converse and work with the world at large. I do not reject this approach in toto; it is my contention that he makes an essentially valid point, but for the wrong reason.

Soloveitchik is correct in assuming that a fundamental gap exists between the metaphysically constituted community and the world at large. He is quite right in taking Liberal Judaism to task for minimizing that gap. As he clearly puts it, "The divine imperatives and commandments to which a faith community is unreservedly committed must not be equated with the ritual and ethos of another community.[7] However, Soloveitchik draws the line of distinction between these two realms at the wrong place. For not only does he place ritual and ethos behind the line of uncommon singularity, but he also includes behind its exclusivity "the axiological awareness of each faith community," namely "its system of dogma, doctrines and values.[8] If this is the case, then Jews are precluded from bringing into any discussions of public morality with non-Jews their theologically informed views of the nature of the human person and society. All these views involve theology. Without this informing basis of discussion, neither Jewish nor Christian authenticity is credible in such an artificially contrived situation.[9]

When these metaphysical or theological concerns are purposely bracketed, secularist criteria of human nature and society must inevitably become the basis of common discussion. And, as we have learned more and more of late, these secularist criteria contradict the views of human nature and society and their consequent values advocated by both Jewish and Christian traditions. We have already seen in our own society how secularist criteria yield values that cannot be accepted by either faithful Jews or faithful Christians in such areas as life and death, the role of the family, crime and punishment, war and peace. If the theological (or metaphysical, to continue Soloveitchik's favored term) foundations of these values and the norms they justify are to be kept hidden, then the only justification left will be a secularist one. When the faithful remain silent, secularism wins by default. Here there must be a logos—a reason—not just an ethos—a habit.[10] There-fore, it is one thing to insist on a strict demarcation between the singular ethos of a faith community and the rational concerns of the world at large (its logos) but quite another thing to operate on a dual truth standard, according to which singular truth and general truth are mutually exclusive. Such contradiction cannot be avoided when the opposing statements are undoubtedly talking about the same things. Thus, for example, the assertion of both Jewish faith and Christian faith that the human person is the image of God directly contradicts secularist notions that the human person belongs to itself (autonomy) or to some larger human or nonhuman whole (heteronomy), even though Jews and Christians can certainly live in peace with those who hold these notions.

Soloveitchik's attempt to protect Jewish singularity leads to an antinomy concerning the secular realm. On the one hand, he writes that "our common interests lie not in the realm of faith, but in that of secular orders."[11] On the other hand, in a note on the use of that very term *secular orders*, he claims to be using it only in the sense of "its popular semantics. For the man of faith, this term is a misnomer."[12] But in a statement issued by his disciples in the Rabbinical Council of America, published as a postscript to his essay, we read the following: "The current threat of secularism and materialism and the modern atheistic negation of religion and religious values make even more imperative a harmonious relationship among the faiths."[13] Now it seems there can be no middle ground between secularism—which inevitably entails atheism in its metaphysics or antimetaphysics—and a moral position related to one's faith. Therefore, even Soloveitchik's disciples recognize that there is no neutrality in a purely secular public stance.

Soloveitchik himself, nevertheless, does refer to God even in this "secular" realm. Thus in proposing that the relationship between Jews and Christians be a "democratic confrontation," he insists "upon one's inalienable rights as a human being created by God."[14] But if the revealed sources of the respective faiths in that God of Jews and Christians are to be kept out of public discourse, are we not left with the God of the eighteenth-century deists, a God most secularists now find at best superfluous in this realm? And is this "God" the *God* of Abraham, Isaac, and Jacob?

Finally, Soloveitchik seems to assume that there are no differences among the various groups of non-Jews who make up the general human background that Jews have to face. Yet Christianity, as we shall see, is considered by Maimonides to be the only scripturally based non-Jewish religion. Rabbenu Tam sees it as a valid form of non-Jewish monotheism; and, according to Menahem Meiri, Christianity (and Islam) is obedient to God's law. Secularism, conversely, although it might be law-abiding on the behavioral level, is hardly obedient to God's law. Therefore, one cannot relate to Christians as one would relate to the secular world at large. Christian anthropology, as it impinges on moral values and norms, can definitely be seen as having a common border with Judaism. Lastly, as a political point, it should be emphasized that if traditionalist Jews refuse to participate in dialogue, then on the political issues in which they cannot help but have an interest—issues such as abortion, homosexuality, war, and so on—Jews far less committed to the authority of the Torah will be "Judaism's spokespersons" by default.[15]

Unlike proponents of the two earlier forms of opposition to Jewish–Christian dialogue, Soloveitchik does take modern secularism seriously. But he has not shown how Jewish participation in the modern world can overcome its dangerous limitations.

## The Secular Context of Jewish–Christian Dialogue Today

The Jewish opposition to dialogue with Christians, just analyzed, does not seem to recognize that Jews and Christians might have a new sense of relationship because the predominantly secular civilization is a threat to both Judaism and Christianity. With the demise of the old characterization of Western civilization as Christendom, in either the political or the cultural sense, both Jews and Christians must ask the ancient question, "How do we sing the Lord's song in a strange land?" (Psalms 137:4). For secularity has threatened them both quite similarly. A common threat has created a new common situation. It is thus inevitable that historically perceptive Jews and Christians should be rediscovering one another. As Jakob J. Petuchowski put it so well, "Neither Jews nor Christians can really afford to be isolationists. In this pagan world of ours, we *together* are the minority 'people of God.' "[16]

Yet Jewish opposition to dialogue still acts as though secularity were not hovering over all of us. Perhaps it is easier to deal with an old, weakened opponent than with a new, more powerful one. Furthermore, Christianity has been a more identifiable opponent than secularism, which has no particular identification as a historical entity. "Secular humanism" is not as identifiable as fundamentalists would have us believe when they sue in the American courts. The enemy here is hard to pinpoint. The opposition to dialogue, and the exaggerated reaction to the residual Christian missionary activity among Jews (unsuccessful as it always has been), might well be displacements of the real anxiety about secularism, against which traditional resources are much harder to find. I also suspect that Christian fundamentalists who assert such things as "God does not hear the prayers of the Jews"—which certainly undercuts any dialogue between Jews who pray and Christians who pray, even if they do not pray together—are similarly displacing their real anxiety about secularism onto an older, more identifiable opponent. For they are far more threatened by those who do not pray at all and who deny the very efficacy of prayer than by those whose prayer is, for them, misdirected.

To be oblivious, then, to the pervasive presence of secularism is to be oblivious to the modern world. The politics of the modern world are secular; secularism cannot be dismissed out of hand by any religious community because political isolation is less and less possible, regardless of the still greater possibility of religious, social, and cultural isolation. Even the most isolationist religious communities have been quite astute in formulating their political agendas and forging their political alliances.

Furthermore, not only is secularism inevitably all around us, but its most immediate political desideratum—international peace—is unavoidably compelling. Therefore, secularism must be faced as both fact and value. In an immediate political sense, one can see some definite value in a nonreligious agenda for dialogue between Jews and Christians. Dialogue on this level involves the logic of what might broadly be seen as a "social contract." As in the social contract constituted by Locke and Rousseau, especially, those entering the contract agree to restrain at least some of their particular interests for the sake of a common compromise.[17] It is clear that any such intergroup agreement to live in peace, not war, whether explicit or tacit, is a desideratum in the world today. The scientific and technological advances of this century have made the world much smaller and have thereby made it less rationally defensible for any particular community to take a totally isolationist stand. We are more and more thrown together in a world over which we have less and less control. Because of this fundamentally inalterable fact of modernity, it seems that all communities, including religious communities, must work out at least a minimal modus vivendi through some type of contracted agreement as the only alternative to hostility and war. For, in this present world, more and more dangerous weapons are available for use in any hostility, and it is unlikely that any hostility can be locally confined for very long.

Nevertheless, although this notion of intergroup social contract is attractive in terms of the most prevalent and immediate concerns of all humankind, it is insufficient for constituting a relationship between Judaism and Christianity and, therefore, between faithful Jews and faithful Christians. It is insufficient because it is based on secularist premises. Anyone who accepts the axiom that peace is better than war could accept this notion of intergroup relationship without being committed at all to either Judaism or Christianity. It seems as though all one need affirm are the possibility and the desirability of some basic political harmony. None of this involves those truths in which Judaism and Christianity, each in its very different way, ground their existence. There can be no talk here of God the creator and sustainer of the universe, God's election of a singular community and revelation to it of unique convenantal responsibilities, God's judgment of both fidelity and infidelity to the covenant, or God's redemption of the world in an act radically transcending finite human accomplishment. This type of secular agreement, which is certainly necessary for the minimal continuity of life and civilization on this planet, seems to require that Jews and Christians bracket the historical character of their respective faiths for the sake of some broader international consensus. The future of civilization seems to require as much.

However, if this type of dialogue-for-the-sake-of-agreement requires an initial bracketing of religious faith, is not faith, in effect, being replaced by something antithetical to it? Can there really be a neutral ground between faith and its absence?[18] The social contract, when universalized beyond a particular historical situation, attempts to constitute an "original position" by autonomous human agreement and from it to derive all rights and responsibilities.[19] The schema of sacred events—creation, election, revelation, judgment, and redemption—which is essential to both Judaism and Christianity, is seen by Jews and Christians as being prior to any interhuman agreement. It calls for human action to be faithfully responsive rather than autonomously initiatory.

To the extent that Jews and Christians participate in civil society and in the increasingly international realms of politics and economics, such bracketing might be necessary. It simply means that no religious community can claim to have a theocratic model from which the answers to each and every political and economic question can be instantly deduced. None of our religious communities and their respective traditions can fully construct a political and economic order adequate to the needs of contemporary life, and we wreak havoc when we try to do so. The Islamic fundamentalism of Iran, based as it is on a monotheistic revelation, provides a cautionary contemporary historical example for both Jews and Christians interested in a pure theocracy. We cannot just turn our backs on the secular world either in a nostalgic demand for a return to the days of old or in a utopian demand for instant redemption. Whatever their spiritual inadequacies, only secular science, secular politics, secular economics, and secular civil and criminal legal systems are currently operative for us. Any attempt to directly uproot them would only worsen, not improve, our already too dangerous world.[20]

Our political and economic needs require this immediately secular sense of common agreement, an agreement integrating goodwill, cooperation, and constructive social planning. Without it, there is no present motivation for any kind of intergroup concord, especially between groups such as Jews and Christians, who have had so many centuries of mutual distrust between them. However, if faithful Jews and faithful Christians are to engage in an authentic and constructive relationship on any level, they must reject the doctrinaire secularist claim that the affirmation of the reality of the secular realm is not only a necessity but the only sufficient source of ultimate value. Faith of any kind cannot coexist with that claim, whether explicit or tacit. It must, therefore, replace it with its own affirmation, and that affirmation must be one that can find a necessary place for the secular agenda, without being subordinate to the assumptions of secularism. That is no small task.

First of all, even the best type of Jewish–Christian relationship is incomplete in terms of bringing about any kind of universal modus vivendi in the world. Even in the West, it can be seriously disputed whether the majority of the people are any longer truly Christians. Moreover, even if they are, their societies have long ceased to be parts of Christendom. They are by no means Christian societies. Therefore, the horizon of the Jewish–Christian relationship must be not only what is between these two communities, but the future of all humankind. Without such a horizon, this relationship is myopic. Each community, in moving toward relationship with the other, must be able to constitute a role for humankind as a whole, and it must be able to do so more compellingly than secularism.

Second, and this point is closely connected to the first, despite the inadequacies of secularism for understanding and developing the relationship between Judaism and Christianity, we cannot simply return to our respective covenants for an immediate alternative to secularist universalism. For these covenants, at least in their original religious sense, are particularistic. Each covenant is made with a particular community and does not seem to be positively concerned with any other. Because covenant presupposes divine election, the covenanted community stands out against all those other communities that have not been so covenanted. Is not covenant, therefore, immediately and ultimately divisive? Does not covenant engender a great sense of solidarity among those within the particular community and an even greater sense of estrangement from all those outside the covenant? This understanding of covenant not only has thwarted the relationship between Judaism and Christianity in the past, but also is used by many secularists today to demonstrate the seemingly counterproductive character of monotheistic religions in general.[21]

Even if the secularist desire for universal agreement no longer leads to rejection of religion per se, after this century's blows to the naive optimism of the nineteenth century, and even if secularists now seek a spiritual dimension for inspiration, does not the tolerance of polytheism or the ahistoricity of the Eastern religions seem more appropriate to this contemporary desire? Considering the history of the relationship between Judaism and Christianity, are secularists so wrong in largely trying to ignore both communities in their legitimate desire for universal justice and peace?

Before discussing our respective covenants as the basis for a good relationship between our communities, we must attempt to discern—through theological reflection at the highest level—whether such a relationship is possible at all. Is such a relationship possible for us if we are to remain faithful to our respective revelations and their traditions? Further, could such a relationship have something to contribute to the quest for justice and peace in this world? Without faithfulness, we will quickly become redundant, stating with complex historical verbiage what secularism can say a lot more simply and convincingly. We will, in effect, be putting our throats out to be slit by Ockham's razor (the theory with unnecessary premises is to be rejected). We will simply become *of the world*. But without a genuine sense of contemporaneity, we will quickly become obscure. We will not even be *in the world*.[22]

To restate the covenant anew today means that it must be seen as entailing the unity and peace that all people of goodwill seek now more than ever before. And it must be done without losing any of the uniqueness of its teaching that has manifested itself in history.

### Phenomenology of Jewish–Christian Dialogue

I have characterized Jewish–Christian interrelationship, taken as a desideratum, as dialogue.[23] Some Jews and some Christians are now speaking to one another in a new way. Despite skepticism and opposition in both communities, this dialogue—often simply called *the dialogue*—is a present reality and one that shows no signs of being abandoned in the foreseeable future. If its religious validity is to be justified, however, affirmation of the value of dialogue must find its place within the respective traditions. The dialogue cannot simply be taken for granted; it is much too revolutionary for that. Rather, it must be carefully defined in order to be justified and in order for it to continue into the future in a constructive way. This requires a phenomenological constitution of the dialogue.[24] The best way to begin is carefully to distinguish between authentic and inauthentic manifestations of it.

In the long medieval period, the relationship between Jews and Christians could not be described as one of dialogue at all—excluding, perhaps, random individual encounters of which we know very little. The only recorded exceptions are those literary interchanges (mostly transgenerational) among Jewish, Christian, and Muslim philosophers on deliberately neutral questions of metaphysics and ethics.[25] Theological interaction, however, was always disputational.[26]

The logic of these disputations usually followed this course. Christians asserted that the covenant that began with Abraham was fulfilled in Jesus. Their basic accusation against the Jews was that the Jews were fixated at a stage of the covenant's incomplete development. Such incompleteness can only be judged inauthentic, and Jews were seen as obstinately refusing to live in the new present *(kairos)* ordained by God from the very beginning.[27] The fact that these charges were most often made in the context of Christian political dominance made them quite compelling to most Christians and to at least some Jews, who were persuaded by them, either for reasons of inner conviction or, more frequently, for reasons of pragmatic expediency. Jews, though, saw Christianity as a distortion of the original covenant, a covenant that Israel alone had preserved in faithfulness to God. Christianity was regarded as disintegrating rather than developing the covenant.[28] Maimonides, as we shall see, boldly suggests that if Christians were given proper instruction in Scripture by Jews, they would see how distorted traditional Christian scriptural interpretation is, and they would actually return to Judaism. And it is worth noting that of those few Christians who were brave enough to seek entry into Judaism in the Middle Ages, many were Christian clerics, whose study of Scripture and quest for its revealed truth led them to conclude that Christianity's basic claims were inconsistent with it.[29] Thus each community spoke to the other, or *at* the other, with a sense of spiritual triumphalism. Christianity, of course, could usually add temporal triumphalism to its claims for itself.

This type of disputational rhetoric has largely disappeared. The predominance of secularism has radically changed the political and cultural landscape. For Jews in the West, *Christian* and *gentile* can no longer be synonyms. Christians can so longer regard Jews as the last holdout against Christianity in the West. The only survival of this type of disputational rhetoric can be seen in the remnants of Christian missionary activity among Jews and Jewish attempts to argue with it on its own terms. The predominance of secularism, however, has made this type of disputational interaction at most a historical sideshow.

Nevertheless, some of the old triumphalism survives today, in more sophisticated garb, to be sure. It survives in attempts of one community to *tolerate* the other community. This tolerance is the attempt to afford the other community a measure of respect, but the basis of this measure of respect is an understanding of the other community that the other community could not accept about itself. Thus Christian tolerance of Jews has usually been based on the notion that even though the Jewish affirmation of the covenant is incomplete in relation to the Christian affirmation of it, this does not mean that Judaism is thereby bereft of the covenant altogether. In other words, Christians are now to be considered the people of God in the fullest sense, but Jews have not been totally removed from that status,[30] for Christian hope for the ultimate conversion of the Jews cannot be based on the denigration of Judaism as spiritually corrupt.

Jewish tolerance of Christianity, although much less well known (even to many Jews), follows quite similar logic. Jewish tolerance of Christianity as legitimate for gentiles (in contrast to the unanimous rejection of the legitimacy of Jewish Christians) is based on the question of whether Christians are faithful to that aspect of the Law that the rabbis took to be binding on all humanity. Are Christians sincerely committed to God's law for the gentiles or not? Considerable medieval Jewish debate centered around this question. Even those Jewish authorities who tended to look on Christian normativity with favor, however, are usually seen as endorsing a view that whatever legitimacy Christianity has, it is because of Judaism. As such, Christianity must be ultimately interpreted by Jews. This logic often emerges when Jewish scholars present "the Jewish point of view" on ethical issues of social concern, such as abortion or capital punishment.[31]

Needless to say, faithful Jews cannot truly recognize themselves in such Christian tolerance of them (although any Jew should prefer it to Christian persecution), and faithful Christians likewise cannot truly recognize themselves in such Jewish tolerance of them. There can be no real dialogue if each side's view of the other is essentially a view of a phantom of its own projection, even if that phantom is more attractive than the ones invented for the medieval disputations. Dialogue must be constituted in such a way that each side can recognize itself in it. The other one standing before me must be discovered with his or her phenomenological integrity. Dialogue has definite preconditions. The abandonment of triumphalism, both overt and covert, is the first such precondition. The tolerance of a subservient religion by a dominant religion (even if only intellectually) is covert triumphalism.

Despite the inadequacies of triumphalism for viewing the other community with phenomenological integrity, it does emerge from a community's confidence in its own truth. Triumphalism is a misapplication of this confidence, to be sure, but when this confidence is still present, the triumphalist error admits of an internally coherent corrective within its own tradition. The tradition's authority is still intact. However, when triumphalism is abandoned too hastily as a historical embarrassment in a pluralistic world, the authority of the tradition is usually compromised in such a way that both the other community and one's own community lose their phenomenological integrity. The precipitous abandonment of triumphalism usually leads to the worse stance of relativism.

Theological relativism, especially when addressing itself to interreligious dialogue, enunciates itself as the counterposition to triumphalism. It correctly senses that triumphalism reflects a morally offensive arrogance, moreover that it seems to lie at the heart of the type of absolutism that is such a menace in the world today. Therefore, the way out is to declare that no religious community *possesses* the truth, that each community must humbly recognize its perspectival limitations in *relating to* the truth. And in this humble recognition, it must see that other religious communities are also related to the truth in a way by no means inferior to its own.[32]

The seeming humility of this approach is, of course, its greatest appeal. But can any religious community maintain its authentic vision of itself if such a view is accepted as foundational?

It is correct to assert that neither Judaism nor Christianity (nor any other religion) can authentically claim the truth as its own original possession. That type of theological arrogance is religiously insufferable.[33] Nevertheless, the doctrine of revelation, which Judaism and Christianity affirm, enables each community to claim that it is *uniquely related* to the truth, that is has received a revelation of the truth from God unlike that of any other community.

As Jews declare before the public reading of the Torah in the synagogue, "Blessed be You Lord Our God, king of the universe, who has chosen us from among all peoples by giving us His Torah."[34] Christianity is no less exclusivistic in its claims. Thus relativism on the part of either Jews or Christians is as inauthentic about its own faith as it is about the faith of the other.

Both Judaism and Christianity base themselves on their election to receive unique revelation from God. The very logic of revelation requires that the community receiving it take an absolute stance toward it in distinction from the revelation claimed by any other community. If, however, all revelations are equally related to the truth, then clearly one cannot take an existential stand on the basis of any one of them to the exclusion of all the others. Rather, one can only stand on the agnosticism common to all. At this point, revelation loses its religious authority. On the basis of this common agnosticism, to root one's life in one revelation as opposed to all others is absurd. Behind revelation, both Judaism and Christianity affirm a God beyond finite understanding; but when that God speaks, his speech has an immediate (if not exhausted) intelligibility: "The Torah speaks in human language."[35] Relativism, by making the authority of any particular revelation absurd, soon abandons the doctrine altogether. In its place, a universal quest for God and truth is put forth. Rather than an objective datum by which God addresses his people, there are multiple subjective efforts to reach an as yet unknown ideal. This theological agnosticism entails moral impotence.

The moral impotence of religious relativism comes out when one faces what for both Judaism and Christianity is the greatest of all God's demands: martyrdom. For if one is to die as a martyr rather than abandon one's own faith for anyone else's, how can one justify this ultimate sacrifice if the other faith is as true as one's own?[36] Even if one's faith is never so tested in extremis, one is to act as though it were.[37] The minority faith is especially vulnerable at this point when such relativism is espoused. For when the ultimate religious answer is that there is no lasting difference, criteria of social and political superiority soon take over. They are closer at hand. Moral authority, and certainly the moral authority of a religious community, depends on its ability to make absolute demands with credibility. If another equally acceptable opinion is presented as such, then a moral vacuum exists in effect.

History, no less than nature, abhors a vacuum. What happens

is that relativists in matters of religion quickly discover absolutes elsewhere. In the contemporary situation, religious relativism is perfectly compatible with secularist absolutism. Revealed religion becomes little more than a matter of custom or taste, something beneath dispute, something of curiosity "to be left rolled up in a corner and whoever wants to study it can study it," as the Talmud puts it.[38] The major moral questions are now left to a totally new tribunal. Thus Baruch Spinoza, who can quite well be considered the first secular Jew, relegated traditional revealed religions *(externos cultus)* to the realm of the private *(quod viri privati officium est),* where they cannot "disturb public peace and quiet," and he assigned "true religion" (that is, philosophically constituted religion) to the public realm. Revealed religions are tolerated only when they concede their public moral authority to the nonrevealed religion of the new secular state.[39] Moses Mendelssohn (d. 1786), the greatest Jewish proponent of tolerance in the Enlightenment, although (unlike Spinoza) a devout Jew all his life (both in and out of the ghetto), relegated Judaism to a level of validity beneath what he called both necessary and contingent truth. Judaism was characterized as "revealed legislation."[40] And although Mendelssohn still spoke about revelation as a reality, it was clearly no longer the source of anything important, either intellectually or morally. It is little wonder that Mendelssohn's vision of Judaism, as relativistic as it was, was such a puny defense against the tide of assimilation in the nineteenth century, which could so easily make Judaism totally irrelevant.[41] Christianity, still having so many adherents, has had to wait, for the most part, until the twentieth century to experience its own irrelevance when relativism leaves the moral necessity for an absolute in essentially secular hands.

It would seem, then, that if Jewish–Christian dialogue is to be authentic dialogue, and a true expression of Judaism and Christianity, it must be constituted so as to carefully steer a course clear between the Scylla of triumphalism and the Charbydis of relativism. Thinkers in each community must *re-search* their own respective traditions to constitute the integrity of the other community and not lose the integrity of their own. The task is formidable because this re-search must be quite radical, working its way back to the roots of the tradition and back out into the present and toward the future. Triumphalism and relativism have been more ready options in this endeavor because they are easier.

The last option to be avoided for the sake of authenticity is more difficult to name than the preceding two. Yet, it seems to me, the experience of the dialogue has produced in at least some of its participants something that could be called religious syncretism. At times, this syncretism seems more unconscious than conscious. Its underlying assumption seems to be that the experience of the dialogue itself is so profoundly original that it has the power to generate new forms of religious life. These new forms are seen as the means whereby, at least to a certain extent, Jews can transcend the limits of historic Judaism and Christians can transcend the limits of historic Christianity. I remember hearing the late Paul Tillich state, at a memorial meeting for Martin Buber in New York in the summer of 1965, that such a mutual transcendence of their respective religious traditions was the basis for his long friendship with Buber.[42] And this mutual transcendence of traditions is possible only as a joint venture.

This syncretistic project manifests itself in several ways. The earliest manifestation, it seems, was in what the late Will Herberg called the "civic religion" of America.[43] This civic religion is actually an attempt to give some sort of religious dimension to the essentially anonymous character of modern secular society. It bears a strong resemblance to eighteenth-century deism, namely the idea that all humankind can recognize a general creator god in nature without any particular historical revelation. For Americans, such a belief has special poignancy in that many of the Founding Fathers of the republic, men such as Franklin, Washington, and Jefferson, were deists.[44] Indeed, the founding document of the American polity, the Declaration of Independence, which mentions "nature's God," was an expression of the deistic theology of its author, Thomas Jefferson. Thus in Americans' celebration of the philosophical foundations of their public life, this civic religion emerged.

Civic religion is designed to "give no offense," that is, to be so historically neutral as not to be based on any one community's revelation. Civic religion is practiced on those occasions when some sort of religious affirmation is called for that will offend practically no one. However, the easy inoffensiveness of civic religion is achieved at the price of essential authenticity.

Its inauthenticity is most clearly seen in what has become a staple of civic religion, the interfaith service. At these exercises—what used to be called brotherhood services—Jews and Christians design an ersatz liturgy that could not be described as Jewish at the expense of Christianity or as Christian at the expense of Judaism.[45] Specifically, Jews avoid mentioning the doctrine of the chosenness of Israel, and Christians avoid mentioning Christ. Such services seem to be the devotions of Jews who have bracketed Sinai and Christians who have bracketed Calvary. Can this be done as the act of Jews qua Jews and Christians qua Christians? Can such holistic immediacy as prayer, which is one's immediate presentation of his or her whole self before God, survive the bracketing of those foundational events that made such self-presentation before God possible? In traditional Jewish liturgy, the declaration of what God has done for Israel is made before petitionary prayer begins.[46] Can we bracket this root of our deepest self when we stand before God, as we can when we stand before our fellow humans? For they see only appearances, but God sees our hearts.[47] Can a Jew truly pray to God as anyone other than the God who chose Israel and gave them the Torah? Can a Christian pray to God as anyone other than the God who revealed himself in Christ? For Jews and Christians, respectively, the events of Sinai and Calvary are total and irreversible. Even though God can be affirmed as creator before these events, and by those who never experienced them, the affirmation of creation by Jews and Christians is mediated by revelation. Neither Jews nor Christians can simply step out of their particular covenants and seek God together in historical innocence as the children of Adam and Eve.

Because these exercises are so basically artificial, they are most often nothing more than the endorsement of the political and cultural status quo of those who have come together to participate in them. They are little different from those innocuous invocations and benedictions that have become de rigueur at public functions in America, from the inauguration of presidents to high-school graduations. Because they are so conformist in both substance and tone, these exercises lack the moral dimension found in Judaism and Christianity, namely the awareness of God, who commands his people and judges them. Such services call to mind that the prophetic critique of ancient worship was that it had reduced God to the level of a mere endorser of the people's own values and had ceased to emphasize God's radical demands.[48]

The second form of religious syncretism seen among some Jews and Christians is not secondary to the experience of an essentially secular reality, as in the case above, but emerges out of experience that can be called essentially religious. The experience of the dialogue has led some Christians, for example, to practice Jewish rituals in a Christian context. I am not referring to the practices of Jews who have actually converted to Christianity and still consider themselves to be religious Jews (the so-called Hebrew Christians or Messianic Jews). Although they pose a special problem for both the Jewish and the Christian communities, that problem is neither an antecedent nor a consequence of the dialogue. What I mean in this case is epitomized by the growing practice of Christian churches celebrating the Passover Seder. Here we see a situation in which a basic Jewish rite is practiced by Christians. More often than not, these churches seek the advice of Jews in their preparations, and often these Jews become participants in the Seder, if not actually the leaders of it.

Such services, from the points of view of both normative Judaism and normative Christianity, are quite problematic. They suggest the constitution of a new religious reality, the celebration of syncretism itself. Maimonides summarized the tendency of the tradition when he cautioned against gentiles performing Jewish rites without the full faith commitment of conversion to Judaism.[49] In other words, the commandments of the Torah are to be performed in the context of the historic covenant between God and Israel. On the Christian side, the Church Fathers warned against "Judaizing," namely Christians practicing Jewish rites.[50] For such practices clearly imply that the historic rites of Judaism and Christianity, respectively, are insufficient for a full relationship with God. When this happens, the dialogue is no longer the relationship of Jews and Christians, in which each one faces the other *from* a distinctive point of origin, one that always transcends the point of meeting *between* them. Rather, the dialogue becomes an encompassing reality in which the Judaism and the Christianity of the participants become moments that are then overcome in a reality whose dynamic is its own momentum.

It is, of course, too early to see where all of this will go. I suspect that just as the interfaith expression of civic religion has been most often a subsequent endorsement of a rather conservative political status quo, this new interfaith expression is becoming a subsequent religious endorsement of a more radical political stance. It seems to find its adherents most often among political radicals such as pacifists and feminists.

However, when the dialogue itself leads to the actual constitution of a religious *tertium quid*, whether it be more conservative or more radical, it can no longer receive an authentic endorsement from either faithful Jews or faithful Christians. For the dialogue to remain a dialogue *between* Jews and Christians, it can only be an expression *from* Judaism *to* Christianity and an expression *from* Christianity *to* Judaism. If the point of origin from which each of the participants comes is subsumed in the foreground of the dialogue itself, then the respective covenantal foundations have been lost. When this happens, Jews and Christians who enter the dialogue no longer have any retort to the criticisms of rejectionists in their own communities.

The argument for the dialogue presented here shall be a theological one. Before such a theological argument can be persuasively formulated, however, it must be able to steer clear of any halakhic proscriptions in its path at the very outset. Halakhah is Judaism's most evident authoritative structure; theology can do its work only within the boundaries of that structure.[51] In the case of Jewish–Christian dialogue, there are no specific halakhic impediments to serious talk with non-Jews. In fact, even the opposition to the dialogue on the part of the eminent halakhist Soloveitchik, as we have already seen, was not based on any specific halakhic objections, but on what he saw as the theological impossibility of members of one faith community being able to discuss matters of faith in a intelligible and honest way outside their own community. It is only when there is the attempt to constitute dialogue as an original religious reality—that is, as a new revelation itself—that halakhic objections can be raised. For this seems to entail the creation of new and highly questionable forms of worship. But I have already indicated that such a constitution is a distortion of the dialogue's true character and intent as well as involving conflict with existing norms in both Judaism and Christianity. Therefore, the theological argument presented here can proceed without fear of direct halakhic contradiction.

## A Jewish Justification for the Dialogue: Methodology

The enunciation of a Jewish justification for the dialogue in the present requires radical research into the sources of Jewish tradition and an empathetic analysis of the Christian partner in the dialogue. These two enterprises are essentially related. The research of the tradition supplies the form of the judgment; the empathetic analysis of contemporary Christianity supplies its content.

Any Jewish treatment of relations with non-Jews must turn to the rabbinic doctrine of the Seven Noahide Laws, the basic moral rules the rabbis saw as binding on all the "children of Noah," that is, on all humanity. We shall examine this doctrine in some detail in Chapter 2. Suffice it to say now, however, that this doctrine brings non-Jews within the purview of Halakhah. For even though dialogue itself is not a halakhic issue, whether Christians accept God's law for them is a major prerequisite for dialogue.

As the criterion for dealing with non-Jews, Noahide law comprises what might be called a normative field. This normative field has two poles, one practical and the other theoretical.[52] From the vantage point of the practical pole, it is concerned with the prohibition of such acts as homicide, robbery, and incest. From the vantage point of the theoretical pole, it is concerned with the beliefs of non-Jews, beliefs that determine for Jews whether the religious practices of a particular group of non-Jews (in our case, Christians) violate the Noahide prohibition of idolatry. Issues that first appear as practical questions, however, eventually entail theoretical questions, and issues that first appear as theoretical questions eventually entail practical questions. In other words, as with all great questions discussed in Jewish tradition, these questions are never purely theoretical or purely practical. They lie at some point or other within the normative field. Thus the judgment of whether or not a particular group of non-Jews can be considered to uphold the prohibition of homicide should ultimately entail an analysis of their beliefs about the nature of the human person, who is both subject and object of the act of homicide. And the judgment of whether or not a particular group of non-Jews are polytheists should ultimately entail an analysis of their religious practices.

Among the Jewish thinkers we shall examine, some made their judgment of Christianity from a more theoretical perspective; others, from a more practical perspective. Maimonides, for example, with his overriding concern with the metaphysical foundations of theology and of law, makes his most forthright statements about Christianity when dealing with the essentially metaphysical question of polytheism. Yet even Maimonides was forced to deal with Christianity within the more practical concern about the moral authority of Scripture and how Christians have accepted it as binding. But Meiri, whose concern is with the practical issue of normativity, still must also be concerned with how religious beliefs have led Christians (and Muslims) to a level of normativity far above that of the ancient pagans with whom the rabbis of the Talmud dealt.

The requirements of judgment about whether the dialogue at present is to be recommended or not for Jews allow us to be selective in our use of the traditional sources. Dialogue is a relationship between finite human persons or, in our case, between finite human communities. As such, it means concentrating on what is truly before us in the present and thereby suspending, for our purposes, anything that does not have meaning for it. Therefore, our judgment will not be overturned if someone should discover that it contradicts the opinion of an earlier authority. For that earlier authority may not be dealing with the same Christian reality with which we are now dealing, he may have based his approach on theoretical assumptions that are his own philosophy rather than traditional Jewish dogma, or his opinion may represent only one tendency within the tradition for which there is a countertendency. As long as a judgment can be developed from a tendency within the traditional sources—that is, as long as there is a reasonable amount of material *out of which* to make such a judgment— its validity can be defended as a legitimate development *of* the tradition. This method is not at all novel; it is the way normative Jewish judgments have always been made.

# 1

# *The Doctrine of the Noahide Laws*

## A Border Concept

Any Jewish constitution of the status of non-Jews, if it is to find a genuine place for itself in the ongoing tradition of Judaism, must constantly and consistently refer to the doctrine of the Noahide laws. This doctrine has been the rubric for the formulation of Jewish views of non-Jews. I have devoted a full work, *The Image of the Non-Jew in Judaism,* to the history, philosophy, and theology of this doctrine; in this chapter, I shall basically summarize the conclusions of that earlier work that specifically pertain to the question of Jewish–Christian relations.

The concept of Noahide law is a border concept that mediates between Judaism and the non-Jewish world in both time and space. The *Noahide* (literally, "son of Noah"), who is the subject of this law, is a designation of both the gentile who confronts Judaism in the present and all humankind before the Torah was given to Israel, separating Israel from all the other nations of the world. The Noahide in the present, then, might be designated as *co-Judaic;* the Noahide before Sinai might be designated as *pre-Judaic.* Because of this dual meaning, the concept of Noahide law has been the one most often used in understanding both the conditions that enabled Judaism to emerge and Judaism's view of what lies directly on its horizon. The former type of understanding might be termed *vertical;* the latter, *horizontal.*

Some treatments of Noahide law have emphasized the vertical aspect more than the horizontal; others have reversed the emphasis. However, since *Noahide* designates both dimensions, no matter how much one's emphasis tends in any one direction, it cannot totally lose sight of the other. Without this dual consideration, one could not be said to be using the concept of Noahide law in a truly cogent way. For our purposes, this means that a Jewish understanding of what constitutes a valid relationship with Christianity entails an understanding of the preconditions for the emergence of Judaism itself. Thus whether one is for the dialogue or against it, the position one takes cannot be Jewishly tangential.

The first explicit presentation of the Noahide laws is in the *Tosefta*, a work commonly believed to have been edited in the late second century of the Common Era. There we read: "Seven commandments were the sons of Noah commanded: (1) concerning adjudication, (2) and concerning idolatry, (3) and concerning blasphemy, (4) and concerning sexual immorality, (5) and concerning bloodshed, (6) and concerning robbery, (7) and concerning a limb torn from a living animal."[1]

## Historical Origins

The rabbis themselves attempted to place the Noahide laws in legal and historical perspective. If this perspective is understood within Jewish history in general and the history of Jewish law in particular, it can help us locate the origin of this doctrine, which greatly determined its course of development.

An early rabbinic source, quoted in the Babylonian Talmud, indicates how the rabbis placed the Noahide laws in a specific legal context.

> Who is a resident-alien *[ger toshab]*? Whoever, in the presence of three rabbinic fellows, obligates himself not to worship idols. This is the opinion of Rabbi Meir. But the sages say whoever obligates himself for the seven commandments for which the sons of Noah obligated themselves. Others say . . . who is a resident-alien? Whoever eats non-kosher meat but who obligates himself to uphold all the commandments in the Torah except the prohibition of eating non-kosher meat.[2]

Thus we see the rabbis identifying the Noahide laws as the minimal prerequisite for naturalized citizenship in a Jewish state.[3] Following the principle of majority rule, the opinion of the sages was codified as the law—namely, that the acceptance of the seven Noahide laws was to be required of resident-aliens.[4]

Another early rabbinic source attempts to place the law of the resident-alien in historical perspective:

> The institution of the Hebrew bondman only applies when the Jubilee applies, as Scripture states, "Until the Jubilee year he shall serve with you" (Leviticus 25:40). . . . Rabbi Simon ben Eleazar says that the institution of the resident-alien only applies when the Jubilee applies.[5]

Thus the institution of the resident-alien—that is, a law-abiding gentile having official status in a Jewish state—has legal force only when the whole Jewish people is in full possession of the land of Israel, which means that all twelve tribes are there together. The above text, then, indicates that this whole institution was preexilic, that it ceased with the destruction of the First Temple in 586 B.C.E.[6] However, it is also certain that the rabbis regarded the Noahide laws as binding even without this full Jewish sovereignty.[7] Hence, the moral authority of these laws survived the inability of Jewish officials either to fully enforce them legally or to fully entitle gentiles to all the political privileges they entailed.

From the first source quoted, it would seem that the Noahide laws are a pre-Israelite institution that was used to constitute the subsequent Israelite institution of the resident-alien. Historical investigation shows, however, that the institution of the resident-alien long preceded the concept of Noahide law. Indeed, the concept of Noahide law, as a recognition of the independence of gentile morality from Judaism, could have emerged only after the time when Jews had political control over any gentiles. For although one can discern all the Noahide laws as operative in scriptural texts describing life before the giving of the Torah to Israel at Sinai, none of these texts or any others in Scripture even remotely implies a specific code for non-Jews sanctioned by Jewish authority.[8]

In Scripture, especially in the Pentateuch, the term *ger*, from the verb *gur* (meaning "to dwell"), is used in a number of different contexts. Sometimes it seems to denote a proselyte—that is, one who has both adopted and been adopted by Judaism. Thus, for example, we read:

And when a *ger* dwells with you and makes Passover for the Lord,
you shall circumcise him, every male, and then he may draw near to
do it, and he shall be like a person native-born on the land. . . .
There shall be one Torah for the native-born *['ezrah]* and for the *ger*
who dwells among you. (Exodus 12:48–49)[9]

At other times *ger* seems to denote a political alien, a sojourner
among the Jewish people, someone with limited rights and respon-
sibilites. Thus, for example, we read: "You shall not abuse a needy
and destitute laborer, whether a countryman or your *ger* who is
in your land in your cities" (Deuteronomy 24:14).[10] Furthermore,
most importantly, Scripture does not explicate exactly how one
becomes a *ger*, either in the religious or in the political sense.[11]

Because of the disparity in the use of the term *ger*, the rabbis
saw it as denoting two different statuses. When the term seemed
to denote a full participant in Jewish religious life, they defined
him as a *ger tzedeq*, a proselyte. When, however, the term seemed
to denote a quasi-citizen of the Jewish polity, they defined him as
a *ger toshab*, a resident-alien.[12]

The preexilic period of Jewish history is characterized by full
Israelite sovereignty and occupation of the land of Israel. Status in
this society was determined by one's relationship to the land.[13]
Full status in preexilic Israelite society presupposed landedness or
official and permanent attachment to cultic shrines, as in the case
of the Aaronide priests.[14] The status of the tribes and of the priests
was determined by patrimony. In such a society, a person without
patrimony would be, in essence, landless; even if he were to pur-
chase real estate, it would return to its original owner by ancestral
right during the Jubilee year.[15] From all of this, it follows that the
*ger toshab* was a non-Israelite citizen living as a resident-alien—a
second-class citizen—under Israelite sufferance.[16] The concept of
such resident-alien status has many parallels in the ancient world,
from the *metics* in Athens to the *peregrines* in Rome.[17]

The neat division of free non-Jews having some formal connection with Judaism into either proselytes or resident-aliens seems to
be a prescription de jure rather than a description de facto. A
good case has been made by a number of modern scholars that
during the biblical, Hellenistic, and even early rabbinic periods,
transition from gentile to fully Jewish status was more of a process
than an event.[18] Indeed, these same scholars have shown, quite
convincingly, that purely religious conversion—namely, a status

resulting from one act of volition alone—was a postexilic innovation.[19] Thus it can be reasonably assumed that generally from the biblical to the early rabbinic period, the *ger toshab* was, in fact, considered a potential Jew.

Moreover, among the Hellenistic Jews living outside the land of Israel, we encounter a group designated as the *sebomenoi*, the "fearers of the Lord."[20] Both Jewish and non-Jewish sources acknowledge the existence of a group of gentiles who observed Jewish religious practices in varying degrees short of full conversion to Judaism. In the Jewish sources, they are usually praised.[21] Non-Jewish sources frequently ridiculed them for adopting the practices of such a strange people, as we can see in the following passage from the second-century C.E. Roman satirist Juvenal:

> Some who had a father who reveres the Sabbath, worship nothing but the clouds and the divinity of the heavens, and see no difference between eating swine flesh from which their father abstained and that of man; and in time they take to circumcision. Having been wont to flout the laws of Rome, they learn and practice and revere the Jewish law.[22]

This process of conversion was complicated by the fact that worship of local deities was prescribed in many places, only native-born Jews being legally exempted from this civic duty.[23]

A number of modern scholars have seen the Noahide laws as originating in the Diaspora as a regimen for these people. For all practical purposes, these *sebomenoi* seem to be the same as the earlier *geray toshab,* only lacking the formal political status of the latter. Their segimen was, therefore, religious and moral in the broad sense.[24]

Aside from the fact that there is no explicit textual evidence for this theory, it is conceptually flawed. For if the process of gradual conversion characterized this group, as it characterized the earlier institution of the *ger toshab,* then why limit their commandments to a mere seven? If gentiles observing laws sanctioned by Judaism are, in effect, potential Jews, such limitation would hamper the process of Judaization. And, indeed, there are two rabbinic texts that seem to prescribe many more commandments for righteous gentiles.[25] Thus the rabbinic doctrine of the seven commandments of the Noahides seems to imply a precise distinction in kind between all the gentiles and the Jews rather than a mere difference in degree between all the Jews and some of the gentiles. The limit of the Noahide laws to seven was taken quite literally in later rabbinic texts.[26]

Some scholars have noted that after the rise of Christianity, rabbinic references to the "fearers of the Lord" virtually disappear. It was from this group that Paul attracted many converts to the new religion. In his discourses in Diaspora synagogues, he repeatedly addresses himself to "God fearers" as well as to native-born Jews.[27] As a result, the rabbis had to emphasize a strict demarcation between Jews and non-Jews. Quasi-Jews, more often than not, became Christians rather than full Jews.

This demarcation could take one of two forms. There were some rabbis of this period who decided that all the gentiles were now cut off from God and the Torah, with salvation of any kind reserved for the Jews. There were other rabbis who decided that salvation was possible for the gentiles, even with no connection to Judaism and the Jews. The following text is the locus classicus of this fundamental dispute:

> Rabbi Eliezer said that none of the gentiles [*kol ha-goyyim*] has a portion in the world-to-come, as Scripture states, "The wicked will return to Sheol, all the nations [*kol ha-goyyim*] who have forgotten God" (Psalms 9:18). . . . Rabbi Joshua said that if Scripture had stated, "The wicked will return to Sheol [namely]: all the gentiles" and was thereafter silent, it would agree with your interpretation. However, since Scripture states. "who have forgotten God," it teaches that there are righteous [*yesh tzaddiqim*] among the nations and they do have a portion in the world-to-come.[28]

The implications of this rabbinic dispute, which took place shortly after the destruction of the Second Temple in 70 C.E. and the beginning of the Jewish–Christian schism, are as follows. According to the view of Rabbi Eliezer, there is an ontological difference between Jews and gentiles. Therefore, the more Jews are described as the people of God, the recipients of the Torah at Sinai, the more the gentiles are described as being separated from God and, thus, without true moral guidance. But according to the view of Rabbi Joshua, the gentiles are as capable of righteousness as the Jews. The criterion of Jewish righteousness is the Torah, with its 613 commandments. The question now became, What is the criterion of gentile righteousness? With the elimination of the "fearers of the Lord" as a recognized group of quasi-Jews, the criterion of gentile righteousness could no longer be *some* of the commandments of the Mosaic Torah per se. As such, a new criterion had to be found. This new criterion, it seems, was the doctrine of the Noahide laws, which we find expressed in the name of rabbinic authorities about two generations after Rabbi Joshua. Nevertheless, it seems that the affirmation of the possibility of *independent* gentile righteousness by Rabbi Joshua laid the theological foundation for the legal constitution of this new doctrine somewhat later.

The Noahide laws provided a minimal conditio sine qua non for a gentile morality that Judaism could recognize as valid, something apart from itself rather than its own potential. Thus the Noahide laws were conceived of as minimal prohibitions only; the positive content of gentile society and culture was of no concern to Judaism as long as it did not contradict these negative limits.[29] This is why the Noahide laws could not have been the criterion for the institution of the *ger toshab* or for the *sebomenoi* of Hellenistic times. The doctrine seems to have arisen after such quasi-Judaism became impossible for the normative Jewish community to tolerate. The strict demarcation that this doctrine presupposes is seen in the following rulings made in second-century C.E. Palestine, when the Jewish—Christian schism was in process, with many gentiles joining the new religion:

> Rabbi Simon ben Laqish said that a gentile who observed the Sabbath is deserving of death [*hayyab meetah*] as it is said in Scripture, "Day and night they shall not cease" (Genesis 8:22). . . . Rabbi Yohanan said that a gentile who engaged in the study of the Torah is deserving of death as it is said in Scripture, "Moses commanded us Torah as an inheritance [*morashah*]" (Deuteronomy 33:4)—an inheritance for us, not for them.[30]

In the Talmud's discussion of this ruling, it is first seen as contradicting an earlier ruling—one, no doubt, reflecting the older theory of pious gentiles as potential Jews to be encouraged in adopting Jewish practices bit by bit—that "a gentile who engages in the study of the Torah is like the high priest."[31] The contradiction is resolved, however, by qualifying the earlier ruling as referring only to gentile study of the seven Noahide laws.

The rabbinic connection of the new doctrine of the Noahide

laws with the antiquarian institution of the *ger toshab* enabled the rabbis to construct a model of normative co-Judaic and pre-Judaic life having connection with a scriptural institution. This theoretical, as opposed to political, constitution of the *ger toshab* led to the development of the Halakhah and the theology of Jewish–gentile relations thereafter.

The concept of a number of minimal, indispensable laws for gentiles might well have risen at the same time that the concept of a number of minimal, indispensable laws for Jews was conceived. In the Babylonian Talmud, we read of the following momentous decision by the Jewish sages:

> Rabbi Yohanan said in the name of Rabbi Simon ben Yehotzedeq that they voted and decided in the attic of the house of Nithzeh in Lydda that for all transgressions in the Torah, if one is told "transgress and do not be killed," one may transgress and not be killed—except for idolatry, sexual immorality and bloodshed.[32]

The historical setting of this decision is during the Hadrianic persecution (ca. 135 C.E.), when the public practice and teaching of Judaism was prohibited by the Romans, on pain of death, as revolutionary activity.[33]

The choice of these three commandments as absolutely indispensable seems to be based on the notion that they are the sine qua non of the relationship with God and fellow humans in this world, that they have a priority over the more specific commandments presented in the Torah by simple divine fiat. Thus the late-medieval commentator Rabbi Joseph ibn Habib wrote about these prohibitions:

> They are grave *[hamurot]*, not only prohibited because of the desecration of God's name in public, for they are not even to be done in private, even at a time when there is no persecution and, thus, no public desecration of God's name is entailed. One should die rather than transgress them because of their own inherent gravity *[homer 'atzman]*.[34]

This definition is important because only Jews are required by the Torah to die rather than desecrate God's name in public. The gravity of these prohibitions, then, transcends the legal question of the conditions that require Jews to die as martyrs.[35]

The universality of the three cardinal prohibitions of idolatry, sexual immorality (incest, homosexuality, adultery, and bestiality), and bloodshed comes out in imaginative rabbinic treatments ('aggadot) of the misconduct of Ishmael and of Esau. Both are presented in Scripture in an unfavorable light. Yet from Scripture alone, it is difficult to surmise just what they actually did to make them morally unacceptable. In two separate rabbinic texts, however, Ishmael and Esau are condemned for transgressing the three cardinal prohibitions.[36] It is important to remember that Ishmael and Esau are pre-Sinaitic Noahides and are also taken to be the founders of leading non-Jewish societies.[37]

Moreover, the Babylonian Talmud records the opinion of the school of Rab that a Noahide is to be punished by death only for violation of three of the Noahide laws.[38] In the ensuing discussion, the prohibitions of sexual immorality, bloodshed, and blasphemy are identified as the three laws in question. Nevertheless, if blasphemy and idolatry are seen as two aspects of the sin of rejecting God,[39] then we see the three cardinal prohibitions of Lydda here as the core of Noahide law. This being the case, the sine qua non for the emergence of Judaism and the sine qua non for the emergence of any acceptable non-Jewish religion and culture are the same. However, as we shall see, the fact that each one realizes itself in a unique way protects each from being reduced to the other and all of them from being reduced to some overarching universal religion and culture.

## Jewish Recognition of the Moral Independence of Gentiles

The question of whether Noahide law is to be enforced by Jews for gentiles or by gentiles for themselves is debated in both rabbinic and medieval texts. If it is ultimately a matter of Jewish enforcement, then Noahide law is essentially an extension of Jewish law for non-Jews—that is, a form of legal suzerainty. If, conversely, it is essentially a non-Jewish responsibility, then Noahide law is something that Jews recognize as obligatory for non-Jews but not something that Jews themselves are obliged to enforce. The former view is more akin to the old concept of the ger toshab; the latter view seems to follow from the newer concept of the

Noahide. The former view implies a legally constituted imperialism. Its intent is clearly external. The latter view seems to imply that lawfulness is not something Jews need to impose on non-Jews but is inherent in created human nature, the same nature that made possible the revelation of the Torah to Israel.[40]

From the perspective of the former view, Jewish interest in Noahide law is prescriptive. As a matter of Jewish enforcement, it presupposes the political power of the Jewish community. The motivation for Jewish interest according to this prescriptive view is clear: a part of Jewish law, for whose enforcement Jews are ultimately responsible, has universal scope. The motivation for the more descriptive view seems to be to discover a point in common between Jews and the non-Jewish world, a world that both precedes them and confronts them.

This difference in judgment regarding the essential meaning of the doctrine of Noahide law can be seen in the following dispute between Maimonides (d. 1204) and Nahmanides (d. 1267), his most insightful and original theological critic.

In presenting the Noahide commandment to establish courts of law, Maimonides employs a scriptural example to emphasize and illustrate the point he is making:

> How are they commanded concerning adjudication [dinim]? They are obligated to install judges and legal authorities in every district and to judge according to these six commandments and to admonish the people. And a Noahide who transgressed any of these seven commandments is to be executed by decapitation. Because of this, all the Shechemites deserved to be executed, for Shechem deserved to be executed for the crime of abduction [that is, robbery] and they saw it and did not judge him.[41]

Maimonides is referring to the abduction and rape of Jacob's daughter Dinah by Shechem, a Canaanite prince, as described in Genesis 34. The brothers of Dinah, Simon and Levi, executed the male Shechemites—but after concluding a treaty with them. Thus they were seemingly guilty of both bloodshed and deception. Nevertheless, Maimonides exonerates them from any culpability inasmuch as they were Jews enforcing Noahide law among non-Jews. Not only were they not culpable, but they are held up as exemplary. They rightfully punished the men of Shechem who, by not doing their duty, even when it involved their own prince, gave their tacit approval to his crime. The sons of Israel were justified, therefore, in executing Shechem for his crime and the Shechemites for their crime of neglecting to adjudicate this grave matter. Thus we have here an example of the general principle that Maimonides laid down earlier in his code—namely, "And so did Moses our master command us from divine authority to force [le-kof] all humankind to accept the commandments of the sons of Noah; and whoever does not accept them is to be executed."[42] In Chapter 3, we shall see how this notion operated in his understanding of the Jewish–Christian relationship.

The question is, Does the text of Scripture paraphrased by Maimonides really exonerate Simon and Levi and hold them up as exemplary? If not, then this case teaches just the opposite, that it is a paradigm for Jewish noninvolvement in the legal and moral affairs of gentiles. It should be remembered that Jacob himself disapproved of the actions of his sons.[43] This is exactly the point Nahmanides makes and builds on in his comment on Genesis 34:13, criticizing both Maimonides's exegesis and the theological assumption underlying it:

> This view is incorrect in my opinion because if it were so, our father Jacob would then have been obligated to be the first one to merit executing them. . . . Why was he angry with his sons? . . . In my opinion, the commandment of adjudication, which was specified for Noahides, not only includes adjudication but, also, such things as the prohibitions of stealing, cheating, etc. . . . like the concept of laws for which Jews are commanded. . . . However, they are not to be executed for failing to fulfill the positive commandment of adjudication. . . . In their law, not acting is not punishable by death.[44]

Nahmanides's basic view of the independence of Noahide law is followed by other medieval Jewish theologians; indeed, the sixteenth-century Polish Jewish scholar Rabbi Moses Isserles saw the basic dispute between Maimonides and Nahmanides in the very section of the Babylonian Talmud in which the doctrine of Noahide law is most extensively discussed.[45]

## The Prohibition of Idolatry

The basic question concerning Christianity that faced all the medieval Jewish authorities, who had to base themselves on the authority of the Talmud, was whether or not Christianity is a form of proscribed idolatry—even for gentiles. This requires that we look at the development of the rabbinically formulated prohibition of gentile idolatry and how it compares with the prohibition of Jewish idolatry and anything resembling it.

As we saw earlier, when the rabbis attempted to connect the new doctrine of Noahide law with the old legal institution of the *ger toshab,* Rabbi Meir was of the opinion that the only requisite for becoming a *ger toshab* was the public renunciation of idolatry. Although the other rabbis saw more than the public renunciation of idolatry as required for this Jewish acceptance of a non-Jew living in their polity, surely none of them disputed this renunciation as the prime requisite. For in the scriptural evidence, idolatry is regarded as a gentile phenomenon that is dangerous to the religious integrity of the people of Israel if tolerated in their midst. Thus if gentiles wished to be domiciled in a Jewish society, they would have to agree to renounce idolatry and worship the one God, even though they did not have to worship in exactly the same manner required of the people of Israel. However, this was a requirement only if they wanted to live in a Jewish society with attendant rights and privileges; it was not considered something obligatory for gentiles per se. For although idolatry is frequently ridiculed in Scripture as nonsense, it is nonsense for only the people of Israel, who are to know better because of the covenant.[46] Gentiles, therefore, cannot be faulted for their own idolatry as long as they do not infect the people of Israel with it.[47]

Thus on the first occasion of idolatry in Israel, after the theophany at Sinai—namely the worship of the golden calf—the scriptural text implies that the "mixed multitude" (*'ereb rab*)[48] referred to simply as "the people" (*ha'am,* Exodus 32:1), tempted the people of Israel to idolatry by stating, "These are your gods O Israel, who brought you up from the land of Egypt" (Exodus 32:4).[49] Furthermore, toleration of the Canaanites was prohibited on the assumption that they would "cause you to sin against Me, for you will serve their gods that this be a snare to you" (Exodus 23:33). This was also the basis of the prohibition of marriages with the Canaanites (Exodus 34:16).[50] This was later extended beyond the Canaanites, when Scripture attributed King Solomon's religious downfall to his tolerance of the idolatrous practices of his pagan wives, who "turned his heart" (1 Kings 11:3–4).[51] The later rabbinic bans on certain forms of social intercourse with gentiles were seen as being for the sake of preventing intermarriage, which was prohibited because it might lead to idolatry.[52]

Finally, it is important to note that when the prophets did condemn the gentiles for their sins, they did not condemn them for idolatry. Thus when Amos condemns Damascus, Gaza, Tyre, Edom, Ammon, and Moab (Amos 1:3–2:2), it is for various forms of treachery against their neighbors, something they themselves would no doubt agree was contrary to their own moral principles, for they had broken agreements they had made with their neighbors, thus violating the universally accepted principle *pacta sunt servanda*. However, idolatry as treachery toward God is never mentioned.[53]

All this follows from the fact that idolatry is considered the supreme act of unfaithfulness to the covenant that God made with Israel. Unfaithfulness involves the substitution of another beloved for the Lord. Because this covenantal relationship between God and Israel is considered by Scripture to be unique, idolatry can only be a sin for Israel. The other nations of the world, bereft as they are of this direct covenantal relationship with the Lord, cannot be morally faulted for unfaithfulness to a covenant in which they themselves are not participants. It is hoped, to be sure, that the gentiles will eventually say, "Let us go and ascend the mountain of the Lord to the house of the God of Jacob" (Isaiah 2:3), but this will not happen until the "end of days" (Isaiah 2:2), when the Lord will make his covenant with Israel irresistible to the gentiles.[54] As the great medieval commentator Rabbi David Kimhi noted in his interpretation of a parallel passage in Micah (4:1–2), in the present pre-Messianic period, when these nations are independent of Israel, the prophet indicates, "Let all the peoples walk each one in the name of its god; but we shall walk in the name of the Lord our God forever" (Micah 4:5). Without the subjugation to Jewish authority that is characteristic of the Messianic Age, even if the gentiles do acknowledge the Lord God of Israel, either individually or collectively, this does not necessarily involve their rejection of polytheism and acceptance of monotheism. It simply means that the mighty acts of God have made a powerful impression on them. Usually, these mighty acts involve Israel.[55]

## The Universal Ban on Idolatry

The great innovation of the new doctrine of Noahide law was that the ban on idolatry was now understood, to a certain degree at least, as being shared by Jews and non-Jews. This necessitated the reinterpretation of a number of scriptural texts, which can be seen in the exegesis of the following verse:

> And lest you lift up your eyes to the heaven and see the sun and the moon and the stars—all the heavenly host, and you be swept away and you worship them, which the Lord has alloted [halaq] to all the peoples under the heaven. (Deuteronomy 4:19)

Undoubtedly, the original meaning of this verse was that God has permitted the gentiles to worship the heavenly bodies because only Israel has a directly covenantal relationship with God. This obvious meaning is expressed by the twelfth-century commentator Rabbi Samuel ben Meir (Rashbam), who did not hesitate to disagree with rabbinic interpretations of Scripture that he believed contradicted the plain meaning of the text.[56] According to him, then, God let the nations worship the heavenly bodies "because he is not concerned with them."

It is obvious that the original meaning of this verse contradicts the Noahide ban on gentile idolatry. This was pointed out by Rashbam's grandfather, the great commentator Rashi, in his comment on Deuteronomy 4:19. Therefore, when the Talmud relates the ancient legend of how the Hellenistic king of Egypt Ptolemy Philadelpus (d. 247 B.C.E.) invited seventy Jewish sages to translate the Torah into Greek (resulting in the Septuagint text), it indicates that the sages did not translate certain verses literally because a literal rendering would lead to erroneous implications. An example is their rendering of Deuteronomy 4:19, which, according to the Talmud, was translated into Greek to read, "which the Lord your God has allotted to them to give light [le-ha'ir] to all peoples."[57]

The present text of the Septuagint, however, contains no such translation but is a literal translation of the Masoretic Hebrew text. Indeed, it is unlikely that the authors of the Septuagint considered idolatry to have been prohibited to gentiles. For the Septuagint (which had become authoritative for most Greek-speaking Jews) prohibited Jews from even ridiculing gentile idolatry, a point that could hardly be made if it was believed that idolatry was proscribed for gentiles.[58]

Although the rabbis now insisted that the ban on idolatry was binding on both Jews and gentiles, they recognized a difference in degree. Concessions were made for an idolatrous cultural residue in non-Jewish culture. Thus the important third-century Palestinian authority Rabbi Yohanan ben Nappaha (who, it will be recalled, also ruled against non-Jewish practice of Jewish rites) stated that "gentiles outside of the Land of Israel are not idolators but are only practicing ancestral custom."[59] It has been pointed out by one insightful scholar that during this period there was a revival of pagan apologetics to counter both Jewish and Christian polemics against idolatry. Rabbi Yohanan, according to this theory, made a sharp distinction between popular idolatry, which was motivated by ulterior considerations, and intellectual idolatry, whose intent was wholly idolatrous. Popular idolatry was found mostly in Babylonia; intellectual idolatry was found mostly in Palestine.[60] Thus much popular idolatry was tolerated simply because it no longer reflected any true conviction.

Rabbi Yohanan gives this distinction a theological basis in the following text:

It is stated: Rabbi Hanina says that one's heavenly constellation [mazal] makes one wise or rich, and that Israel has its own constellation. Rabbi Yohanan said that Israel does not have its own constellation. Rabbi Yohanan said that we know that Israel does not have its own constellation from the verse, "Thus says the Lord, do not learn from the ways of the nations, and from the heavenly signs [u-me' otot ha-shamayim] do not be afraid, for the nations are afraid of them." (Jeremiah 10:2)[61]

On the surface, Rabbi Yohanan seems to be repeating the old doctrine that monotheism is required of the Jews, whereas the gentiles are permitted to be polytheists. However, the key to understanding this statement of Rabbi Yohanan is his choice of the scriptural proof text. The heavenly bodies are called "signs"; that is, the nations of the world approach God through the mediation of nature, even through the symbolization of created nature in images. Israel, because of its unique historical relationship with God, must approach him directly through revealed commandments.[62] Here we see the beginnings of the notion, which was greatly developed in the Middle Ages, that the difference between Israel and the rest of the nations of the world is not that Israel worships the one God and the gentiles worship *other* gods altogether. Rather, the difference is that Israel worships God directly, for the covenant makes that direct relationship with God the only acceptable one for them. The nations of the world, being outside this direct covenant with Israel, are not wholly separated from God but are farther removed from him. Therefore, they are justified in approaching him through visible intermediaries, which are now seen as functioning symbolically.

The notion that gentile idolatry is not necessarily polytheistic in principle was prevalent in Hellenistic Judaism. Following the Septuagint, Josephus and especially Philo prohibited Jewish ridicule of pagan cults because their ultimate intent is not in essential opposition to monotheism.[63] This view goes back to the very beginnings of Hellenistic Judaism, to the Septuagint and to the Greek *Sirachides*. Thus when Deuteronomy 32:8 states, "He sets up the borders of the peoples according to the number of the people of Israel," the Septuagint renders it as "according to the number *[kata arithmon]* of the angels of God."[64] In other words, the nations of the world are under indirect divine governance; they are under the rule of God's appointed messengers. Ben Sira reiterated this notion when he wrote, "To every nation he set up a governor *[hegoumenon]*, but Israel is the portion of the Lord" (17:7). Somewhat earlier, Malachi, the last of the literary prophets, wrote, "From the rising of the sun to its setting, my name is great among the nations. And in every place offerings are presented unto my name" (1:11). The Talmud notes that this verse refers to the fact that even gentile idolators acknowledge one supreme God *(Elaha d'Elaha)*.[65] All this was perhaps best expressed by the tenth-century poet-philosopher Rabbi Solomon ibn Gabirol (Avicebrol), whose work was heavily influenced by Neoplatonic metaphysics, with its emphasis on gradations in being, in his philosophical poem "The Royal Crown" *(Keter Malkhut)*:

> Yet is not Thy glory diminished by reason of those that worship aught beside Thee, for the yearning of them is to draw nigh Thee. But they are like the blind, setting their faces forward on the King's highway, yet still wandering from the path."[66]

# 2

# The Status of Christianity in Medieval European Halakhah

## Rabbenu Jacob Tam

Even those segments of the Jewish community in medieval Europe that were not interested in any relationship with Christians that could be termed remotely dialogical could not avoid political and economic relations with them. These Jews were living within and under Christendom. However, political and economic relations were essentially different.

In the realm of politics, the Jewish community was related to the various Christian states in which it was officially allowed to dwell as a tolerated minority community. Jews as individuals were not citizens of these host states in any legally recognized sense; they were, rather, members of a separate community that had formal relations with the host state *as a community*.[1] The task for Jewish thinkers was to show how such relations, and the forfeiture of full Jewish sovereignty that they presupposed, could be justified on the basis of Judaism. Such justification was not at all difficult because Jews had long experience living within and under other political systems as, more or less, *imperium in imperio*. Already in the third century of the Common Era, the Babylonian authority Mar Samuel of Nehardea formulated the seminal legal principle, "the law of the ruling authority [*malkhuta*] is the law."[2] This principle, about which a huge literature had developed over the centuries, basically conceded Jewish sovereignty in large areas of civil and criminal law when that was the price of toleration of the Jewish community by the non-Jewish host society.[3] The twelfth-

century French authority Rabbi Samuel ben Meir (Rashbam) justified this politically expedient legal principle as follows:

> All the levies and taxes and legal procedures enacted by kings in their
> kingdoms are binding as law *[dina]*. For all the subjects of the king-
> dom freely accept *[mirtzonam]* the statues of the king and his enact-
> ments. Therefore, it is totally legal *[din gamur hu]*. Thus, one who
> takes property, when it is according to the king's law *[hoq ha-
> melekh]* that obtains in the municipality, does not do so as a robber.[4]

Rashbam's remarks are in the form of a comment on the locus
classicus of the seminal principle of Mar Samuel. He was, however, speaking about his own Jewish community in Christian France
as much as he was about Parthian Babylonia in the days of Mar
Samuel. In both cases, the Jewish community was able to contract
with its non-Jewish host society based on this type of compromise,
something every contract, social or private, entails. This relation,
however, was between two societies, leaving aside situations in
which Jews and non-Jews were directly involved in litigation between private parties. Furthermore, the contract had nothing to
do with the particular religion of the host society.

Interaction between Jews and Christians on the economic level
was, of course, far more frequent. Ancient proscriptions against
benefiting from or being benefited by idolatry or anything associated with it had to be reinterpreted, because European Christians
posed a different set of legal problems from those presented by
Romans or Parthians. This can be seen in the radical reinterpretation of the following proscription: "Three days before the holy
days *['eedayhem]* of the gentiles, it is prohibited to do business
with them, to lend them objects or borrow objects from them, to
lend them money or to borrow money from them, to pay debts to
them or collect debts from them."[5] The standard reason for this
sweeping prohibition is that all these activities contribute in some
way or other to the idolater's acknowledgment of his god on the
holy day.[6]

In an important medieval gloss on this text, a question is raised
about contemporary noncompliance with this prohibition. Jews were
doing business with gentiles even on the very days of the gentile
religious festivals.[7] It is further pointed out that not only are the
Christian festivals mostly days commemorating their saints *(ha-*

*qodashim),* but they have an additional holy day once a week, namely Sunday.[8]

The first suggested justification for the popular practice is based on the principle of the second-century Palestinian authority Rabbi Yohanan, which we examined in Chapter 1. It will be recalled that Rabbi Yohanan observed that gentiles living outside the land of Israel are no longer committed to idolatry per se but are practicing its rites only as ancestral custom.[9] However, it is quickly pointed out that this would not apply to the prohibition of dealing with them on their festival day itself, according to the Talmud.[10] The implication seems to be that even though these gentiles are not idolators, on the festival day itself, when they are actually performing the ancient idolatrous rites, the very performance of them will inevitably entail some conviction, even if it is mostly sentimental. One might see a contemporary illustration in the feelings of many "cultural" Christians who participate in Christmas or Easter rites. Although they are not regular churchgoers and would not confess Christian faith in any other context, in the heightened emotional atmosphere of these holy days, surrounded by the symbols of their ancestral faith, some conviction does inevitably emerge, however momentary and fleeting.

Christianity had to be viewed in a different light if Jewish economic relations with Christians were to be justified by Jewish law. Its adherents had to be considered something other than idolators, and Christianity itself had to be considered something other than idolatry.[11] The pragmatic justification of the avoidance of Christian enmity *('aybah)* was quickly dismissed as insufficient to justify the total disregard of the ancient proscription.[12] It was not a profound enough justification. The final and complete justification is because "concerning the gentiles among us, it is established for us that they do not serve idols." The Talmudic precedent cited for this dispensation, however, deals with dispensation of only an individual gentile from the stigma of idolatry generally associated with other gentiles.[13] The medieval use of this precedent dispenses an entire community. This dispensation is much more radical than that of Rabbi Yohanan, since most medieval Christians really did believe in Christianity, whereas most of the gentiles outside the land of Israel during the time of Rabbi Yohanan were assumed not really to believe in their ancient religions anymore. The twelfth-century French authority Rabbenu Jacob Tam (Rashbam's younger brother) further limits the actual prohibition to dealing in articles for specifically religious purposes *(taqrobet)*. Elaborating on this leniency, the author of this long gloss states that even if we do consider Christians to be idolators, all of them donate money for these religious purposes, and money has no earmarks. It is thus impossible to specify what money is actually being used for these purposes.

The fact is, however, that Rabbenu Tam considered Christians not to be idolators *because* Christianity is not idolatry. The ancient gentiles with whom Rabbi Yohanan was concerned, on the contrary, were not idolators *in spite of* their ancestral religions. Rabbenu Tam's point of view is enunciated in other contexts as well.[14]

Ancient Jewish law prohibited Jews from either drinking or deriving monetary benefit from the wine of non-Jews. The assumption was that wine is an article closely associated with idolatry, and, even if we do not know for sure that the wine was actually dedicated to a pagan god, it is probable that the gentile having contact with this wine had idolatry on his mind because of this close association.[15] Later in the rabbinic period, another reason was given for this prohibition of non-Jewish wine: involvement with it might lead to too much social intercourse with non-Jews, which could lead to intermarriage, which could ultimately lead to actual apostasy.[16] Here the connection with idolatry (for Judaism, apostasy to any other religion by a Jew is tantamount to idolatry)[17] is even less direct.

No Jewish authority at that time actually permitted Jews to drink non-Jewish wine. If Christians per se are no longer considered idolators, however, then it is inevitable that the strictures against benefiting from wine that they had made or come into contact with would be relaxed. Thus Rabbenu Tam permitted Jewish benefit from gentile wine just short of actually drinking it.[18] This ruling was occasioned by the fact that the wine trade was an important part of the economy of his time and place, and Jews were already heavily involved in it. In this permission of what was already widespread Jewish practice, Rabbenu Tam had precedent in the opinion of his grandfather, Rashi, who himself based his opinion on an even earlier opinion of the post-Talmudic Babylonian authorities *(ge'onim)*.[19]

It would seem that if Christians are no longer considered idolators, there should be no reason to prohibit Jews from drinking their wine. Indeed, when the view of Rabbenu Tam and his grandfather and brother, among others, was reported to his nephew, Rabbi Isaac (Ri), he assumed that they had permitted the actual drinking of gentile wine. However, when Rabbi Isaac inquired of his uncle whether this was indeed his conclusion, Rabbenu Tam denied the charge, claiming that the student who had reported this was confused.[20] Nevertheless, Rabbenu Tam was hard put to justify his distinction between drinking gentile wine and only benefiting from it monetarily. Logically, one should either be permitted both acts or be forbidden both acts inasmuch as both prohibitions are based on the same reason.[21] This is the point Rabbi Isaac persisted in making, citing a variety of precedents. The only answer Rabbenu Tam and his disciples could finally come up with is that the practice of dealing in gentile wines was so widespread that it would be practically impossible to stop it.[22] However, it was continually emphasized that the truly pious avoid all contact with gentile wine whatsoever.[23]

What emerges from all this discussion is that Rabbenu Tam and those who followed his point of view were involved in a deep paradox. On the one hand, they did not regard Christians as idolators. On the other hand, Christians were not Jews either, and, although economic intercourse with them was necessary, social intercourse was feared as an opening to Jewish assimilation into the larger Christian civilization.

Rabbenu Tam's rulings simply stipulate that contemporary Christians are not idolators. The rulings might be termed strictly legal; that is, they are concerned with behavior and its consequences. But Rabbenu Tam went further than that and indicated his theological reasons for this legal stipulation. This comes out in his treatment of the question of non-Jewish oaths. Here the theological considerations must be examined because judicial oaths involve a commitment made before God to another human being. It is essential to determine just what one's religious intention is under these circumstances.[24]

The Talmud had presented the following ruling, which clearly proscribed Jews from entering into any business partnerships with gentiles because of the probability that the gentile would be required to take an oath: "The father of Samuel said that it is forbidden ['asur] for a person to set up a partnership [shuttfut] with

a gentile lest the gentile become obligated to swear an oath
[*shebu'ah*] by his god. And the Torah stated, 'it shall not be heard
on your mouth' " (Exodus 23:13).[25] In the context of the Talmudic literary unit in which this statement is brought, the first half
of the scriptural proof text is brought; "And the name of other
gods you shall not cause to be remembered." Thereafter, the Talmud brings an earlier rabbinic ruling that "this verse is a prohibition [*'azharah*] . . . not to occasion [*ve-lo vigrom*] others to
vow by its name that they might fulfill the vow in its name."[26]
These "others" are gentiles.[27] This ruling, then, prohibits a Jew
from being even an indirect cause (*gerama*)—that is, from even
creating the occasion—for a non-Jew to swear by his or her deity.
The earliest prohibition, however, seemed to prohibit a Jew only
from requiring such an oath—that is, acting as a direct cause for
a non-Jew to do so, but not where the non-Jew does so at his or
her own initiative.[28]

Faced with this absolute prohibition, Rabbenu Tam reinterprets
the status of its non-Jewish subjects as follows:

> Nevertheless, in this age they all swear by their saints [*qodashim*] to
> whom they do not ascribe divinity [*'elohut*]. And, even though they
> mention God's name along with them, and their intent [*kavvanatam*]
> is for something else, nonetheless, their awareness [*da'atam*] is of the
> Maker of heaven and earth. Even though they associate [*shemisht-
> tatfin*] the name of God and something else, we do not find that it is
> forbidden to indirectly cause [*ligrom*] others to perform such associ-
> ation.[29]

In short, if gentiles are permitted to acknowledge God through
mediation, then as long as God is the ultimate object of their concern, they may swear by these intermediaries and not transgress
the Noahide prohibition of idolatry. Furthermore, Jews may enter
into business associations with them in which this type of oath
might very well be required at some point during the course of the
relationship.

The reinterpretation of Rabbenu Tam centers around the term
*shuttfut*, "partnership." In the Talmudic text, partnership refers
to the relationship between the Jew and the non-Jew. In Rabbenu
Tam's radical reworking of it, it now refers to the non-Jew's relationship with God, a relationship that admits a third party as
intermediary. Jews are prohibited from approaching God through

any such intermediary because of the strictly immediate covenantal relationship with God. Rabbenu Tam's main theological point, then, is that the fact that gentiles lack this convenantal immediacy does not eliminate them from a relationship with God altogether. This is the case as long as they ultimately intend the Lord God, maker of heaven and earth. Christians clearly fall into this category, and, because they do, Jews can respect their moral commitments when they are grounded in their religious commitments.

A good case can be made, however, that Rabbenu Tam's leniency in the area of oaths is limited to the invocation of saints by Christians. It has been pointed out that this limitation is based on the distinction that Christians themselves made between *adoratio* (devotion to the Godhead per se) and *veneratio* (secondary veneration of the saints).[30] Rabbenu Tam could not, therefore, extend this leniency when the Trinity or any of its persons is invoked, because such an oath entails an intention of a direct participation in the Godhead itself by the person so named. Nevertheless, later medieval halakhists (and, for Jews, the Middle Ages do not begin to end until the French Revolution in 1789), who considered themselves very much within the Ashkenazic tradition of Rabbenu Tam, extended this leniency even to the use of the Trinity in Christian oaths.

They were able to do so because the term for "partnership" *(shuttfut)*, which originally denoted a simple interhuman contract and then was taken to denote the relationship between God and the Christians mediated by their saints, was now seen as being interchangeable with a related term, *shittuf*, which in philosophical Hebrew denotes an *interdivine* relationship.[31] The Trinity, of course, is precisely such an interdivine relationship. We now see three steps in a process of legal and theological development of the Jewish view of the Christian relationship with God: (1) where it is totally illegitimate, (2) where its secondary aspects (veneration of the saints) are legitimate, and (3) where its primary aspect (adoration of the Trinity) is legitimate.

One can explain this last shift in meaning in one of two ways: More conservatively, the shift can be seen as being caused by the fact that most later-medieval halakhists were often quite ignorant of the Jewish philosophy of the earlier Middle Ages and were often anatagonistic to it. This was especially true of the Ashkenazim in northern Europe, who, moreover, did not know the Arabic background of those Hebrew philosophical terms that had become common Jewish parlance. They could easily confuse the term *shittuf* (denoting an interdivine relationship) with *shuttfut* (now denoting an extradivine relationship) and assume that both meant the same thing.[32] Furthermore, many of them knew much less about Christianity than had Rabbenu Tam. Finally, it is assumed that these rabbis were far more pragmatic than theological and that their overall project was to facilitate Jewish economic survival in Christian societies.

The problem with this conservative approach is that it assumes that these halakhists, who under all other circumstances scrupulously examined the phenomena they had to judge, were here much less scrupulous—downright careless, in fact. Moreover, the area of idolatry and everything connected with it is one of the most stringent and inflexible areas of Jewish law.[33] Nevertheless, these rabbis did skirt the issue of the Trinity altogether and based their legitimization of Christianity on Christian biblicism (as did Maimonides, as we shall see in Chapter 3) and on the Christian affirmation of the doctrine of *creatio ex nihilo*. Rabbi Moses Rivkes, a seventeenth-century Lithuanian Talmudist, epitomized this whole approach when he wrote:

> The rabbis of the Talmud meant by the term "idolators" the pagans who lived in their time, who worshipped the stars and the constellations and did not believe in the Exodus from Egypt and in the creation of the world out of nothing. But the nations under whose benevolent shadow we, the Jewish nation, are exiled and are dispersed among them, they do believe in the creation of the world out of nothing and the Exodus from Egypt and in the essentials of the Faith *[u-be'iqqray ha-dat]*, and their whole intention is toward the Maker of heaven and earth, as other authorities have said . . . these nations do believe in all of this.[34]

In the first mention of belief in the Exodus and creation, the sequence is important. For in the thirteenth century, the antiphilosophical Spanish Jewish theologian Nahmanides asserted that belief in creation can only be an extension of belief in actually experienced miracles, the greatest of which was the Exodus. It cannot be inferred from ordinary experience, as some philosophers assume.[35] Thus the legitimization of Christianity rests on its biblicism. Yet when Rabbi Rivkes mentions Christian belief in "essentials of the Faith," the Trinity does not seem to be seen as a counterexample to this proposition. How could he avoid it when it seems to contradict the designation of Christianity as affirming scriptural doctrine?

I would radically suggest that the reason for this avoidance is the great influence of the Kabbalah, which arose after the time of Rabbenu Tam. Kabbalistic theology, as Gershom Scholem never tired of pointing out, began as a revolt against the Aristotelian and Neoplatonic metaphysics of early medieval Jewish philosophy. This was first and foremost a revolt against the philosophical notion that any relations predicated of God are totally external to the actual divine being, which entails that the inner life of God, being absolutely unitary, is inpenetrable. The Kabbalistic revolt asserted an association of multiple factors within the Godhead itself. These ten parts of the divine inner life, the *sefirot* (literally "spheres"), although not ultimately independent, are real enough to constitute an interdivine relationship, a relationship that the revelation of the Torah alone made partially penetrable by the Jewish people. Much of Judaism was now reinterpreted as a participation in the Godhead, which itself is a prior field of participating parts.[36]

Although Kabbalah captured the imagination and conviction of large masses of Jews, it always had its enemies. One of these enemies was the fourteenth-century halakhist Rabbi Isaac ben Sheshet Parfat (Ribash). Writing about certain Kabbalistic prayer techniques, he pointed out:

> Even in the main prayer of the eighteen benedictions *[shemonah 'es-reh]* they intend each of the benedictions to be to a separate divine sphere. And all of this is very strange for those who are not kabbalists like them and who think this is a belief in divine multiplicity *['emunat sheniyut]*. Once I heard one of those involved in philosophy *[ha-mitpalsim]* speak contemptuously about the kabbalists saying, "the idolators believe in the Trinity and the kabbalists believe in a tenfold God!" . . . Is it not better to pray directly *[stam]* to the Lord, may he be blessed, with intention *[be-khavvanah]?*[37]

The enemies of Kabbalah thus regarded the logic of its theology as indistinguishable from the logic of the Trinity.

Defenders of the Kabbalah have, of course, attempted to counter these charges.[38] However, none of their arguments is very convincing. The fact is that the acceptance of much of Kabbalah, both consciously and unconsciously, made a strictly metaphysical rejection of Christian Trinitarian claims less plausible. For anti-Trinitarian arguments could easily be turned into anti-Kabbalistic arguments. The differences between Judaism and Christianity, then, would have to be drawn in terms of the theology of revelation and the authority of the Law. Similarities between Judaism and Christianity could be asserted on the grounds of biblicism alone. All this would have been impossible, I think, without the influence of Kabbalah on all of Jewish life and thought. It is no accident that those Jewish thinkers in the nineteenth century who polemicized against the "mythical" aspects of Christian theology were precisely those rationalists who venerated Maimonides's philosophical theology, with its absolute "monotheism," and who detested Kabbalah as a regression in Jewish spiritual and intellectual progress.[39]

The acceptance of Rabbenu Tam's basic thesis that gentile monotheism need not be as strict as Jewish monotheism, plus the prevalence of Kabbalah among Ashkenazic halakhists, made difficult any compelling anti-Trinitarian argument (except, of course, for Jews, on strictly convenantal grounds) either halakhically or theologically. On halakhic grounds, it was very difficult to convince any Jew not extremely learned in Christian doctrine that there was any real difference between the veneration of the saints and the adoration of the persons of the Trinity. On theological grounds, as we have just seen, any anti-Trinitarian argument could easily be turned into an anti-Kabbalistic argument. In European Sephardic communities, however, despite the prevalence of Kabbalah there, too, the halakhic arguments against Christian Trinitarianism would still be invoked, because most of the halakhists there followed Maimonides's halakhic thesis about the univocal prohibition of any intermediacy between God and man as idolatry, whether for Jews or for gentiles. Most of the halakhists there did not accept Rabbenu Tam's double standard for the prohibition of idolatry. Furthermore, in many of these communities, Christian missionary efforts directed toward the Jews were both intense and on a high enough intellectual level to require Jews to formulate a theological refutation of all their claims. This was especially so in Spain before the expulsion of 1492, where conversionary efforts were most intense, and after 1492 in those Sephardic communities, such as Amsterdam, where Marranos returning to a full and open practice of Judaism were eager to divest themselves of pro-Christian opinions of any kind and influenced their fellow Jews with their anti-Christian zeal.

The view of Christianity developed by Rabbenu Tam and his successors is not a precedent for Jewish–Christian dialogue in any direct sense. For it seems to assign to Christianity an explicitly inferior status in relation to Judaism. Judaism is an immediate relationship with God; Christianity is a mediated relationship with God. Yet in its attempt to assign legitimacy to Christianity on its own terms, this approach clearly avoids the type of triumphalism that makes dialogue impossible. Furthermore, it constitutes a common moral area, namely that of trust of each other's oaths, with the recognition that the Jewish and Christian parties can approach it from different theological bases. In the phenomenology of this common moral area, the fact that Jews regard Judaism as religiously superior to Christianity (and Christians vice versa) is not the issue. There can be an area of common social interaction without either religious community surrendering its own truth claims to the other theologically. Such surrender would be a form of relativism, which had to wait for the modern world to become fully manifest.

Finally, it must be noted that as much as Judaism claims to be a more immediate relationship with God than Christianity, so does Christianity claim to be a more immediate relationship with God than Judaism. Thus Paul wrote:

> Having then this hope, I speak with great openness, and not like Moses "who placed a veil on his face" [Exodus 34:33] so that the children of Israel not gaze at its fading. For their minds were weakened. Indeed, until this very day that same veil makes them ignorant whenever the old Covenant is read for it is not removed, only by Christ is it lifted.[40]

This is understandable because each community can view the other's relationship with God only externally. They both can view it from only a human perspective. Thus what the other community believes to be the divine extension *into* the human world appears from a human perspective to be a separate entity altogether, something projected *between* man and God. From this human perspective, the mediating factor appears as something independent. But for Judaism, the Torah is God's self-manifestation over and above his commanding will.[41] For Christianity, Christ is God's manifestation. Nevertheless, the Torah is not the content of the relationship with God for Christians, and Christ is not the content of the relationship with God for Jews. Therefore, for each community to recognize that what *appears* to mediate the relationship with God for the other community is *not* an idol is the most that can be done without surrendering to relativism. This seems to be the enduring theological point that can be inferred from the view of Rabbenu Tam and those who followed in his tradition. It has great significance for a Jewish constitution of the Jewish–Christian dialogue.

## Rabbi Menahem Ha-Meiri

The approach to Christianity taken by the fourteenth-century Provençal halakhist Rabbi Menahem Ha-Meiri, much more than that of Rabbenu Tam, is based on the fact that Christians (and Muslims) have a moral code that fully complies with the Noahide laws. As such, they are considered generically different from the pagans to whom most Talmudic legislation concerning gentiles pertains. Thus Meiri comments on the locus classicus of the Noahide laws in the Babylonian Talmud as follows: "Every Noahide whom we see, who accepts upon himself the seven commandments, is one of the pious [*me-hasiday*] of the nations of the world and is in the category of the religious [*ba'alay ha-dat*] and he has a portion in the world-to-come."[42]

By "acceptance" (*qabbalah*), Meiri clearly means acceptance of the seven Noahide laws as divinely ordained commandments. However, he did not constitute the relation between Christian morality and Christian belief theologically, as did Rabbenu Tam (incompletely, to be sure), nor did he do it more philosophically, as did Maimonides.[43] Rather, Meiri simply emphasized a historical relation between Christian morality and Christian denial of idolatry. Historically, he is convinced, the two go together. For him, Christians (and Muslims, whom he always links with Christians in this respect) are those who are of "the nations bound [*ha-gedurot*] by religious laws [*be-darkhay ha-datot*] and who have renounced [*u-shemudot*] polytheism."[44] Sometimes he mentions lawfulness before the renunciation of idolatry; sometimes he mentions it afterward.[45] But gentiles before the rise of Christianity and Islam are members of "the earlier faiths" *(ha'emunot ha-qedumot)*.[46] Meiri's interest seems to be more pragmatic than theoretical; that is, the gentiles' theology can be generally justified if their observance of Noahide moral law can be seen specifically. And following Maimonides's definition of divinely revealed law as that law which correlates political and theological concerns, Meiri designates the ancient pagans as unacceptable precisely because their law had no such correlation but was totally mundane in its scope and intent: "And the other Torahs of the ancient nations and their laws *[vedatayhem]*: their subject matter is only concerned with political conduct and human statutes *[nimusim]* set down by men . . . and according to their law this is totally sufficient."[47]

Meiri emphasizes the Christian and Muslim advance from this limited aspect of human normativeness in a number of places when speaking of the gentiles of his day. Because of this, Meiri was in the forefront in removing certain civil liabilities that gentiles had had in earlier Talmudic law.[48] For he explained that whatever civil disabilities there were for gentiles in Talmudic law, even in that period they had applied only to idolators. Whereas at that time it had been assumed that a gentile was eo ipso an idolator unless proved to be a law-abiding "Noahide," in Meiri's time it was now to be assumed that the masses of Christians and Muslims, *because of* Christianity and Islam, were considered to be law-abiding collectively.

Meiri's emphasis on the religious acceptance of the Noahide laws by Christians especially, who accept them from the text of the Hebrew Bible itself, is quite important. It indicates that when non-Jews accept aspects of Judaism for themselves, Jews are to respect them for it. This goes back to an early rabbinic legend that when God gave the Torah to Israel, they were to write it on stones so that the nations of the world could send messengers and take as much of it as they wanted.[49] However, another rabbinic legend, probably later, emphasized that the nations of the world could not keep even the Noahide laws, much less other aspects of the Torah of Israel.[50] Thus when they do accept these laws, they are seen as doing so out of prudence rather than piety and are considered to be now in the category of those "who are not commanded but do practice the commandments."[51] It would seem that Meiri wants to return to the older rabbinic teaching that encouraged non-Jews to borrow various aspects from Judaism voluntarily. This can be seen in his treatment of Rabbenu Tam's permission of women to voluntarily practice commandments that they were not actually commanded in the Torah.[52] He writes, "for, after all, such a person is in the category of religious law *[bi-khllal ha-dat]* as, for example *[ke-gon]*, women."[53] Although women are the case in point in Rabbenu Tam's ruling, Meiri sees the principle as broad enough to include other examples as well. That is the force of his "for example." It obviously includes non-Jews, as can be seen by his use here of the very same justification he used elsewhere for Christianity and Islam.

Meiri was a Jewish refugee from France in the expulsion of 1306, but there is evidence that during his adult life in Provence, Jews had good relations with Christians there and were treated well by them.[54] That is important. For when Jews are being persecuted by Christians because of their adherence to Judaism, Jews can hardly be expected to have much regard for Christian morality. Thus Rabbenu Tam, who apparently lived under much greater Christian persecution of Jews, deals with only the Christian negation of idolatry. But Meiri, who, at least in his adult life, experienced a less oppressive Christian atmosphere, has a more broadly positive view of Christians and Christianity. Jewish respect for Christian normativeness had to suppose some degree of Christian respect for Jews and Judaism.

For this reason, it seems, medieval Jewish attempts to legitimize Christianity as somehow derivative from Judaism never turned to the most obvious ancient precedent, the Samaritans. The Samaritans, too, observed many Jewish practices, and there are examples in the Talmud of respect for Samaritan practice of some of the commandments.[55] But the Samaritans (like the Muslims, but unlike the Christians) claimed that the Jews had a distorted version of the Torah. Moreover, the Samaritans were relentless enemies of the Jewish people, especially of the Temple in Jerusalem.[56] Like the later anti-Jewishness of some Christians, which would crop up again and again in history, Samaritan anti-Jewishness was based on the delegitimization of Judaism and the Jewish people.[57]

From this, an important lesson can be learned by Jews, and by Christians as well, about the dialogue. Recognition of the religious legitimacy (which is not the same as the religious equality) of the other community is a necessary but not *the* sufficient condition of the dialogue. In other words, the dialogue is more than but never less than a mutual recognition of each other's religious legitimacy. As this study shows, that requires hard theological work. Without such recognition, there can be no dialogue at all, or dialogue can only be a pretext for covert proselytizing. With it, however, the dialogue has a chance, and the type of democratic society that Jews and Christians can envision, in which both can contribute to its moral foundation, might very well be the dialogue's most cogent raison d'être. For this new enterprise, Rabbenu Tam and Meiri, without intending to do so, to be sure, laid important groundwork.

# 3

# *Maimonides's View of Christianity*

## The Present Legal Status of Christianity

When examining Maimonides's view of Christianity, whether in his specific legal judgments or in his more theological reflections, it is important to remember that he always views Christianity together with Islam. Clearly, for Maimonides, Christianity and Islam are related to Judaism in an altogether different way from any other non-Abrahamic religion. Maimonides lived his entire life in Muslim societies: in Spain, in North Africa, and, finally, in Egypt. His knowledge of Christianity was not the result of firsthand experience, as was his knowledge of Islam; he had learned about Christian doctrine and practice secondhand.[1]

It is usually assumed that Maimonides's practical view of Christianity was altogether negative, that, in contrast to Islam, he regarded Christianity as a form of proscribed polytheism, even for gentiles. Early in his career, in his commentary on *'Abodah Zarah*—the tractate of the Mishnah dealing with idolatry and the restrictions on Jews in their relationships with idolators—Maimonides makes this categorical statement about Christianity and Christians:

> Know that this Christian nation, who advocate the messianic claim, in all their various sects [*le-khol shinuy kitotayhem*], all of them are idolators. On all their festivals it is forbidden for us to deal with them. And all Torah restrictions pertaining to idolators pertain to them. Sunday is one of their festivals. Therefore, it is forbidden to deal with believers in "the messiah" on Sunday at all in any manner

whatsoever; rather, we deal with them as we would deal with any idolators on their festival.[2]

Shortly thereafter, Maimonides extends the prohibition even further:

> Therefore, one must know that any one of the cities of the Christian nation that has in it a place of worship [bamah], namely, a church, which is, without a doubt, a house of idolatry: through that city one must not intentionally pass, let alone dwell there. But, the Lord has turned us over into their hands that we must sojourn in their cities against our will in order to fulfill Scripture's prediction, "you will serve there gods that are the work of human hands: wood and stone" (Deuteronomy 4:28). If this is the law pertaining to the city, all the more so does it apply to the house of idolatry itself, that it is minimally forbidden to look at it, let alone go near it, all the more so to actually enter it.[3]

These two passages must be seen together in order to understand the basis of Maimonides's judgment. If Christians simply believed in a Messiah whom the Jews could not accept for valid objective reasons—namely, he did not restore Jewish sovereignty in the land of Israel and rebuild the Temple in Jerusalem—that would not suffice for judging them to be idolators. However, for Maimonides, the fact that they employ icons in their worship seems to indicate the inevitable consequence of their erroneous Messianic belief.

In his code of Jewish law, *Mishneh Torah,* Maimonides simply reiterates his judgment about the idolatrous status of Christianity without repeating the reasons he gave in his earlier work.[4] In another passage there, dealing with the restrictions on Jews in relation to the use of non-Jewish wine, he makes the following distinction:

> The resident-alien [ger toshab], namely, one who has accepted the seven Noahide laws, as we have already explained: his wine is forbidden to drink but it is permitted to derive monetary benefit from it [muttar be-haniyyah]. . . . Such is the case with all the gentiles who are not idolators, like these Muslims ['elu ha-yishma 'elim] . . . so rule all the post-talmudic authorities [he-ge'onim]. But, as for even the nonsacramental wine [stam yaynam] of those idolators, it is forbidden to derive monetary benefit from it.[5]

Here it is assumed, following the Talmud, that even the ordinary wine of the idolators—that is, wine that we do not know was actually dedicated to a god *(yayn nesekh)*—probably has the taint of idolatry in some way or other.[6] And in this case, it is clear that Maimonides is contrasting the nonidolatrous Muslims with the idolatrous Christians. Regarding the Muslims, the only reason for prohibiting Jews from drinking their wine is the weaker Talmudic reason that drinking the wine of the gentiles will be an occasion for too much social intimacy, which might lead to intermarriage.[7] Furthermore, as we have seen, although the literal legal status of the resident-alien *(ger toshab)* was regarded as inapplicable in any situation short of full Jewish sovereignty in the land of Israel, it remained the rubric for dealing with any gentile or group of gentiles who were neither idolators nor full converts to Judaism *(geray tzedeq)*. Muslims, but not Christians, fall into this category, according to Maimonides. Indeed, they seem to be the only non-Jewish religious community that does.

## The Present Theological Status of Christianity

Maimonides's negative view of Christianity was expressed not only in a legal context, where his main point had to be based on the actual practice of Christians (all the Christian groups of his day: Catholic, Orthodox, Armenian, Ethiopic, and Coptic) of using icons in their churches. As a theologian, he took equally strong exception to Christian Trinitarianism. In his great work of philosophical theology, *The Guide of the Perplexed,* Maimonides writes of monotheism:

> God's being One by virtue of a true Oneness, so that no composition whatever is to be found in Him and no possibility of division in any way whatever—then you must know that He, may He be exalted, has in no way and in no mode any essential attribute, and that just as it is impossible that He should be a body, it is also impossible that He should possess an essential attribute. If, however, someone believes that He is one, but possesses a certain number of essential attributes, he says in his words that He is one, but believes Him in his thought to be many. This resembles what the Christians say: namely, that He is one but also three, and that three are one.[8]

Maimonides is able to make a more convincing case for a necessary connection between polytheism and idolatry than for a necessary connection between mistaken Messianism and idolatry. After all, Jews, too, have had cases of mistaken Messianism, and they did not bring idolatry in their wake.[9] Polytheism, however, posits a multiplicity in God, and, for Maimonides, such multiplicity presupposes a material element in God.[10] From this presupposition, it is clear how the use of icons became part of the worship based on this type of theology. Indeed, Maimonides even regards the designation of any physical attributes in God, by Jews, as having idolatrous implications.[11]

In addition to being a form of polytheism, Christianity is unacceptable because it has compromised the integrity of Mosaic prophecy.[12] It has abrogated the authority of most of the commandments of the Torah and has placed Jesus on a higher level than Moses. In making this point, Maimonides implicates Islam as well as Christianity, although he can find no fault with Islamic monotheism per se. Acceptance of the truth and primacy of Mosaic prophecy is almost as important as acceptance of monotheism and rejection of polytheism and idolatry. Mosaic prophecy is the most original and most pure manifestation of monotheism. Any contradiction of this original and pure monotheistic prophecy can only render the subsequent prophecy false.

However, in this recognition that there can be derivative prophecy and that that derivative prophecy is also outside the Jewish people, Maimonides sets two criteria, one philosophical and the other historical. And these criteria make for a more complex view of Christianity.

The philosophical criterion is that the normative thrust of any authentic prophecy be such that it establishes a political order in which practical excellence is linked with theoretical excellence. Theoretical excellence, for Maimonides, is increasing knowledge of the truths about God and God's relationship with the universe. In *The Guide of the Perplexed* he stipulates,

> If, on the other hand, you will find a Law all of whose ordinances are due to attention being paid . . . to the soundness of the circumstances pertaining to the body and also to the soundness of belief—a Law that takes pains to inculcate correct opinions with regard to God . . . and with regard to the angels, and that desires to make man wise, to give him understanding, and to awaken his attention,

so that he should know the whole of that which exists in its true form—you must know that this guidance comes from Him, may He be exalted, and that this Law is divine.[13]

This, as scholars have pointed out, is Maimonides's version of the ideal polity envisioned by Plato and interpreted by the Muslim philosopher Alfarabi.[14] Platonic *nous* ("intellection"), the highest form of knowledge, now becomes *nebu'ah* ("prophecy").

It would seem, however, that Christianity would not qualify as a source of divine law inasmuch as Maimonides has designated its theology as polytheistic. Nevertheless, when discussing the historical preconditions for the reign of the true Messiah, earlier in *Mishneh Torah*, Maimonides includes Christianity along with Islam. There he writes:

> But there is no power in man to apprehend the thoughts of the Creator of the world. . . . Thus these words of Jesus of Nazareth and this Arab [Muhammed] who came after him were only to prepare the way for the Messiah-King and to order *[le-taqqen]* the whole world to serve the Lord altogether, as it says in Scripture, "For I shall unite all the peoples into a pure speech, all of them to call upon the name of the Lord and to serve Him with one shoulder." (Zephaniah 3:9)[15]

Christianity and Islam base themselves, to a certain extent, on earlier Jewish monotheistic claims, and Maimonides is apparently asserting that what is derivative *from* Judaism is also potential *for* Judaism's full earthly culmination in the reign of the Messiah-King. If that is the case, however, then Christianity (like Islam) cannot be a form of idolatry. For if it were (no different from any other form of idolatry, as Maimonides stated earlier in his commentary on the Mishnah), how could it possibly "prepare the way for the Messiah-King"?

In this notion of Christianity and Islam as derivatives of Judaism, Maimonides followed the lead of the eleventh-century Spanish theologian Rabbi Judah Ha-Levi. In his theological dialogue *Kuzari*, Ha-Levi depicted a pagan king—a philosophical monotheist—who attempts to find the true religion. After interrogating both a Muslim theologian and a Christian theologian, he finally and reluctantly interrogates a Jewish theologian. After a brief discussion with him, he chooses Judaism over both Christianity and Islam for himself as well as for his people, because the latter two religions are at best derivative from Judaism. Since both Christianity and Islam grudgingly admit Judaism as their source, the king concludes that Judaism is the original and most authentic monotheism.[16] It is the only one that has remained pure and unadulterated by pagan additions and distortions. In so arguing, Ha-Levi, and Maimonides after him, reversed the successionist claims of both Christianity and Islam—that they are the true fulfillment of what was a primitive beginning in Judaism. Rather than improvement, as the Christians and the Muslims claimed in their anti-Jewish polemics, succession is the dilution of the original revelation. The only reason this historical fact is not more widely known is the present political impotence of the Jewish people. The world does not take them seriously because of it. Indeed, that is why the king of the Khazars consulted Christian and Muslim theologians first and was reluctant even to bother consulting a Jewish theologian. For a pagan, lack of worldly power entails lack of religious importance.

Ha-Levi, before Maimonides, also posits the monotheistic potentiality—the messianic preparatory role—of Christianity and Islam:

> The nations merely serve to introduce and pave the way for the expected Messiah, who is the fruition, and they will all become his fruit. Then they will revere the origin which they formerly despised. . . . Consider not their abstention from idolatry, and energetic declaration of the unity of God.[17]

This passage, to be sure, is part of a polemic against the claims of superiority of Christianity and Islam. Yet, like Maimonides after him, Ha-Levi sees Christianity and Islam playing a preparatory role as part of God's mysterious plan for world history. And although the full details of God's plan are beyond human ken, the "nations" about which Ha-Levi speaks cannot be polytheistic idolators. They can be only Islam and Christianity, inasmuch as they are the only ones that claim to be monotheistic. No other nation at that time fits this description. Christianity and Islam are still in a state of monotheistic potentiality, but not monotheistic actuality precisely because they are imperfect. Their religious beliefs and practices are sometimes positive and sometimes negative in the context of pure monotheism.

Indeed, the test of the most effective monotheism is not only the purity of its belief, but also the unified political and personal order it creates. This order is to be singularly monotheistic in its intentionality. Here Maimonides was convinced of the practical superiority of the Torah over any other form of revealed legislation. In addition, Judaism has the longest experience as a monotheistic community. Thus Maimonides continued his discussion of how Christianity and Islam prepare for the Messiah-King and his exalted reign—how they prepare for it but are by no means equal to it:

> How is this so? The whole world is already filled with the words of [their] messiah and the words of the commandments, and these words have spread to the farthest islands and among many obstinate *['arlay leb]* peoples, and they discuss these words and the commandments of the Torah. They say, "these commandments were true *['emet hayu]*, but are already invalid *[batlu]* today, and are not meant to be perpetual *[nohagot le-dorot]*." . . . But when the true Messiah arises and will triumph and be uplifted and exalted, all of them will immediately return and comprehend that their ancestors misled them.[18]

The error of the Christians and the Muslims, for Maimonides, is that they assume that the Torah's authority is passé and that a monotheistic community and culture can be constituted without it. Yet despite their political power—as contrasted with the political impotence of the Jewish people—they have not been able to bring about social and political unity and harmony, which should be the practical outcome of monotheism. It is important to note that Maimonides saw the Messiah-King as a political ruler who will be able, without supernatural intervention, to effect universal monotheism by putting the Torah into full practice and having full authority.[19] He seemed convinced that if the Jews had the necessary political power, monotheism would become the pervasive political norm the world over. The Messianic failure of Christianity and Islam indicates that their versions of monotheism cannot effect a unified and harmonious world order. They have not superseded Judaism, as they themselves claim, but have only diluted its original message and missed its great monotheistic strength. In the days of the true Messiah, however, all the peoples will accept Judaism as the purest and most comprehensive monotheism. Those peoples who have always been pagans will accept it as something genuinely new. Christians and Muslims will return to their true spiritual origins in Judaism. In the meantime, there will be certain insightful individual Christians and Muslims who will anticipate this Messianic reality and convert to Judaism here and now.

## Christian Biblicism

It would seem that Maimonides ranked Islam higher than Christianity on theological grounds. Nevertheless, in at least one specific area, he expressed a preference for Christianity over Islam. When asked whether or not the Talmudic ban on teaching gentiles any more of the Torah than the seven Noahide laws still applied, Maimonides answered in the affirmative on the following grounds:

> It is permitted to teach the commandments to Christians [notzrim] and to draw them to our religion, but this is not permitted with Muslims because of what is known to you about their belief that this Torah is not divine revelation ['aynah min ha-Shamayim] . . . but the uncircumcised ones believe that the version [nosah] of the Torah has not changed, only they interpret it with their faulty exegesis. . . . But when the Scriptural texts shall be interpreted with correct exegesis ['al ha-perush ha-nakhon], it is possible that they shall return to what is best ['el ha-mutab]. . . . There is nothing that they shall find in their Scriptures that differs from ours.[20]

It is clear that Maimonides meant that *anything* in the Hebrew Bible may be taught by Jews to Christians. For the question was: "Is every Jew obligated to refrain from teaching anything [dabar] from the commandments [min ha-mitzvot] except the seven commandments or what is based on them, or not?" Furthermore, "correct exegesis" seems to encompass most of postbiblical Judaism as well. Muslims, as opposed to Christians, having rejected the Hebrew Bible as authentic revelation in its present form, will not be moved by scriptural proofs, as would Christians. Moreover, Maimonides explicitly stated that the purpose in teaching Scripture to Christians is to attract them to Judaism; it is "possible" ('efshar) that they will convert to Judaism if exposed to such proper teaching by good Jewish teachers.

Maimonides regarded both Christians and Muslims as paving the way for the universal reign of the Messiah, which will be coeval with the restoration of full Jewish sovereignty and the full hegemony of the Torah in the land of Israel. This will be the final triumph of monotheism. In his code, Maimonides spoke of the divinely mandated duty of Jews "to force [le-kof] all humankind to accept the commandments given to the Noahides."[21] He emphasized, however, that only those "who want to convert [ha-rotzeh le-hitgayyer]" are to be accepted as full converts to Judaism.[22] Whereas the acceptance of the Noahide commandments is to be seen as a political necessity, something that Jews should enforce whenever and wherever they have the power to do so, conversion to Judaism can only be a matter of inner conviction.

In this responsum about the Christians, Maimonides also emphasized that when Jews have political power over gentiles, study of the Torah by such gentiles should be contingent on their potential for conversion. That can be enforced, but conversion itself can only be a matter of persuasion. Furthermore, Maimonides clearly believed that the conversion of both Christians and Muslims to Judaism is a desideratum that Jews ought to encourage and facilitate as much as possible. Thus in his enumeration of the 613 commandments of the written Torah, which was his preamble to his full codification of the written Torah, oral Torah, and subsequent rabbinic legislation, Maimonides explicitly states:

> The ninth positive commandment is one which He commanded us to sanctify the divine Name, which is what He said, "and I shall be sanctified in the midst of the people of Israel" (Leviticus 22:32). The essence of this commandment which we are commanded is to publicize [le-farsem] this true faith in the world, and we should not fear any harm.[23]

Although Maimonides's traditional basis for this statement is the Talmudic ruling that a Jew is required to die for the true faith rather than convert to *any* other religion, the Talmud does not mention that one is to risk even death in publicizing the true faith *in the world*.[24] It seems, rather, to be dealing with a situation of Jewish passivity—namely, when gentiles come upon Jews who then refuse to convert to *their* faith. Maimonides, conversely, is talking about a situation of much greater Jewish activism; Jews are to take great risks in bringing non-Jews to the true faith. And, indeed, there were great risks for members of a tolerated minority to attempt to convert members of the dominant Christian or Muslim majority to Judaism. Maimonides himself did not live in a

Christian society where what he was advocating would pose a real political problem, but it seems that his questioner about the propriety of teaching Torah to Christians did live in Christendom. Moreover, Maimonides himself was quite encouraging of conversion to Judaism by Muslims. However, his approach to Muslims was different from his approach to Christians. With Muslims, he emphasized philosophical monotheism and how Judaism, both in doctrine and in practice, was its superlative manifestation in human history.[25] With Christians, however, he emphasized the study of the Hebrew Bible, their "Old Testament," as the appropriate means to that end. With Muslims, that approach would do more harm than good. The fact that these Christians are not pure monotheists now, as are the Muslims, does not seem to detract from Maimonides's high esteem for their biblicism.

## Maimonides's Philosophical Constitution of Christianity for Judaism

One could, of course, simply leave the matter at this point and conclude that in terms of his philosophical theology, Maimonides preferred Islamic monotheism over Christian Trinitarianism; but in terms of what we might call his historical theology, he preferred the Christian canonization of the Old Testament over the Muslim rejection of it and total replacement of it as sacred Scripture with the Quran. Nevertheless, we can infer that Maimonides did have a unified approach even here.

As far as Maimonides is concerned, the study of Scripture in and of itself is no guarantee of the philosophically demonstrable monotheism he considers the foundation of all true religion. For the nonphilosophical study of Scripture leads one to accept its anthropomorphism literally. And Maimonides saw anthropomorphism as the ideational corollary of polytheism and the ultimate basis of idolatry. It is the theologically unacceptable limiting of the transcendence of God.[26] Christianity is, for him the prime example of the error of such anthropomorphism, both in its original doctrine of the Incarnation and in its related doctrine of the Trinity. Thus although Christian study of Scripture has immediate practical value, on the theoretical level it requires a philosophic hermeneutic to reveal its esoteric truth (sitray Torah).

On the theoretical level, Islamic monotheism is clearly superior to Christian Incarnationism and Trinitarianism. Furthermore, although historical revelation enabled the people of Israel to emerge as the original monotheistic community, historical revelation is not the conditio sine qua non of monotheism. Because it is immediately true *(ratio per se)*, monotheism can be attained by philosophical means, although when it comes to the apprehension of most people *(ratio quoad nos)*, who are not philosophers, monotheism requires historical revelation.[27] Christians have such a historical revelation. They may not be true monotheists in theory, but they have accepted practical monotheism in their acceptance of the Hebrew Bible as the word of God. In their case, the proper exegesis of Scripture, learned from Jewish teachers, no doubt, will (it is hoped, but not necessarily) correct their faulty doctrines about God. Ultimately, they will be brought by such instruction to Judaism itself. Yet Christianity is only historically derivative and philosophically in a state of potentiality in relation to the truth. Judaism is historically original and philosophically in a state of much greater actuality. That is why it is clearly superior to Christianity. Its superiority lies in the fact that it alone has preserved the correct monotheistic exegesis of Scripture, based on a theology that rejects philosophically untenable Incarnationism and Trinitarianism. Nevertheless, even this new halfway status of Christianity in Maimonides's jurisprudence and in his theology represents a development away from his earlier more negative opinion. He could no longer consider Christianity to be an idolatry like all others, as he once did. The implications of that development must now be explored.

## The Appropriation of Maimonides's Theology

As it stands, Maimonides's view of Christianity does not provide any substantial precedent for the constitution of the Jewish–Christian dialogue in the present and for the future. The dialogue presupposes some point of commonality, some point where Jews and Christians can face each other as equals but without bracketing their respective religious identities, as secularism demands. Yet for Maimonides, as he himself explicitly stated his own position, there seems to be no such point of commonality between Jews and

Christians. Judaism is at all times to be presented as the superior religion. And although, as Maimonides's thought developed, Christianity is no longer seen as idolatry pure and simple, it is still regarded as derivative and potential Judaism at best. Clearly, no true Christian could possibly recognize himself or herself in this characterization. Considering the disputational climate in the Middle Ages, which largely determined relations between religions, Maimonides's view of Christianity can be regarded as, at most, a generous concession to an inferior faith. Furthermore, most Jews—especially those religiously committed to Jewish tradition—would find Maimonides's attempt to turn them into missionaries to the gentiles in general, and to Christians in particular, foreign to their own self-understanding.[28]

However, just as Maimonides himself reworked scriptural and rabbinic materials, finding implications in them that their original authors would not or could not develop, I intend to do the same here with the implications of Maimonides's own theory. This use of Maimonides's view of Christianity is one that he himself would not have made; it presupposes a fundamental change from the scientific paradigm current in his time.[29] The appropriation involves drawing a new implication from Maimonides's apparent judgment of Christian legitimacy, which seems to be based on the criterion of practical reason as distinct from theoretical reason. This requires us to begin by looking at one of the most serious debates in modern Maimonidean scholarship.

Most modern scholars have assumed that Maimonides, as the Aristotelian that he usually was, regarded theoretical reason as superior to practical reason.[30] Practical reason in this philosophical scheme is regarded as the necessary human prerequisite for sustained contemplation, which is the essential activity of theoretical reason. Theoretical reason is superior to practical reason because, for Aristotelians such as Maimonides, it is what we today call astrophysics. Its proper object is the heavens and the principles of causation behind their regular motion. The supreme causal principle—taken as a real prime entity *(archē)*, not just an abstract formula—is God, the Unmoved Mover, the supreme object of cosmic attraction. The teleology seen in the purposiveness of human action is thus not something projected onto the cosmos by humans, but is a human participation in the real purposiveness of the cosmos itself. That is why it is truly natural.[31] Adding to this

Aristotelian metaphysics of teleology the Neoplatonic designation of God as the source of all being, which are emanations from him, gives one the picture of Maimonides's approach to God.

In Maimonides's time, theoretical astrophysics had an inherent spiritual superiority that it could not have today, even in the light of its impressive contemporary accomplishments. The heavens, as the proper object of this physics/metaphysics, were taken to be inherently superior to any sublunar object. Their matter was considered to be essentially different from sublunar matter. The matter of the heavens was seen as being indestructible, and the circular motion of the heavenly bodies was seen to be perpetual motion, as opposed to the linear, terminable locomotion of sublunar entities—that is, the earth and all that it contains. This earthly motion involves constant exertion *(bia)* and is ultimately exhausted.[32] It is weighted down by inertia. That is why Aristotle saw true human fulfillment *(eudaimonia)* in the theoretical life whose proper object is the eternal heavens in orbit around God, their Prime Mover.[33] This theoretical life alone, by virtue of its exalted object, is worthy of ultimate human concern. Aristotle was convinced that this was the only opportunity for the human person to become godlike, functionally at least. All this was possible because the heavens were taken to be the model for human achievement in that they were both intelligible and intelligent. Moreover, their intelligent attraction to God became, for a Jewish Aristotelian such as Maimonides, a philosophical constitution of traditional Jewish angelology.[34] Thus Maimonides, who was often so quick to interpret anthropomorphic scriptural passages figuratively, took the verse, "the heavens declare *[mesapprim]* the glory of God" (Psalms 19:2) absolutely literally.[35]

When Galileo and Newton, however, showed that the laws of physics are no different in the heavens from what they are on earth, that gravity is thoroughly universal, this fundamental distinction between theoretical reason and practical reason lost its original sustaining foundation. The heavens were still intelligible; in fact, their quantification by the increasingly mathematical physics gave them a far more complex intelligibility than they had possessed in Aristotelian/Ptolemaic physics. Nature's intelligibility was understood as being greatly enhanced once it was removed from the earlier teleological limitations.[36] But the heavens were no longer regarded as intelligent. They lost their privileged personal status and ceased to be exemplars for intelligent human action. Man, not the angelic heavens, was now the highest intelligence in creation.[37] And if the idea of creation was rejected, too, then man alone was the highest intelligence qua *causa noumenon*.[38] In other words, human action was now based either on God's will (theonomy) or on man's will (autonomy). Nature was no longer authoritative qua heteronomy.

Building his new metaphysics on what he considered the ruins of the old physics and its metaphysics, Kant concentrated on the new exalted human subject. Since the old contemplative ideal was lost in this fundamental shift of scientific paradigms, Kant could only see practical reason—that is, man's status as a self-legislating moral being—as replacing it as the source of authentic human dignity.[39]

Assuming this line of development in the history of philosophy, it would seem that Maimonides's theories of nature as the norm should have gone the way of those of Aristotle and Ptolemy in this area. That would have been true, indeed, if one continued with the usual assumption that Maimonides followed Plato and Aristotle in constituting the relation between theoretical reason and practical reason as that which is higher over against that which is lower and for its sake. However, at the very end of *The Guide of the Perplexed*, Maimonides seems to remove practical reason from its subordination to theoretical reason. Drawing on a rabbinic interpretation of the scriptural verse "Let not the wise one glory in his wisdom. . . . but let him glory in this, that he understands and knows Me" (Jeremiah 9:22–23), Maimonides writes:

> For when explaining in this *verse* the noblest ends, he does not limit them only to the apprehension of Him, may He be exalted. For if this were his purpose, he would have said: *But let him that glorieth glory in this, that he understandeth and knoweth Me*, and have stopped there; or he would have said: *that he understandeth and knoweth Me that I am one . . .* or something similar.[40]

After indicating the insufficiency of theoretical reason alone, he continues by emphasizing practical reason and excellence:

> But he says that one should glory in the apprehension of Myself and in the knowledge of my attributes, by which he means his actions. . . . In this *verse* he makes it clear to us that those actions that ought

to be known and imitated are *loving-kindness, judgment,* and *righteousness.* He adds another corroborative notion through saying, *in the earth*—this being a pivot of the Law. For matters are not as the overbold opine who think that His providence, may He be exalted, terminates at the sphere of the moon and that the earth and that which is in it are neglected.[41]

More conservative scholars have argued (and I have also argued along with them) that Maimonides is emphasizing here only the importance of practical reason and excellence, that they not be in any way neglected or belittled.[42] He is not asserting that they are superior to theoretical reason and excellence in the full scheme of things. Rather, he is arguing that the two must be closely coordinated in any complete human life and in any complete human society. Here he is seen as closer to Plato's correlation of politics (the sphere of practical reason) and metaphysics than to that of Aristotle.

However, more radical scholars, especially the neo-Kantian philosopher and Jewish theologian Hermann Cohen (d. 1918) and some of his disciples, have insisted that Maimonides is indeed, at long last, emphasizing the theological superiority of practical reason and excellence over theoretical reason and excellence in human existence. In other words, they regard Maimonides here as a proto-Kantian.[43] And if I were inclined in their philosophical direction, I could see a new Kantian designation of a religion of practical reason in which Judaism and Christianity would have a unique historical relationship. Moreover, the old closeness between Judaism and Islam (at least in Maimonides's mind) would be considerably less inasmuch as it is based on theoretical reason as constituted by the old metaphysics. And that theoretical reason on which so much of Maimonides's constitution of monotheism is founded is now seen as having been subordinated by Maimonides late in his theological career. Finally, what Maimonides himself subordinated, Galileo and Newton undercut, and Kant buried.

This is reading more into Maimonides than he himself actually said, however, and it is based on a philosophical perspective that cannot constitute either Judaism or Christianity, each in its own phenomenological integrity. For it takes the practical remnant of Maimonides's philosophical theology as a precedent for autonomous ethics, when actually, by its stress on biblicism, his theology reasserts the traditional idea of a theonomous ethics coming from revelation. This reading cannot constitute an authentic dialogue *between* Judaism and Christianity inasmuch as it places them *into* the context of a larger philosophical whole. And this larger philosophical whole, as we shall see, is one that collapses into secularist universalism, which makes any religion based on historical revelation redundant. Only Maimonides's separation (but not yet his constitution) of practical reason and excellence from their grounding in Platonic political theory and Aristotelian metaphysics, both at the end of the *Guide* and in his responsum on Christianity, is useful for our attempt to constitute the Jewish–Christian dialogue. For in so doing, he was asserting more authentically traditional Jewish doctrine.

Maimonides's appreciation of Christian biblicism, which can be only a practical excellence not intimately related to his notion of theoretical excellence, can now be seen as transcending all of his theoretical philosophy and theology. They can now be seen to be counterproductive, for both philosophical and theological reasons. Practical reason is no longer ultimately justified because it is a precondition for a now impossible contemplative ideal in a philosophical sense. And the primacy of practical reason and excellence has a long tradition in both Judaism and Christianity.[44] Therefore, if it can be shown that the common biblicism of Judaism and Christianity—especially in the doctrines of creation and human nature—provides the basis for a common constitution of morality, then we have a true basis for the Jewish–Christian dialogue. This is my own appropriation of an essential insight of Maimonides in a way that he would not and could not do. I do not claim to be "Maimonidean" in any strictly derivative sense. However, the procedure is justified in that Maimonides—like any authentic theologian—was not devising his own doctrine but interpreting what he understood as Judaism's truth.[45] As such, he was committed to a truth larger than his own thought. Moreover, he donated his own thought about it to an ongoing, often unpredictable, theological process of which we are heirs—albeit not the final heirs. In Chapter 6, I shall further develop this insight of Maimonides and another insight about the possibility of revelation, for the sake of constituting the Jewish–Christian dialogue in the present and for the future.

# 4

# The Quest for the Jewish Jesus

## The New Jesus of Nineteenth-Century Historicism

Until the twentieth century, the history of the Jewish–Christian relationship, in the area of theological discourse, was essentially disputatious. Each community disputed the claims of the other from its own dogmatic base. Even when there was a degree of acceptance of the existence of the other community, that existence was relegated to a decidedly inferior status from that same dogmatic base. No area of commonality was constituted wherein the two communities could face each other as equals.

When Judaism and Christianity faced each other disputatiously, the primacy of the Law in the Jewish relationship with God was inevitably contrasted with the primacy of Christ in the Christian relationship with God. Christians saw Christ as having fulfilled and transcended the Law and as having brought the Church, as the body of Christ, along with him.[1] Jews saw Jesus and his followers as having usurped the Law's proper power and authority for themselves.[2] The contrasting claims were mutually exclusive. It was dogma against dogma with no middle position possible. At this level, the only way out of the impasse would be if the Torah could be regarded as other than "the Law" of Jewish dogma and Jesus could be regarded as other than "the Christ" of Christian dogma. It was nineteenth-century historicism that made such an antidogmatic intellectual move possible.

Christianity, in its German liberal Protestant form, with its desire to be at the cutting edge of the contemporary culture *(Kultur-*

*protestantismus),* became enamored of historicism before Judaism did. Indeed, it set the tone for Liberal Judaism to follow: "Wie es sich Christelt, so juedelt es sich" ("like Christian, so Jewish"), as Heinrich Heine had so accurately quipped. In 1835, the German Protestant theologian David Friedrich Strauss published his revolutionary study, *The Life of Jesus.* In this controversial work, Strauss epitomized what Albert Schweitzer would later call "the quest of the historical Jesus." It was an attempt to discover a human Jesus apart from the Christ preserved and developed in traditional Christian dogma. This reflected historicism's wish to discover the past *wie es eigentlich gewesen* ("as it really was"), as opposed to its preservation within *Heilsgeschichte* ("salvation history"). Of course, as Schweitzer pointed out in his monumental assault on this whole project, it was in truth an attempt to reconstruct a Jesus more acceptable to religion's "cultured despisers" (in the words of the title of the seminal nineteenth-century liberal Protestant work of Friedrich Schleiermacher) rather than an attempt to discover the "original" Jesus, whoever he was. It was, then, a contradiction in terms—namely, a historical attempt to overcome history. Along these lines, Schweitzer wrote: "It is not given to history to disengage that which is abiding and eternal in the being of Jesus from the historical forms in which it worked itself out, and to introduce it into our world as a living influence. It has toiled in vain at this undertaking."[3]

Nevertheless, despite its historiographic flaws, this whole project did have the effect of releasing the person of Jesus from its confinement to traditional Christian dogma for the new, more anthropocentric culture in Western civilization. By so doing, it enabled the adherents of that culture to maintain their link with Christianity's central figure in a radically altered cultural context. And if Christians could now see Jesus in this decidedly new non-Christological light, could not Jews follow suit? In fact, it would be easier for them, inasmuch as they had never been related to Jesus as the traditional Christ of the Church. Could not this de-dogmatized Jesus indeed be the common ground for Jews and Christians in this new age? Could not this new humanized Jesus function for liberals in both communities as a common cultural image still having power and influence? For if Jesus need no longer be the Christ of the Church, then his reconstruction along human lines must inevitably lay renewed stress on his role as a Jewish teacher.[4]

The efforts of Christian scholars to discover a more human Jesus were definitely not part of any attempt to establish common cultural or intellectual ground with Judaism. In fact, the new, more secular emphasis on Jesus's ethical teaching often led to a new denigration of Judaism as "legalism," as opposed to the Christian ethics of love. The old theocentric triumphalism of Gospel over Law, faith over works, now became the new anthropocentric emphasis of ethics over law. In this move, the influence of Kant's subordination of religious doctrine to practical (ethical) reason is apparent and was often explicitly acknowledged.[5] In following this line, liberal Protestant thinkers had a double-pointed prong with which to put down Judaism and Roman Catholicism on the grounds that they were both essentially legalistic ("heteronomous" in the pejorative Kantian sense). Thus Adolf von Harnack, the most important German Protestant Church historian in the late nineteenth century, wrote in his most widely read book:

> Jesus opens up to us the prospect of a union among men, which is held together not by any legal ordinance, but by the rule of love. . . . It is a high and glorious ideal. . . . It ought to float before our eyes as the goal and guiding star of our historical development.[6]

More often than not, the Jewish reaction to this new Christian polemic was to counter its claims to ethical primacy with what were considered to be superior Jewish claims in that area. In making these counterclaims, Liberal Jewish thinkers usually did not deal directly with the newly reconstructed Jesus of liberal Protestant theology. Not requiring a "historical Jesus" for these counterclaims, they could simply address the Christian claims themselves in the present in terms of their immediate truth for the present. Since the contemporary culture asserted that its value lay in its universalism, the project of these Jewish polemical responses to the new Christian triumphalism was to argue that the essence of Judaism was more truly universalist than the essence of Christianity. Harnack's 1900 book, *Das Wesen des Christenthums (The Essence of Christianity)* elicited Leo Baeck's 1905 response, *Das Wesen des Judenthums (The Essence of Judaism)*. Clearly, the establishment of dialogue was not the intent of either liberal Christian or Liberal Jewish thought at this time and place.

## Interest in the New Jesus Among American Reform Jews

It is primarily in early-twentieth-century America, where some Jews and Christians were beginning to develop a new relationship with each other in the context of democracy, that we see an attempt to reconstruct a "Jewish" Jesus as a religiocultural element in this relationship. This seems to reflect the greater inroads of secularism in American society at that time. Furthermore, American Protestantism was far more flexible and less doctrinally closed than contemporary Protestantism in Europe, especially in Germany.

This was primarily a phenomenon among some American Liberal or Reform thinkers, but it could not have taken place without what this American form of Judaism had already inherited from Liberal Judaism in Europe. The old impasse between the two communities was based on the conflict between the Torah as the Law presented by Judaism and Jesus as the Christ presented by Christianity. Therefore, if Jesus had been de-Christologized, as it were, then the Torah had to be delegalized. Along these lines, Liberal Jewish thinkers had constantly emphasized that the very word *Torah* in Hebrew means "teaching" *(Lehre)* or "guidance" rather than "law" *(Gesetz)* in the strict sense of the term.[7] They often pointed out that the equation of *Torah* with *law* was the result of the Greek translation of it as *nomos,* beginning in the Septuagint. By pointing this out as a foreign mistranslation, they hoped to show that they were returning to the purer and more authentic Jewish origins.[8] This was an attempt to separate and elevate the "essence" of Judaism from Halakhah (Jewish law). Thus Kaufmann Kohler (d. 1924), probably the most influential American Reform theologian in the early twentieth century, wrote that "the Torah as the expression of Judaism was never limited to a mere system of law."[9] And in fact, the limitation of Judaism to law in the narrow sense is traceable to Spinoza, who wanted to make Judaism totally irrelevant, and Moses Mendelssohn, who wanted to make Judaism of secondary importance in relation to the new secular society and culture. Those committed to Judaism's primacy, however, would certainly admit that Judaism is more than a system of law—more but not less.[10] Kohler, however, is saying something much more radical. For he continues this thought by speaking of the Torah

> with its twofold aspect as *law* and *doctrine*. As *law* it contributed to the marvelous endurance and resistance of the Jewish people, inasmuch as it imbued them with the proud consciousness of possessing a law superior to that of other nations . . . it permeated Judaism with a keen sense of duty. . . . At the same time it gave rise to ritualistic piety, which, while tenaciously clinging to the traditional practice of the law, fostered hair-splitting casuistry and caused the petrification of religion in codified Halakhah.[11]

Kohler is distinguishing among three elements: doctrine, law, and Halakhah. By "law," he obviously means *moral law* as opposed to "ritualistic piety." Therefore, the essence of Judaism is, for him, ethics and theology (universal law and doctrine), not specifically Jewish law qua Halakhah.

One result of this process of liberalization in Judaism, as developed by some American Reform thinkers, was to see the de-Christologized Jesus as an important *teacher* of this delegalized Jewish *teaching*. He could now be the basis for Christians who had risen above traditional Christian dogma to relate to Jews who had risen above traditional Jewish dogma. In the old disputatious context, Christ kept Christians away from Jews in much the same way as the Halakhah kept Jews away from Christians.

The strategy of the American Reform thinkers who wanted to reevaluate the Jewish relationship with Jesus was to attempt "to divorce the religion of Jesus from the religion about Jesus, and on this basis, to justify his relevance for Judaism."[12] This overall project usually involved several distinct points.

The first point was to raise the question in the light of a new era of tolerance and mutual understanding between Jews and Christians in democratic societies. A number of Reform thinkers emphasized that Jews had been loath to deal with the personality and teachings of Jesus in earlier times because they were so severely persecuted by Christians in the name of Jesus. However, with all the optimism of the *Zeitgeist* of the late nineteenth and early twentieth centuries, it was proposed that the relationship with Christians in general and the person of Jesus in particular need no longer have these painful associations. Thus the Reform rabbi Stephen S. Wise—probably the best-known rabbi in America at the time—emphasized the radically different context for approaching this whole subject. In 1925, before a large audience in Carnegie Hall in New York, Wise enthusiastically endorsed a recently translated Hebrew biography of Jesus by the Jewish historian Joseph Klausner, saying:

> It marks the first chapter in a new literature. Such a book could have never been written a few years ago. You all know what would have happened to the Jew who would have dared to express his opinion based on facts—of Jesus a few years ago. Thank God the time has come when men are allowed to be frank, sincere and truthful in their beliefs.[13]

Even in those optimistic days of the 1920s many Jews in America questioned whether the situation between Jews and Christians had changed all that much. Many critics, including a number of his fellow Reform rabbis (over and above the more predictable denunciations of Orthodox rabbis and Yiddish-speaking secularists), reacted strongly, charging Wise with naiveté, sensationalism, and downright ignorance of past and present Jewish history. For them, Christianity was so saturated with anti-Semitism that Jesus could have no positive connotations for Jews at all.[14] Since the Holocaust, in which so many Christians had acquiesced in Nazi genocide of the Jews and Christian doctrine seemed to lend itself so easily to Nazi distortions, this wariness of a new relationship with Christians—whether directly involving the person of Jesus or not—has increased in many Jewish quarters.

The second point in the attempt to reconstruct a Jewish Jesus closely follows the first. For underlying this optimism about new possibilities for the Jewish—Christian relationship was the fact that the dogmatism, coming from both sides, that had hitherto separated Jews from Christians, was giving way to a new, more enlightened rational universalism. Several liberal Christian publications in the 1920s emphasized that a new relationship was possible because "liberal Jews are showing an appreciation of the teachings of Jesus much more readily than might be expected when it is considered that they are compelled to penetrate to the meaning of his words through the thick maze of prejudices by which so many Christians have obscured that meaning."[15] In other words, "Liberal Jews" and "unprejudiced Christians" can find common ground together when Jesus is seen as superlatively human (contrary to traditional Judaism) and less than divine (contrary to traditional Christianity). In Europe, a Liberal Jewish thinker of the caliber of Hermann Cohen had already made much the same point. But Cohen and others like him in Europe spoke in much more guarded tones. Virtually no reciprocal sentiment was being expressed there by even the most liberal Christian thinkers.[16] In America, as we have just seen, some liberal Christians were talking about Jesus in a way with which at least some Liberal Jews could identify. Indeed, at times they were doing so in an effort to establish a new, friendlier relationship with Jews. This, no doubt, explains why statements of American Jews on this subject were so much more enthusiastic; indeed, some bordered on rhapsody. Here, for example, is Kaufmann Kohler, whose more sober theological position we just examined:

> Judaism . . . waits for the tie when all life's deepest mysteries will have been spelled and to ideals of sage and saint, that of the seeker of all that is good, beautiful and true will have been joined; when Jew and Gentile, synagogue and church will merge into the church universal, into the great city of humanity whose name is God is there.[17]

Clearly, Kohler and others like him did not desire the simple assimilation of Judaism into Christianity, as was charged by a number of Orthodox critics (whose animosity toward anything Reform made their charges less than credible).[18] Rather, they were convinced that a new universal age was at hand—especially in America—and that a new picture of Jesus would be a helpful component therein, just as the old picture of Jesus as the Christ crucified by the Jews impeded any such universalism.

The third point in the attempt to reconstruct a Jewish Jesus, in fact, had little to do with the Jewish–Christian relationship at all. This was the attempt to see a de-Christologized Jesus as a proto-Reform Jew.[19] Just as liberal Protestant thinkers projected Jesus's struggles with Jewish legal authorities (especially the Pharisees) onto their struggles with Protestant orthodoxy (and, even more so, with Roman Catholic orthodoxy), so did some Reform thinkers project Jesus's struggle onto their struggle with that segment of Jewish traditionalism they characterized as "Orthodoxy," with all the negative connotations of that word. Thus, Joseph Krauskopf, a prominent American Reform rabbi around the turn of the century, predicted that "when the Jew shall have completely cast away his obstructive exclusiveness and ceremonialism and the Christian his christology, Jew and Gentile will be one."[20]

This statement seems to be directly in the interest of the new universalism discussed before. However, it appears that Krauskopf's remarks were directed more at his own Jewish parishioners of 1901, many of whom considered themselves emancipated from just such "obstructive exclusiveness and ceremonialism." For the project of Reform Judaism at that time, especially in the United States, where it had become far more radical than its contemporary *Liberales Judenthum* in Germany, was to emphasize Judaism as "Ethical Monotheism" and to eliminate as much of distinctly Jewish ritual as possible, just short of risking confusion with Unitarianism. It is a sign of how assimilated the congregants of these American Reform rabbis had become that this Jewish antitraditionalism had to employ the person of Jesus as one of the main points in its presentation for Jews. In other words, it had to import an image from the non-Jewish culture into what was essentially an inter-Jewish polemic. The conservative Talmudist Louis Ginzberg (d. 1953), after hearing a sermon of a radical Reform rabbi about Jesus, shortly after his arrival in America from Germany around 1900, is reported to have remarked that "he recognized he was in a synagogue," despite the de-Judaized liturgy, "for Jesus was no longer a fashionable subject in church."[21]

If this de-Christologized Jesus is accepted, it marks a break with both Judaism and Christianity to such an extent that dialogue between them becomes a new monologue containing them instead.

The Reform rabbis whose views we have just briefly examined were for the most part popular preachers and not systematic thinkers. Yet some of their points were presented in a more philosophical way by a renowned modern Jewish philosopher, Martin Buber, who made dialogue the very cornerstone of his thought.

## Martin Buber's Jesus

Martin Buber (1878–1965), the best-known Jewish thinker in this century in the West, was often accused by fellow Jews of having more to say to Christians than to Jews. The charge is basically false. Even when Buber addressed himself to the immediate concerns of Christians, he did so as a Jewish thinker speaking out of Judaism as he understood it. Nevertheless, a statement such as the following one about Jesus, if not explored in terms of its proper place in the overall context of Buber's thought, seems to lend credence to this common Jewish charge against him:

> From my youth onwards I have found in Jesus my great brother. That Christianity has regarded and does regard him as God and Saviour has always appeared to me a fact of the highest importance which, for his sake and my own, I must endeavor to understand. . . . I am more than certain that a great place belongs to him in Israel's history of faith and that this place cannot be described by any of the usual categories.[22]

Clearly, Buber does not mean to understand Jesus *either* as he has been understood in traditional Christian theology *or* as he has been ignored in traditional Jewish theology. The rejection of the traditional Christian understanding is explicitly made in his acknowledgment of it and by his reference to his project being "for his [Jesus's] sake and my own." With this juxtaposition of Jesus and himself, Buber replaces the traditional Christian understanding of the relationship with Jesus as being totally subordinate to the relationship with the Christ. For if Jesus is his brother—albeit his "great brother"—then *both* Jesus *and* Martin Buber are similarly related to God, who is now *their* father directly. And with his rejection of the "usual categories" for understanding Jesus, Buber replaces the traditional Jewish understanding of Jesus as a Messianic pretender, one who is to be ignored by Jews because he did not fulfill the Jewish Messianic requirements, especially the political requirements. These requirements were seen by Maimonides and other medieval Jewish authorities as being part of the Law. Hence, in his double replacement of Christianity's and Judaism's views of Jesus, Buber is attempting to transcend the limitations of the respective laws of both communities. His attempted reconstruction of Jesus should therefore be seen in the context of his views on law in general and specifically on the role of law in the human relationship with God.

In an address to a Christian audience, Buber stated of the Law that "my point of view with respect to this subject diverges from the traditional one; it is not a-nomistic, but neither is it entirely nomistic."[23] When considered in the light of Buber's fundamental distinction between the I–thou relationship and the I–it relationship, this statement is not as vague or even as self-contradictory as it appears.

In the I–thou relationship, the bond is directly between two persons; in the I–it relationship, there is a less direct bond between a person and a thing (that is, a subject–object relationship). Law, which as a structured code is expressed in the third person rather than in the second person ("thou"), by its very nature pertains to only the I–it relationship. Buber sees the reduction of the relationship with God to the level for the subject–object relationship as a threat to the integrity of both Judaism and Christianity. He concludes his remarks to this Christian audience with the words, "whenever we both, Christian and Jew, care more for God himself than for our images of God, we are united in the feeling that our Father's house is differently constructed than our own human models take it to be."[24] These remarks to Christians are not to be taken as patronizing or hypocritical, for Buber also said quite similar things to Jews. "Images" and "human models" may particularly suggest a critique of Christianity, especially in its use of visual symbols. However, Buber does not mean just visual images, but any objectification or structuring of the direct relationship with God. In this sense, his critique is directed as much to Judaism as it is to Christianity.

Although Buber regards the directly personal I–thou relationship as the epitome of human consciousness and the *only* authentic relationship with God, he does not utterly reject the impersonal I–it relationship. He is fully aware that in our ordinary conduct in society and the natural world, this relationship is a human necessity, even if not as desirable as the higher I–thou relationship. In fact, his only qualification in this acceptance is that the I–it relationship not be so extended that the I–thou relationship is reduced to I–it's categories.[25] Furthermore, because both relationships involve purposeful human action, both entail commandments. However, because the I–thou relationship is so spontaneous as to admit of no a priori structure, the commandments it entails cannot be known in advance of the direct encounter with the thou, especially the divine Thou. The commandments emerge anew from each new encounter.[26] Commandments here can be only ad hoc.

But because the I–it relationship is fundamentally an ordered one, the commandments it entails must admit of a priori structure; that is, they must be systematized in a code of law. As such, unlike I–thou commandments, I–it commandments are mediated by a universal propositional structure that stands between the person commanding and the person responding. Thus we can see here, paraphrasing the Talmud, the following syllogistic form of an I–it commandment—that is, a law: [27]

1. [All] who rise to pray must do so after having been in a serious frame of mind [*kobed ro'sh*].
2. Being engaged in the study of codified law [*halakhah pesuqah*] is an example of being in a serious frame of mind.
3. Reuben has been engaged in the study of codified law.
4. Therefore, Reuben may rise to pray.

Here we see that before Reuben may address God, he must judge himself as an individual to be a member of the universal class of "serious-minded*ness*," of which being engaged in the study of codified law is one of several accepted examples. [28] For Buber, I–thou directness is precluded by any such universal propositional judgment. Reuben's prayer can be an I–thou act only if it is his immediate second-person response to God's presence here and now alone.

In this sense, then, Buber is neither an anarchist nor an antinomian, at least not in the strict sense. He is not an anarchist because an anarchist denies the validity of *law in society*, regarding even human society as requiring the constant spontaneity of the I–thou relationship. Buber, no doubt, regarded this as dangerous romanticism. [29] He is also not an antinomian in the strict sense because he affirms the normative character of God's presence to human creatures. That presence, for him, is most definitely authoritative. What Buber vigorously rejects, however, is the ordering of the *present* I–thou relationship with God by the structure of law, which can only be *from the past*. [30] In his paradigmatic work *I and Thou*—the work on which everything he subsequently wrote is commentary—he says:

What is it that is eternal: the primal phenomenon, present in the here and now, of what we call revelation [*Offenbarung*]? . . . Man receives, and what he receives is not a "content" [*einen Inhalt*] but a presence *[eine Gegenwart]*. . . . I neither know of nor believe in any revelation that is not the same in its primal phenomenon. I do not believe in God's naming himself or in God's defining himself before man . . . that which reveals is that which reveals. That which has being is there *[Das Seiende ist da]*, nothing more *[nichts weiter]*.[31]

Buber denies neither commandment *(Gebot)* nor law *(Gesetz)*; what he denies is any durable relation between the two. Commandment is only in the realm of the I–thou relationship; law is only in the realm of the I–it relationship. These relationships are distorted only when one constitutes commandment within the I–it relationship or law within the I–thou relationship.

Jesus, for Buber, is a paradigm of the I–thou relationship with God. And since dogma is a form of law, Buber wants to release Jesus from the confines of both Christian and Jewish dogma. The former makes too much of him, and the latter too little. Jesus's personality is directly normative and, therefore, nonsystematic. This is how Buber presents Jesus as such a paradigm:

> And to anticipate and choose an image from the realm of unconditional relation *[der unbedingten Beziehung]*: how powerful, even overpowering is Jesus's I-saying, and how legitimate *[rechtmaessig]* to the point of being a matter of course *[selbstverstaendlichkeit]*: For it is the I of an unconditional relation in which man calls his You "Father" in such a way that he himself becomes nothing but a son. . . . I and You remain; everyone can speak the You and then become I; everyone can say Father and then become son; actuality abides.[32]

In his reflection on Judaism and Christianity *(Two Types of Faith)*, Buber clearly wants to claim Jesus as a primary teacher of the type of Judaism he considers to be a truly authentic response to God's revelation. In so doing, he performs a colossal tour de force by categorizing both Paul and the rabbis as essentially legalists, when they are usually seen as absolute antagonists, resting on antithetical theological foundations. He wants to remove Jesus from their respective authority and traditions and place him together with at least some of the Pharisees, whom he regards as more spontaneously spiritual than either Paul or the rabbis. He calls this "Old Testament belief and the living faith of post-biblical Judaism" as well as "the Jesus of the Sermon on the Mount" as "opposed to Paul."[33]

In discussing Paul's use of the Septuagint translation of Genesis 15:6—"And he believed in the Lord and he [God] accounted it to him [Abraham] as righteousness"—Buber connects Paul with the rabbis as well as with philosophically expressed Hellenistic Judaism:

> Paul found in his Greek Bible at this point something which is immersed in a different atmosphere . . . instead of the divine consideration, deeming, ratification, there has come into being an attributing, a category in *the judicial computation* of items of guilt and innocence against each other and in connexion with this. . . . The rightness of conduct which justifies the individual before God . . . *a limitation* common to Alexandrian and contemporary rabbinical Judaism.[34]

For Buber, Jesus is a representative of one type of Pharisaic piety, whereas "rabbinical Judaism" represents another type. Thus of the Sermon on the Mount, he writes that "it is only the sublimation of a Pharisaic doctrine from a definite point of view . . . the great and vital lineage of this doctrine is unmistakeable."[35]

In what seems a definite reaffirmation of his commitment to Judaism—something required of any faithful Jew when he or she becomes favorably impressed by either Jesus or Christianity—Buber emphasized that he considered the Christian dogma of Christ a barrier to a more direct relationship with God. For all his affinity with Jesus, he is advocating *imitatio Jesu* only within the context of his version of biblical-Pharisaic faith—not as the Church advocates *imitatio Christi* within the context of a new religion. Thus right after quoting the statement of the Swedish Christian theologian Nathan Soederblom that "one may at times feel a doubt about the Godhead of God, but not about the Godhead of Christ," Buber swiftly resounds with the exclamation, "Christ, not God!"[36] Indeed, that is what he must have meant when, in his address to a Christian audience (a missionary society to the Jews, no less), examined before, he spoke about the relationship with God himself as being "differently constructed than our human models take it to be."[37] It seems as though Buber believed that Jesus as the Christ was an obstructive model constructed by Paul and the Church after him. And, of course, halakhic Judaism, too, is such an obstructive human religious construct.

Finally, in an address to a Jewish audience in Israel, Buber assured his listeners that his great concern with Jesus was a Jewish, not a Christian, concern:

> I firmly believe that the Jewish community, in the course of its renaissance, will recognize Jesus; and not merely as a great figure in its religious history, but also in the organic context of a Messianic development . . . whose final goal is the Redemption of Israel and the world. But I believe equally firmly that we will never recognize Jesus as the Messiah Come, for this would contradict the deepest meaning of our Messianic passion.[38]

This is actually Buber's most conservative statement on the subject of Jesus. For if our main interest in Jesus is "in the organic context of a Messianic development," and if the goal of that development is "the Redemption of Israel and the world," then, clearly, the recognition of Jesus's role *in the world,* at least, was already acknowledged by Rabbi Judah Ha-Levi and Maimonides, as we have seen. This acknowledgment was no doubt known to Buber, and was probably known to at least some of the educated people who came to hear him both in Europe and in Israel.

## Law and History

The approach of the American Reform rabbis and of Buber to the person of Jesus are similar in that they presuppose rejection of the Law—Halakhah—as the indispensable norm of the Jewish relationship with God. Both also presuppose that Jesus can be seen apart from his role as the Christ, the indispensable norm of the Christian relationship with God. Both, therefore, attempt to transcend historic Judaism and historic Christianity. They differ, however, in that they approach the person of Jesus from opposite directions.

For the Reform rabbis, the traditional Christ of Christianity is too individual to be normative after the Enlightenment. Following Kant, any norm must be totally generic—that is, able to be universalized—in order to be morally binding. That is the very essence of law. Religion's only rational justification is a moral one; therefore, any religious figure must be an exemplar of universal moral law in order to be authoritative. Indeed, Kant himself characterized Jesus as as perfect an *example* of a man well-pleasing to God as one can expect to find in external experience (for it be remembered that the *archetype* of such a person is to be sought nowhere but in our own reason). . . . And the presence of this archetype in the human soul is in itself sufficiently incomprehensible without our adding to its supernatural origin the assumption that it is hypostatized in a particular person.[39]

As true sons of the Enlightenment, the Reform rabbis wanted to see Jesus as an exemplar of the universal morality they believed to be the essence of Judaism. Thus they understood the relationship with God as essentially lawful, but that law was not the traditional Law of Judaism, which bases its authority on God's revelation to and covenant with the singular people of Israel, beginning at a definite point in history. It goes without saying that that law would not be Christ as the basic norm of the Church as a historical community.

However, not only can this approach to Jesus not be the basis for dialogue between traditional Jews and traditional Christians who insist on remaining related to God within their respective traditions, but it is even questionable whether the universal morality they advocated requires the affirmation of the transcendent God of Scripture at all. It would seem that secularism can posit the same morality they posit, and it can do so without the dogmatic adhesion of affirming the transcendent God of Scripture, whose covenant ensures human freedom but can hardly coexist with human autonomy. In other words, not only is their approach, based as it is on the rejection of the authority of the Law, questionably Jewish, but it is also questionable whether the very God they affirmed is anything more than a projection of human idealism.

Buber's approach, however, might be considered questionably Jewish for the same reason, but it is certain that he affirms the transcendent God of Scripture. His approach, unlike theirs, cannot be accused of being ultimately reducible to secularist universalism. On the contrary, for Buber, the traditional Christ of Christianity is too generic to be religiously normative. In other words, instead of being an I directly related to the divine Thou, Jesus as the Christ has become a he who mediates between the human I and the divine Thou. But an I–thou relationship, by definition, cannot be mediated by anything.[40] If it is, it becomes a less personal I–it relationship. In the I–thou relationship, every I and every thou is an individual suí generis. Each can only address *(ansprechen)* the other. But each cannot express *(aussagen)* the other, for such expression requires placing the other in a general class of some sort, a class whose individuals all bear a common noun.[41] Thus the Trinity, the doctrine that follows from the doctrine of the Incarnation in Christianity, posits a class within the Godhead itself. The divine persons are related to one another, and human creatures must relate to the whole class, not just directly to God the Father.[42]

By so arguing against both Halakhah and Christ, Buber poses a challenge to the constitution of anything generic in the relationship with God in both Judaism and Christianity. As such, his challenge is far more profound than that of the American Reform rabbis. His religious challenge goes to the heart of both religious traditions and their generic institutions. And it is these institutions that must antedate the dialogue if it is to be truly an *interfaith* reality rather than a syncretistic substitute for the respective traditional faiths themselves.

Buber's objection, then, is against a constitutive role for law in the relationship with God in either Judaism or Christianity. It is as much a challenge to Christianity as it is to Judaism, because Christianity did not reject the role of law in the relationship with God. Contrary to the view of romantics in every age, Christianity did not substitute for the Law of Judaism a spontaneous, unstructured faith. Christianity, as well as Judaism, affirms the role of both logos and ethos in the life of faith. Not only is this manifest in Roman Catholic doctrine,[43] but even the greatest Protestant theologian of this century, Karl Barth, confirms the role of structure/law in Christianity: "the Christian life is an ordered life . . . a life determined and regulated by its basis, its power and its essence, and cannot be a life at the mercy of chance or individual will."[44] Barth then goes on to specifically reject "a religious enthusiasm which wishes to submit Christian life . . . simply to the dictates of the conscience of every individual."[45]

Christianity's difference with Judaism is about *which* law most directly relates one to God: the law of Moses and his heirs in the Halakhah, or the law of Christ and his heirs in the Church. Each community regards its law as more directly relational than the law of *any* other community. Furthermore, both Judaism and Christianity affirm that redemption, like revelation, is ultimately dependent on God's grace, not man's works.[46] Works are commanded as a faithful response to the grace of revelation and the grace of redemption hoped for. They are not their causes in any necessary nexus.[47] Not being caused by human works, they cannot be conceived of as human projects whose fulfillment can be calculated.[48]

I cannot counter Buber's challenge from the Christian side of the Jewish–Christian relationship, although I can sense what it might be. I shall counter it instead from within my own understanding of Judaism.

In dealing with Buber's objection, we must look at the relation between commandment *(Gebot)* and law *(Gesetz)*, the relation between *mitzvah* and *Halakhah* as basic categories in Judaism. According to Buber, the two terms are mutually exclusive. A commandment, as a direct call from the divine Thou to the human I, cannot become a law.[49] It cannot become a prescription to a collective entity whose duration is structured by tradition. And a law ceases to be law if taken as a commandment. Franz Rosenzweig, Buber's younger (and more traditional) colleague, basically accepted Buber's distinction between commandment and law, but attempted to argue that the two are not mutually exclusive and that an act can be both commandment and law if one experiences it as revelation.[50] Even Rosenzweig still approached the whole question from a subjective standpoint, however. For him, the question is: How can a person elevate a traditional norm up to the level where that person hears the voice of God directly commanding it to him or her? Conversely, I would approach the question first from an objective standpoint, because my personal experience is not sufficiently foundational to serve as a criterion of what God's commandment is and what it is not. For me, the question is: How does a commandment become part of a legal system (that is, how does it become generic) and still not lose its capacity to carry the original voice of God, who ordained it?

Classical Judaism certainly does not regard commandment and law as mutually exclusive, but as necessary components of a continuum. Therefore, the question to ask is: What would a commandment be without law? I would answer that a commandment without law could only be an individual's relationship with God at a single time and place, a relationship to the exclusion of all others across time and space. But even Buber himself was not satisfied with this reduction, as is evident in his sharp polemic against

Kierkegaard's individualistic constitution of faith.[51] If this is the case, what prevents this private commandment from being in truth a projection onto God of one's own autonomous will? Only a commandment perpetually binding on others as well as on oneself in community—that is, one taken as law—transcends one's private isolation in time and space. And because tradition is an ongoing process, the law cannot be taken as the projection of even the collective at any one time and place. It is constantly adapting itself to speak to unforeseen situations.[52] Here we see the necessarily heteronomous component of the commandment. A Jew is to do God's will in the context of the people of Israel and its authority as it extends across time and space.[53] Thus law is the objective requirement of commandment. Buber, however, confuses revelation, which is public and perpetual *(ledorot)*, with a prophetic oracle, which is individual and temporary *(lesha'ah)*.[54]

The great danger that the commandment behind the law will be silenced has always been seriously recognized. "Those who grasp the Torah do not know me" (Jeremiah 2:8). When this happens, and all too frequently it does happen, when the commandments are seen as law only—"a human commandment learned by rote" (Isaiah 29:13)—when the commandments become solely heteronomous, then the Jewish legal system withers from within. Personal inwardness, an awareness of the *theonomous* character of the Law, is itself a requirement of the Law. However, when the Law seemed to have become a heteronomous institution, God graced the Jewish people with prophets and, later, with pietistic movements, such as Hasidism in the eighteenth century, to act as correctives to this basic distortion of the revealed Torah.[55]

The fundamental question of the Law—of any law, for that matter—is the moral question that only the individual can ask himself or herself: Why am I to obey this law? Why is it good and to be done? To that question, it seems there can be only one of four answers.

1. I obey this law because my own will is the only sufficient good; hence, the law can be obeyed only if I made it (autonomy). The law, then, constitutes my relationship with myself.
2. I obey this law because my own will is not sufficiently good; hence, the law can be obeyed only if it is my participation in a

prior social order (heteronomy qua positive law). The law, then, constitutes my relationship with a collective.

3. I obey this law because my own will and the will of any society are not sufficiently good; hence, the law can be obeyed only if it is my participation in a prior universal order (heteronomy qua natural law). The law, then, constitutes my relationship with nature.

4. I obey this law because the only sufficient good is what the Creator has revealed as good; hence, that law can be obeyed only if it is God's will (theonomy). The law, then, constitutes my relationship with God.

(I eliminate law as obeyed out of fear of external punishment, since that is not a moral motive.)[56]

If the law of the Torah is obeyed because of its intrinsic ground, then that can only be because God's voice is to be hearkened to out of love; that is, all these specific laws are commandments of the beneficent Creator. Not only may one elevate traditional law to the level of commandment, as Rosenzweig insisted in his polemic against Buber, but one *must* do so, for inward intention *(kavvanah)* is what enables observance of the commandment to be a faithful response to the voice of God, who commanded it. "The commandments themselves require inward intention" is the final judgment of Jewish law.[57] Inward intention is the subjective requirement of the commandments, just as normativeness is their objective requirement. Without the inward response of the members of the religious community of Israel, the whole raison d'être of its life is absent, and it degenerates into what Professor Abraham Joshua Heschel used to call "religious behaviorism."[58] Therefore, both the objective and the subjective components of the commandments are required. Without the objective component, the commandments can too easily become individual projections; without the subjective component, the commandments can too easily become mere behavior.

The proper constitution of the commandment is a precondition of the dialogue. It alone enables the dialogue to be an extension of an authentically Jewish and an authentically Christian life. Both Jews and Christians must obey the commandments as God has revealed them to their respective communities. Only fidelity to the commandments enables Jews and Christians to engage in the dialogue with their respective identities intact. They will not then expect from it either too little or too much. Neither the Reform rabbis nor Buber, it seems, actually constituted a durable dialogue between Jews qua Jews and Christians qua Christians.

# 5

# *Franz Rosenzweig's Theology of the Jewish–Christian Relationship*

## The Personal Background

Even more after his death than during his too brief lifetime, Franz Rosenzweig (1886–1929) has become for some of the most theologically serious Jews today the consummate personal model. Through his personal legacy as well as his actual writings, he has become their guide in the rediscovery of the authentic voice of Jewish tradition to speak to our present situation in the world. Rosenzweig was a most extraordinary man, whose impressive legacy must always be treated with utmost respect.

Rosenzweig is a personal model in a number of areas. His rediscovery of a vital Judaism after a semiassimilated, Jewishly indifferent youth, and after a near conversion to Christianity as a young but mature man, has made him the personal model for some Jews who desire to overcome the modern world for the sake of the God of Israel—to overcome it, but not to negate it. His ability to lead a life of faithful courage, joy, and intellectual creativity during an increasingly debilitating terminal illness provides a personal model for some who face similar—though often lesser—terrors in their own lives. His translation (with Martin Buber) of the Hebrew Bible into a new German idiom was a real exegesis—that is, bringing the inner meaning of the text *(exagein)* out of the Hellenized and Christianized "Bible German" of Luther and Mendelssohn and bringing German readers out of their Germanness into the spirit of the Hebrew text.[1] For this reason, he has become a personal model for similarly minded translators today, who see their work as facilitation of a true interaction between the ancient text and the contemporary reader.

Finally, and for our purposes most importantly, his personal dialogues with serious and thoughtful Christian believers, such as Eugen Rosenstock, have been taken by some as the model for the Jewish–Christian dialogue today. In fact, there are those who see contemporary Jewish–Christian dialogue as inconceivable without its Jewish beginnings in Rosenzweig.[2]

There is little doubt that Rosenzweig's dialogues with Rosenstock (an assimilated Jew who had converted to Christianity out of genuine religious conviction at the age of sixteen) were authentic and exciting personal encounters and that they were of a very impressive intellectual quality. There is also little doubt that Rosenzweig's theory of the Jewish–Christian relationship was largely a conceptualization of what emerged from these dialogues. Indeed, it is perfectly consistent for a thinker such as Rosenzweig, who was deeply influenced by Kierkegaard, to write *out of* his own unique experience—"existentially," we would now say—rather than attempt to jump over that personal experience to speak *sub specie aeternitatis*. The question for us now, in our attempt to constitute the Jewish–Christian dialogue in the present and for the future, is whether Rosenzweig is able to give us a theory of the Jewish–Christian relationship helpful for its constitution as an authentic dialogue.

Because Rosenzweig's theory of the Jewish–Christian relationship emerged from his dialogues with Rosenstock (and to a lesser extent with another thoughtful Jewish convert to Christianity, his own cousin Rudolf Ehrenberg), it will be most helpful for us to use as much of the written record of these dialogues as possible as the context for examining key sections of Rosenzweig's central work, *The Star of Redemption*.

This correspondence and the first draft of *The Star of Redemption* were being written simultaneously while Rosenzweig was serving in the German army at the Balkan front during World War I. Eugen Rosenstock (-Huessy) long survived Franz Rosenzweig and was actively cooperative in the publication of their correspondence in the 1930s and the publication of an English translation of the letters in the 1940s, and he expressed his own significant insights well into the 1960s. It is therefore important to compare his views with those of Rosenzweig. If a dialogue takes place between two active participants coming toward each other from different directions, are not the views of both important in assessing the theory that emerges from what took place between them? Indeed, we should here ask again the question I posed as a guiding point in the introduction: Can each participant recognize himself in the characterization of the other one, and can each participant's characterization of himself be seen as consistent with the characterization of his own particular religious tradition?

## The Background of Philosophy

In order to understand Franz Rosenzweig's constitution of the Jewish–Christian relationship, one must first understand how the spiritual journey of his life—in the sense of *itineris mentis*—can be seen as consisting of three stages: (1) the movement from philosophy to revealed religion, (2) the movement to Christianity as seemingly the only viable revealed religion today, and (3) the movement to Judaism as the only viable revealed religion for the Jews and Christianity as the only viable revealed religion for the rest of humanity. The first of these three movements sets the stage and the agenda for the second and third.

Modern philosophy, beginning with Descartes, became more and more preoccupied with the conscious subject as the fundamental point of reference. For Rosenzweig, what began with Descrates culminated with Hegel. It was Hegel who saw the dialectic of history leading toward the full integration of the subject and the object. Rosenzweig was convinced that philosophy, in the sense of an all-inclusive system, was impossible after Hegel because Hegel's system was the system of all systems based on the independence of reason and the drawing of the full consequences of that independence. Revealed religion, which for Rosenzweig is the only religion worthy of the name, seemed to have been drawn into reason's circle by Hegel.[3] However, revealed religion is based on the self-presentation of the transcendent God. In Hegel's system, nevertheless, revelation had to be finally overcome *(aufgehoben)* precisely because the final emergence of reason—or *spirit*, in Hegel's preferred terminology—negates all external transcendence.[4] Reason's final emergence is the ultimate triumph of immanence. Rosenzweig saw this triumph especially in Hegel's total rejection of Kant's notion of the *Ding an sich*, the thing itself, which stands behind all appearances as a surd that reason cannot include in its privileged circle of comprehension.[5] Indeed, for Hegel, in the fulfillment of Spirit/Reason, nothing will be itself *(an sich)* anymore, but everything will function within the conscious whole *(fuer sich)*. Everything will find its full and final place within Spirit/Reason. Thus Spirit/Reason alone will be both by itself and for everything else in itself *(an und fuer sich)*.[6]

Rosenzweig was not so naive as to think that other philosophical systems had not been constructed subsequent to Hegel's and, indeed, in spite of it. In fact, one of his teachers was Hermann Cohen, who had constructed such a system based on a "return to Kant," that is, a return to Kant away from Hegel. However, none of these systems, even Cohen's, had the philosophical appeal of Hegelianism, which seemed to provide the method for dealing with all the concerns of the conscious subject.[7]

There was, however, one concern that Hegelianism, as the epitome of the philosophical project, could not include in its circle—in fact, could not deal with it at all—and that is the unique personal situation of the subject as a mortal being aware of the imminence of his or her own death. Rosenzweig begins his *Star of Redemption* with this unequivocal assertion:

> All cognition of the All originates in death, in the fear of death. Philosophy takes upon itself to throw off the fear of things earthly, to rob death of its poisonous sting, and Hades of its pestilential breath. . . . For indeed, an All would not die in the All. Only the singular can die and everything mortal is solitary. Philosophy has to rid the world of what is singular.[8]

Rosenzweig's direct refusal to accept the supremacy of philosophy has special force when it is remembered that it was written in the trenches by a soldier during World War I—a war in which there seemed to be no reason for the continuing slaughter of so many lives on all sides. Indeed, many have seen this as the historical stimulus for rejections of Hegelian-style idealism as diverse as the theology of Karl Barth, the philosophy of Martin Heidegger (with whom Rosenzweig himself seemed to sense a commonality of concern),[9] and the poetry of T. S. Eliot.

In Rosenzweig's own case, the broken circle of philosophical finality required that the erstwhile philosopher jump out of it, not into the abyss of nihilism but into an affirmation of the very transcendence that Hegelianism was supposed to have finally overcome philosophically. Indeed, Rosenzweig characterized this quest in the words of the ancient Greek philosopher Archimedes, who, in looking for a point to move the whole world, exclaimed, "Give me a place to stand *[dos moi pou stō]!*"[10] And for Rosenzweig, the quest for a transcendent standpoint was best initiated by Kierkegaard, who correlated the mortality of the individual human person with his or her own sinfulness. Thus writing about Kierkegaard, Rosenzweig said "That fulcrum was the peculiar consciousness of his own sin and his own redemption *[eigenen Erloesung]* on the part of Søren Kierkegaard himself or what might ever happen to be his first or last names."[11] It is clear that in identifying with Kierkegaard's quest, those "first or last names" were most immediately meant to be "Franz Rosenzweig." It seems, then, that the quest for transcendence could only be a quest for God to be satisfied by revelation, not philosophy, and to be fulfilled by redemption, not idealism. In the existential sense, Rosenzweig saw the alternatives as faith à la Kierkegaard or nihilism à la Nietzsche, whom Rosenzweig characterizes as "that daredevil climber, up to the steep pinnacle of madness, where there was no more onward *[wo es kein Weiter mehr gab]*."[12] Thus just as Hegel wanted revealed religion to be overcome by philosophy, so Rosenzweig wanted philosophy to be overcome by revealed religion. And just as Hegel saw this overcoming of revealed religion as a going-through-and-beyond, so Rosenzweig saw the religious overcoming of philosophy required at that hour.[13] Almost thirty years later, Eugen Rosenstock characterized the initial intellectual bond between himself and Franz Rosenzweig as "their enmity towards the idols of relativism."[14] By "relativism," he seems to mean any philosophy that subsumes the singular individual into a larger whole rather than directly relating him or her to God, who is the sole transcendent absolute.

## From Revelation in General to Christian Revelation

Because Rosenzweig sees religion as solely that which is founded on revelation, one cannot understand his movement from philosophy to religion as a movement simply from atheism to theism.

Rather, he must be seen as moving from a detached ahistorical position to an affirmation of historical revelation, indeed to that which centers all history. There are here only three possible options—certainly only three possible options for a Western intellectual circa 1913—Islam, Judaism, or Christianity. Not only was Islam not a real cultural possibility at that time and place, but Rosenzweig questioned the originality of the revelation it proclaimed, considering it to be a "parody" of Jewish and Christian revelations.[15] As for Judaism, at that time and place, Rosenzweig regarded it as having lost its power to authentically speak to anyone.[16] He did not yet really know it from within his own personal experience. That left Christianity, and in Eugen Rosenstock, Franz Rosenzweig found a brilliant living witness to the present power of Christian revelation. During their period of intense face-to-face dialogue in the summer of 1913 in Leipzig, Rosenstock intellectually convinced Rosenzweig of the existential untenability of any philosophical relativism and personally showed him the Christian alternative. At that point, Rosenstock brought his Jewish friend to the very threshold of the Church.

Yet it seems as though Rosenzweig had a premonition that Christianity might not be the only alternative; otherwise, why did he insist on postponing his actual conversion until he had spent the High Holy Days of Rosh Hashanah and Yom Kippur as a Jew? Is not this ambivalence evident when, in writing to his cousin Rudolf Ehrenberg (a recent convert to Christianity himself, who must have been happy that his cousin would soon be joining him in the Church), he states, "I could turn Christian only *qua* Jew— not through the intermediate stage of paganism"?[17] Why make a detour through Judaism when it is, at best, only Christianity's preexistent past, a past long overcome? If Rosenstock was to be his model for entry into Christianity, clearly Rosenstock's conversion out of an assimilated family background at the age of sixteen was a conversion from "paganism," not Judaism in any real sense. It seems that Rosenzweig wanted to experience something more direct even than the inspiring example of Rosenstock.

By now it is well known that Rosenzweig, after spending Rosh Hashanah in Kassel with his parents, to whom he announced his plans of imminent conversion (earning a warning from his mother, despite her own lack of observance, that apostates were not welcome in their Liberal synagogue), spent Yom Kippur of 1913 in a traditional synagogue in Berlin. He came away from that experience transfigured.[18] He never mentioned the experience, which is quite consistent with his later view of revelation as an ineffable event.[19] But, clearly, something Jewish witnessed itself to him as revelation, or at least an echo of revelation, something more powerful than what had showed itself in Rosenstock's Christian witness. Rather modestly and cryptically, Rosenzweig simply announced to Rudolf Ehrenberg, "So I remain a Jew *[Ich bleibe also Jude]."*[20] Of course, he did not mean "I am remaining the Jew I have been heretofore." A few years earlier, Rosenzweig had told his parents that "we are Christian in everything" and that "it would have been entirely out of the question" for Rudolf's brother Hans, who had just converted to Christianity, "to become a Jew."[21] By "remaining" a Jew, Rosenzweig meant a return to an archetypal Jewish self within, a self he was just beginning to discover. Indeed, the continuing process of inward discovery would be the leitmotif of Rosenzweig's theory of Judaism and of his role as teacher of similarly returning Jews in Frankfurt-am-Main in the early 1920s.[22] An authentic Jewish voice of incredible power and attraction had been reborn on Yom Kippur of 5674 (1913).

## A New Constitution of the Jewish–Christian Relationship

If Rosenzweig were like so many other "returnees" to Judaism *(ba'alay teshubah)*—the kind we meet more frequently today—he should simply have turned his back on both philosophy and Christianity and quickly worked his way into Judaism by living and thinking the most insular Jewishness possible. Rosenzweig, however, was too much of a philosopher to discard philosophy's methods, if not its pretensions, and he was convinced that a Jew had to look out on the world from his Jewish standpoint and constitute it for himself. And for Rosenzweig, that world could only be a Christian world. Revelation can only be either Jewish or Christian. All other religions are not based on historical revelations, and Islam (most unfairly) he considered a mere parody of Judaism and Christianity.[23]

Rosenzweig chose *The Star of Redemption* as the title for his magnum opus both because of its geometric image of the correlation of six independent points and because of its astronomic image of a body that burns continuously at its core and sends out rays from its surface. These two images of the star supply the bare outline of Rosenzweig's theological scheme in this work.

From the title of his work alone, it is clear that Rosenzweig's ultimate concern is with redemption *(Erloesung)*, for which revelation is its proximate background and creation its more remote background. Creation is constituted as God's relationship with the world; revelation, as God's relationship with man; and redemption, as the final and complete conciliation between God-related-man and God-related-world. This final and complete conciliation, for Rosenzweig, will involve the direct relationship of everything with God.

Although he insists on the basic distinctions among God, man, and the world—as opposed to the Hegelian reduction of all three to Spirit/Reason (the height of consciousness)—Rosenzweig sees redemption as the final and complete overcoming of the present separation between Judaism and Christianity. What he has done, it seems, is to transfer his old Hegelian logic from philosophy to theology. For whereas God, man, and the world are to be taken *an sich* (independently by themselves), creation and, especially, revelation are to be taken *fuer sich*, for the sake of redemption.

It is only against the horizon of redemption that one sees how Rosenzweig constitutes the present relation of Judaism to Christianity and Christianity to Judaism in the context of revelation. Thus Rosenzweig writes:

> Before God, then, Jew and Christian both labor at the same task. He cannot dispense with either. He has set enmity between the two for all time and withal has most intimately bound each to each. . . . The truth, the whole truth *[die ganze Wahrheit]* thus belongs to neither of them nor to us. . . . And thus we both have but a part of the whole truth. But we know that it is in the nature of truth to be im-parted *[zu teil zu sein]*, and that a truth in which no one had a part would be no truth.[24]

And then Rosenzweig goes on to justify these differences, based on the present particularity of truth, stating:

> The "whole" truth, too, is truth only because it is God's part *[Gottes Teil]*. . . . Thus both of us, they as much as we, we as much as they,

are creatures precisely for the reason that we do not see the whole truth. Just for this we remain within the boundaries of mortality. Just for this—we remain *[bleiben wir]*.[25]

Two important points emerge from this last statement. First, God himself, unlike Hegel's God, is still transcendent even at the culmination of history in redemption. God is not overcome at the end.[26] That is why what is for us the *whole* truth is still only God's *part*. Second, Jews and Christians must remain in their particularity until the end. That particularity is not only the general human condition of finite mortality, but also the present limitations of both Judaism and Christianity in relation to the final redemption. This, I believe, is the force of his *bleiben wir*. For it will be recalled that in writing to Rudolf Ehrenberg in 1913 about his not converting to Christianity after all, Rosenzweig simply stated, "Ich bleibe also Jude." When these two statements are now combined, we see that this remaining a Jew for him means both a return to his archetypal Jewish self and a refusal to see either Judaism or Christianity as the redemptive culmination of history. Only at that culmination will Judiasm and Christianity have fulfilled their respective historical roles and both be overcome by a truly redeemed world. For this reason, it is vital that Jews remain Jews and Christians remain Christians until the end. Any attempt to blur this distinction can be regarded as only pseudo-Messianic. It would seem, then, that there is no room in this theological scheme for conversion in either direction—although conversion of Jews to Christianity (as exemplified by Rosenstock and the Ehrenberg brothers) was the far more pressing problem at hand.

Whereas the relation between present revelation and future redemption is symbolized by the geometric image of the six points of the star, the roles of Judaism and Christianity are symbolized by the astronomic image of the star both burning at its core and sending out rays from its surface. For Rosenzweig, Judaism's self-absorption is symbolized by the burning core; Christianity's worldliness is symbolized by the rays sent forth from the star's surface. It is clear that the primacy in this relation belongs to Judaism: "The rays go forth only from the fire; and flow unresisted to the outside. The fire of the core must burn incessantly. Its flame must eternally feed upon itself. It requires no fuel without."[27]

Following the logic of this image, the burning star per se *(an sich)* does not require the rays at all. The star still burns even if the rays are blocked in the process of extension. The rays, however, do require the continuous burning at the star's core. If that fire goes out, the rays cannot by themselves *(an sich)* perform their function, even if nothing external blocks them. They must be related to the core *(fuer sich)*. Stating this relation in another way, Rosenzweig returns once again to geometric imagery and writes about Judaism's "eternal life" and Christianity's "eternal way":

> Eternal life and eternal way are as different as the infinity of a point and the infinity of a line. The infinity of a point can only consist of the fact that it is never erased; thus it preserves itself in the eternal self-preservation of procreative blood. The infinity of a line . . . consists of the very possibility of unrestricted extension. . . . Christianity, as the eternal way, has to spread even further. . . . Christianity must proselytize.[28]

In other words, following this geometric logic, the line presupposes the point, for a line is an infinite extension of points; but the point does not presuppose the line. It is self-sufficient.

Over and over again, employing all sorts of imagery, Rosenzweig emphasizes Jewish inwardness and the absence of an authentic Jewish need to expand in numbers or in earthly power. Judaism's self-sufficiency is by no means absolute, however, but is so only in relation to Christianity. Christianity has not overcome Judaism. The tour de force here is the way in which Rosenzweig counters Christian claims that Christianity has overcome Judaism, that is, "fulfilled" its promise in such a way that the continued and separate life of the Jewish people is not necessary. Yet even though Judaism might well be self-sufficient in relation to Christianity, it is not self-sufficient in relationship with God or in terms of the total redemption of the world.

Rosenzweig's notion of Jewish self-sufficiency as a "community of blood" *(Gemeinschaft des Bluts)*[29] is not to be confused with racism, which regards such a racial bond as absolute.[30] This elected blood community is eternal only because of its relationship with God, who ever transcends it and the nations alongside it. Thus a passage that states "it is this rooting in ourselves, and in nothing but ourselves, that vouchsafes eternity"[31] should be seen in the light of a passage that states:

The Jew alone suffers no conflict *[Zwiespalt]* between the supreme vision which is placed before his soul and the people among whom his life has placed him. . . . The Jew's myth, leading him into his people, brings him face to face with God who is also God of all nations. The Jewish people feels no conflict between what is its very own *[dem Eigensten]* and what is supreme *[dem Hoechsten]*; the love it has for itself *[zu sich]* inevitably *[unmittelbar]* become love for its neighbor.[32]

Jewish inwardness and unworldliness are the result of the continuing Jewish relationship with God. That is where Judaism's self-sufficiency lies. Just as the Lord is the only one *(einzig)* for the Jewish people, so the Jewish people is the only unique *(einzig)* people for God.[33] About the Lord, it is stated, "Hear O Israel: the Lord is our God, the Lord alone *['ehad]*" (Deuteronomy 6:4); about Israel, it is stated, "Who is like Your people Israel, a unique nation *[goy' ehad]* on earth" (1 Chronicles 17:21). This similar meaning of the Hebrew word *'ehad* is employed in a well-known passage in the Talmud. There it is noted that the *tefillin*, which a Jew binds on his arm and head daily—and which have been seen as a symbol of Israel's being forever bound to God—contain these words (among others): "the Lord alone." In a bold metaphor, it is asserted that God, too, binds himself to Israel with *tefillin*. And in God's *tefillin* are found the words, "a unique nation on earth."[34] Whether Rosenzweig, whose knowledge of rabbinic sources at this time was still small, knew this particular Talmudic passage, I cannot say. But he has, nevertheless, presciently paraphrased it.

Picking up once more Rosenzweig's comparison of Judaism to a spatial point and Christianity to an extending line, one can see the geometric function of the point as immediate, whereas the line's function is mediated; it must go through a series of points in its extension. That is its very definition. Thus Rosenzweig characterizes the way of Christianity as "centrifugal."[35] Rosenzweig uses this logic to characterize the Jewish relationship with God as immediate, whereas the Christian relationship with God is mediated by Christ. Here in *The Star of Redemption,* he is again conceptualizing what he originally asserted in dialogue, both with Rudolf Ehrenberg and with Eugen Rosenstock.[36] To Ehrenberg, he wrote in 1913, after having decided to "remain" a Jew:

We are wholly agreed as to what Christ and his church mean to the world: no one can reach the Father save through him. No one can reach the Father! But the situation is quite different for the one who does not have to reach the Father because he is already with him. And this is true of the people of Israel (though not of individual Jews).[37]

By "individual Jews," he may very well have meant Ehrenberg himself (and Rosenstock), that is, a Jew by blood who went out looking for a mediated relationship with God in Christianity, when God was already his Father immediately simply by virtue of his birth as a Jew.[38]

Here Rosenzweig is basically asserting—although I am reasonably sure that at this stage of his education in Judaism he was yet unaware of the precedent—what Rabbenu Tam had asserted more than eight centuries earlier, that Christians are monotheists even if their monotheism is mediated. For them, this is acceptable; for Jews, it is not. Rosenzweig's Jewish instincts again made him prescient, as it were, about the actual content of Judaism, so much of which he was later to discover for himself firsthand.

To Rosenstock, whom Rosenzweig no doubt regarded as a more powerful Christian adversary than Ehrenberg, he was even more pointed. To him, Rosenzweig wrote several years after 1913 that

> any and every Jew feels in the depth of his soul that the Christian relation to God . . . is particularly and extremely poverty-stricken and ceremonious; namely, that as Christians one has to claim from someone else, whoever he may be, to call God "our Father." To the Jew . . . what need is there for a third person between me and my father in heaven?[39]

And finally, in *The Star of Redemption,* most pointedly, he attributes the Christian need for the intermediacy of Christ in the God—man relationship to the fact that Christianity is still "on the way"; that is, it has not yet overcome the pagan origins of its gentile adherents.[40]

## The Relationship Between Judaism and Christianity in the Present

The relationship between Judaism and Christianity on the horizon of the final redemption will be a relationship in which both will converge and be simultaneously overcome.[41] Their differences will be negated in a third, as yet unemerged, historical reality—indeed, in history's very culmination. It is clear, however, that the distinction between the two communities must be maintained until then. However, for Rosenzweig, even here and now their roles are not totally separate. Each community performs a vital function for the other, even in the preredeemed world.

Concerning Judaism's vital role for Christianity, whether addressing his Christian dialogue partners directly or only in thought, Rosenzweig is quite explicit. By remaining faithful to its own immediate relationship with God, Judaism saves Christian expansion from degenerating into pagan conquest, that is, expansion for its own sake alone.[42] In order for the rays of the star to maintain their connection with their original source in Jewish revelation and their final goal in redemption, there must be a living Jewish people with its living Judaism. Without Judaism as Christianity's everpresent basis, the rays of the star will be unable to continue shining. They will be like starlight we see today, which astronomers tell us is from stars that died tens of thousands of years ago. Rosenzweig emphasizes, therefore, Christianity's continuing need for Judaism. It cannot overcome Judaism without destroying itself. Christianity has a true need to affirm Jewish transcendence. Without that affirmation, Rosenzweig warns that "this champion certain of victory, always faces the danger of having the vanquished draw up laws for her. Sent to all men, she must nevertheless not lose herself in what is common to all men."[43]

Playing on the Christian doctrine of the Trinity, Rosenzweig sees Christianity as entailing a threefold danger from which only a living Judaism can save it:

> That the Spirit leads unto all ways and not God; that the Son of man be the truth, and not God; that God would become All-in-All and not the One above all—these are the dangers. . . . Thus they are dangers which Christianity never overcomes [*nie hinaus kommt*]—spiritualization of God, apotheosis of man, pantheification of the world.[44]

Judaism alone saves Christianity from gnosticism in all its guises.[45] Gnosticism, by asserting that earthly existence is unredeemable, so spiritualizes the Christian Gospel as to take it right out of history. (Jewish gnosticism has the same effect on Judaism.) Gnosticism is the ultimate denial of creation as God's relationship with the world and revelation as God's relationship with mortal human creatures in history.

To be sure, the Church has recognized the danger of the gnostic distortion of its truth, especially when it rejected the early attempt of Marcion and his followers to remove the Hebrew Bible (the Church's "Old Testament") from the Christian canon.[46] However, for Rosenzweig, Christian biblicism alone is not enough. For even if the Church retains the Old Testament as its sacred Scripture in its liturgy and authoritative teaching, without the living presence of the Jewish people and its Judaism, the message of the Old Testament and the Gospel accounts of the Jewish Jesus can be quickly allegorized away.[47] In fact, Rosenzweig goes so far as to assert that the Jews are the closest link Christians have to Christ himself. Without that connection to the real Jesus, paganism reclaims Christians back to their natural gentile origins.[48] Rosenzweig emphasizes that regression by showing the ambivalence of the Germans about their new Christian identity—an ambivalence about whose eruption into nihillistic violence and extermination shortly after his death in 1929 Rosenzweig was once again uncannily prescient:

> The nations have been in a state of inner conflict ever since Christianity with its supernatural power came upon them. Ever since then, and everywhere, a Siegfried is at strife with that stranger, the man of the cross [des gekreuzigten Mannes], in his very appearance so suspect a character. . . . This stranger who resists the continued attempts to assimilate him to that nation's own idealization [Wunschbild].[49]

That this Christian-but-still-pagan ambivalent consciousness should erupt in hatred of the Jews is, for Rosenzweig, to be explained by the fact that it is the Jewish source of Christianity that forces the Christian to turn away from his naturally pagan instincts.[50] For this reason, Christian hatred of Jews seems inevitable at any point short of the final redemption. Rosenzweig apparently believed that Jews have to accept that pre-Messianic historical fact. The service that Judaism performs for Christianity must go largely unappreciated; indeed, Jews can hardly expect any such appreciation while Christianity is still "on the way," a way that is not at all smooth but involves constant obstacles to be overcome.[51]

Rosenzweig is not as explicit in spelling out Christianity's present necessity for Judaism as he is in spelling out Judaism's present necessity for Christianity. Perhaps this is because in *The Star of Redemption* and in his earlier letters, he was still addressing himself to Christians, especially to Jewish converts to Christianity such as Rudolf Ehrenberg and Eugen Rosenstock. He had to argue against their triumphalist Christian notion that even Jews could find an authentic relationship with God in the present only in Christianity. Nevertheless, there are some less explicit passages in which Rosenzweig does see Christianity as a necessity for Judaism.

In *The Star of Redemption,* Rosenzweig seems to set the theological stage for Jewishly affirming Christianity's present necessity in the following passage, heavy with Hegelian overtones:

> What does this mean to root one's self? It means no more and no less than that one people, though it is only one people *[als Einzelnes],* claim to constitute All. For whatever is individual is not eternal because the whole *[das Ganze]* is outside it. It can only maintain its individuality *[Einzelheit]* by becoming a part of that All. An individual entity which in spite of its individuality strove for eternity, would have to take the All into itself.[52]

Following Hegel quite closely, Rosenzweig here refuses to acknowledge the self-sufficiency of any particularity in history. Either it must be included in some greater whole, or it must become a greater whole itself, thereby including everything else in it. Rosenzweig is too much of a Hegelian to accept any permanent dualism in history. In line with the second option, of becoming itself a greater whole, Rosenzweig emphasizes the status of the Jewish people as the unique people *(eine Volk)* rather than as a nation among others *(Volk unter Voelkern).*[53] In this sense, he is emphasizing the key designation of Israel as the unique people of God in the Sabbath afternoon prayer *(tefillat minhah),* where in the whole service "the fervor which compels the coming of the Kingdom is at its greatest intensity."[54] Within this intensity, Rosenzweig asserts that we know "the eternal union of God with his people and of his people with mankind."[55] Earlier, Rosenzweig had emphasized the incompatibility between eternity and mere particularity:

> But this does not hold when a people refuses to be merely an individual people and wants to be "the one people" *[das eine Volk].* Under

these circumstances it must not close itself off within borders, but include within itself such borders as would, through their double function, tend to make it one individual people among others. And the same of its God, man, world.[56]

In other words, Judaism must reconstitute the basic relationship among God, man, and the world. In this reconstitution, Judaism is now "man," and Christianity is "the world." And both are related to God by virtue of their respective revelations. The Lord is thus God of all nations.

The necessity of Christianity for Judaism, then, is that it has the capacity to include all nations in the revealed relationship with God. Judaism cannot perform this redemptive function for itself. Were it to try to do so, it would lose the unique intensity of its present relationship with God. This is the main thrust of Rosenzweig's ongoing polemic with Liberal Judaism, as epitomized by the universalism of Hermann Cohen. By attempting to move from the uniqueness of Judaism to the generality of the world, it inevitably loses itself in apologetics.[57] It is not Judaism's task to engage in disputes with Christianity based on universalist criteria; it is Judaism's task to recognize the indispensable universalistic ministry of Christianity for the sake of the final redemption. By moving from paganism to the more immediate relationship with God, Christianity already contains the world within itself. Its worldliness is authentic as long as Judaism holds its beginning and end with God for it. That same worldliness, however, would be inauthentic for Judaism because it would involve the incorporation of the world per se *(an sich)* into itself, and that is something that was not originally there or meant to be there.

## Is Rosenzweig's Jewish–Christian Relationship a Jewish–Christian Dialogue?

In Rosenzweig's constitution of the Jewish–Christian relationship, the particular origin (Judaism) of a universal process retains its particularity until the separation between the two is overcome at a higher level—a higher level as yet wholly future. That future point will be redemption. The logic here, as we have seen, is obviously Hegelian. Three questions about this relationship must be answered:

1. Can Christians recognize themselves here as authentically characterized by this Jewish theologian?
2. Is the emphasis on Jewish unworldliness valid, especially for purposes of the present and the foreseeable future?
3. Did Rosenzweig himself truly intend the relation he constituted between Judaism and Christianity to be a dialogical relationship?

Rosenzweig's contrast of the elements to be related is based on Jewish unworldliness as immediately opposed to Christian worldliness. And even though he was fully aware that much of "the world" is not Christian but pagan, he seems to have seen the world becoming more Christian as Christianity continued its mission to the world.[58]

Was this historical judgment true in 1916? Is it true now? Christians themselves have responded negatively to Rosenzweig's assumption that Christianity is less particularistic than Judaism. Furthermore, the world is not becoming more Christian but less so. Worldliness, which for us now means secularism, is equally threatening to both Christianity and Judaism. Rosenzweig apparently overemphasized Christianity's present historical power and influence. Indeed, in his writings, he often uses the terms *Christentum* ("Christianity") and *Christenheit* ("Christendom") interchangeably. They are, however, historically distinct. *Christendom* is the term characterizing European civilization as a Christian civilization, whereas *Christianity* is the religion based on the faith assumption of God's incarnation in the body of a particular man, Jesus of Nazareth. Whereas Christianity transcends European civilization, which is but a moment in history, Christendom does not. There is no more Christendom, neither is it all likely to reemerge in the world at hand.[59] Dorothy Emmet, translator of the Rosenzweig–Rosenstock correspondence into English, wrote in her preface, "It was perhaps easier to see Christianity in this way in 1916 than in 1945. Today Christianity also is being persecuted in many parts of the world, and we can nowhere speak with confidence of its triumphant progress toward the conquest of civilization."[60] A few years after that, Stalin asked his paradigmatically modern question, "How many divisions does the Pope have?" However, even in 1916, Eugene Rosenstock himself was no more optimistic about the power of Christian worldliness. Rather, he pointedly wrote back to Rosenzweig the following: "So beside Christianity and Judaism there stands today a third factor, which has come down from Rome, namely, the imperialism of the nations. . . . I charge you with confusing Christianity with the nations."[61] And Rosenstock indicated shortly before this retort to Rosenzweig that "this paganism is now dominant in all the Churches, insofar as science aspires to live 'without presuppositions."[62] Since faith is *the* great presupposition, the scientific attitude, when seen as proceeding from a neutral stance, threatens the religious communities themselves from within. And it is the scientific attitude, understood as such, that secularism has always claimed as its true foundation. Rosenstock and, to a lesser extent, Dorothy Emmet thus rightly accuse Rosenzweig of having misread the historical times: the trend is away from Christian faith (or any faith, for that matter), not toward it. Christianity, like Judaism, can only nurture its own singularity and hope that it will not be engulfed by secular worldliness.[63]

Finally, can any Christian be expected to accept the primacy of Judaism for his or her own relationship with God? If a Christian were to accept this primacy, then why should that Christian not actually become a Jew? Conversion to Judaism is always a possibility, but it is a possibility Rosenzweig does not even mention. How could he? Such mention would provide a strong counterexample to his own elaborate theological constitution of the Jewish–Christian relation. It is perfectly understandable that the Christian Rosenstock must react most negatively to the Jewish–Christian relation that Rosenzweig is suggesting. In fact, in the same letter in which he identifies contemporary paganism with what we call "scientism," he writes, "Do you understand why I am so far from finding in Christianity the Judaizing of the pagan? That from which Christ redeems is exactly the boundless naive pride of the Jew, which you yourself exhibit."[64] No religion can maintain itself very long, demanding as it must the absolute loyalty of its adherents, and at the same time regard itself as in any way subordinate to another religion. Rosenstock's reaction thus seems far more justifiable than Rosenzweig's suggestion to him or to any Christian.

Rosenstock was highly critical of Rosenzweig's seeming equation of Christianity with worldliness, but both he and Rosenzweig were negative about Jewish attempts to be worldly, which for both

of them meant Zionism. Rosenstock sees Zionism as a real threat
to the very Jewish-particularism-in-relationship-with-God that Rosenzweig had been so strongly asserting. For him, it would seem,
Zionism is nothing less than Judaism's own pagan potential.[65]
Moreover, it would also seem that Rosenstock's point is more for
the sake of countering Rosenzweig's theology than out of any concern for Judaism per se. Rosenzweig, it is important to consider,
does not reject this basic assumption. He only claims that Rosenstock has overestimated its danger for the survival of Judaism. For
him, Zionism is only something "that belongs throughout to the
series of messianic movements that are eventually being produced
in Judaism, all more or less grand self-deceptions."[66]

As Rosenzweig's own Jewish identity developed, his attitude
toward Zionism changed from outright rejection to ambivalence.[67] Nevertheless, for our concern here, Rosenzweig's rejection
of Zionism is a necessary corollary of his basic distinction between
Jewish self-sufficiency and Christian worldliness. For this reason,
his anti-Zionism is almost the opposite of that of his teacher, Hermann Cohen, and most of the other adherents of Liberal Judaism
at that time. They rejected Zionism as contrary to Judaism's true
universalism, whereas Rosenzweig—and here he was remarkably
close to many of the Orthodox—rejected it as contrary to Jewish
particularism. That is, it was a Jewish attempt to assimilate collectively rather than individually, to be a nation like all the other
nations of the world.[68]

Rosenzweig was correct that Zionism—in both its secular and
even its religious forms—can present itself as a pseudo-Messianism.
It can indeed attempt to be seen as the final redemption or its
immediate and inevitable potential. One can have strong theological objections to such pretense without, however, being at all
opposed to the state of Israel.[69] Nevertheless, Zionism can also be
seen, as it was by Rosenzweig's later colleague Martin Buber, as a
unique opportunity for the Jewish people to nurture and develop
its own singular life and destiny. As Buber put it at the beginning
of his main work on Zionism, "So long as one understands 'Zion'
simply as one more nationalistic idea, one does not recognize its
unique meaning."[70] Furthermore, to simply leave the worldliness
of politics to the Christians, or to any other group of non-Jews,
for that matter, is an invitation to be dominated and, thus, a threat

to the very physical survival of the Jews themselves. The near destruction of all of European Jewry in the middle of this century readily testifies to just that.

In our own time, as distinct from Rosenzweig's Zionism's project of a Jewish state in the land of Israel has become a historical reality. It is a fact for the Jews and for anyone else who is related to the Jews in any way. No one, whether Jew or non-Jew, can now speak of Jewish unworldliness and still be speaking about the reality and the real concern of the overwhelming majority of the Jewish people today. That being the case, since Rosenzweig's characterization of Christianity-in-relation-to-Judaism is dependent on this assumption of Jewish unworldliness, its rejection largely eliminates his constitution of the Jewish–Christian relationship in the present and for the foreseeable future.

Finally, it should be pointed out that although some later Jewish and Christian thinkers have seen the Rosenzweig–Rosenstock exchanges as being the model for Jewish–Christian dialogue, neither Rosenzweig nor Rosenstock was at all optimistic about them. Rosenzweig spoke about the "enmity" *(Feindschaft)* between Judaism and Christianity at all times before the final redemption.[71] Moreover, he denies any positive area of common interaction between the two faiths in the present. And is not the constitution of such a common area alone what makes dialogue possible? Indeed, when discussing what connects Judaism and Christianity, Rosenzweig inevitably uses the word *Verhaeltnis,* which denotes a formal relation, rather than *Beziehung,* which denotes a direct personal bond.[72] Thus even in his exchange with Rosenstock, Rosenzweig explicitly denies this common presupposition of Jewish–Christian dialogue per se:

> The art of the Synagogue does not enter into living relation with *[lebendigen Zusammenhang mit]* other art, nor Jewish theology with Christian theology, and so on; but Jewish art and theology, taken together, build up the Jews into a united whole and maintain them in their form of life . . . and only then do they work as a ferment on Christianity and through it *[durch es hindurch]* on the world.[73]

This passage should be compared with a passage in *The Star of Redemption* in which Rosenzweig sees any such "living relation" *(Zusammenhang*—literally "hanging together") only within the organic Jewish community *(Gemeinde),* specifically in the close relationships between the generations.[74] Clearly, relationships within the community are closer than those between communities, but Rosenzweig seems to deny *any* direct commonality between Judaism and Christianity in the present.

Rosenstock, too, did not see his exchanges with Rosenzweig, personally significant as they were for both men, as a dialogical model for Jews and Christians per se. In an introduction to the original German edition of the letters, published in 1935, he emphasized that such an atypical exchange would never be possible in the present. Furthermore, he characterized their face-to-face exchanges in the summer of 1913 in Leipzig as not between Judaism and Christianity at all, but between revelation-based faith and philosophical faith.[75] Finally, in 1968, for an introduction to a new publication of the English translation of the letters, Rosenstock admitted that "a Jew and a Christian momentarily put aside their insoluble enmity," and that "in their enmity towards the idols of relativism . . . the Jew and the Christian found a cause in common."[76] In other words, their coming together was because of a common enemy rather than because of a common position.

In the present, Judaism and Christianity still have a common enemy. Secularism, by proclaiming its self-sufficiency, makes no place for either Judaism or Christianity. However, an authentic dialogue must have a common-situation-between and not just a common-threat-without. It must have this if it is to be sustained and to sustain the engagement of its participants. For this reason, what transpired for Rosenzweig and Rosenstock together is an important *via negativa* for Jewish–Christian dialogue itself. It is an important ground-clearing operation because, after all the historical accidents are put aside, the precariousness of both Judaism and Christianity in the secular world is still much the same for us now as it was more than seventy years ago for them. However, clearing ground is not yet standing up and positively building something new together. If there are Jews and Christians who believe in that possibility, then they must go beyond what Franz Rosenzweig and Eugen Rosenstock were able to accomplish in their brief time together.[77]

# 6

# A New Theology of Jewish–Christian Dialogue

## The Covenanted Community and the World

The authentic relationship between Jews and Christians in the dialogue is a relationship between persons whose faith is already nurtured from within their own religious communities.[1] No matter how visible the life of that singular religious community is to others, it can never be for an outsider what it is for an insider. For that life can be directly understood only by one who has made a total commitment to be one with that historical community. That is its only true context. It can only be an act of *insight*. Thus no Christian, no matter how well versed in Judaism, can ever directly understand the covenantal intimacy of the Sabbath without first literally becoming a Jew.[2] Similarly, no Jew, no matter how well versed in Christianity, can ever directly understand the covenantal intimacy of the Eucharist without first literally becoming Christian. These areas of covenantal intimacy lie too far within for them to be jointly perceived by jews and Christians who share a border. The respective laws of Judaism and Christianity have recognized this elementary fact and have ruled accordingly.[3] For this reason, Jews are to be related to other Jews more intimately than they are to be related to non-Jews. The former relationship is more singular; the latter, more general.

An analogy with the difference between a person's relationships with his or her own family and those with the larger society might prove useful for purposes of description. Originally, one's immediate family is one's world. Every adult man is often seen as one's father; every adult woman, as one's mother. When one learns to distinguish between his or her own father and all other men, between his or her own mother and all other women, then the singular relationship with one's own family becomes more intense precisely because it is differentiated against a more general human background. And just as one's own familial relationship calls for the constitution of the more general background of the human world, so one's own covenantal relationship calls for the constitution of the more general background of the human world that is not part of one's own covenant. This is how Jews can intelligently constitute the role of Christians for themselves and how Christians can do likewise for Jews. Each is part of that larger background for the other. However, because I can see only from the perspective of my own Judaism—that is, the Judaism in which I am a total participant—I can attempt this theological constitution only from the Jewish side of the dialogical relationship. And I can only hope that in my understanding of Christianity, Christians will recognize themselves in a way they can accept. My task, then, is to see how Christians stand before me against the wider background of the world.

## The Logic of the Relation of the Singular and the General

At this point, theological reflection involves the logic of the relation between the singular and the general. I use these terms rather than the more usual *universalism* and *particularism* because they are more elemental, and therefore their use entails less philosophical prejudice than the familiar universal–particular dichotomy. In reality, of course, the relationship is between the more-singular and the more-general; no real singularity is without some generality, and no real generality is without some singularity. There are a number of ways to see this relation. Our desire for the constitution of the dialogue in the present and for the future will determine which way is to be preferred.

First, the relation between the singular and the general can be seen whereby the general is governed by the singular. The history of Roman law provides a good example. Originally, Roman law was the business of those who were part of the city of Rome. It was the *ius civile*, the city's law. When Rome extended its range of political dominance over areas that could not be included in its own polity directly, lest that polity's power become too diluted, it developed the institution of *ius gentium*, the law of nations. This law was more general than the *ius civile* because its subjects were persons under Roman rule but with whom Roman citizens were to be less intimately related. Because they inhabited the same political and economic world as the Roman citizens, some sort of relationship had to be constituted with these resident-aliens *(peregrines)*, but it had to be more general in the interest of maintaining Roman dominance over foreigners.[4] What we see here is the triumphalism of the singular over the general in such a way that, at best, these foreigners are formally tolerated by the ruling power. As the Roman imperial experience showed more and more clearly, the subtleties of adjudicated tolerance were often more politically expedient than simple conquest. Nevertheless, the true integrity of these "others" was not the concern of the political system that enacted *ius gentium*. For it was a Roman official who adjudicated this law *over* these resident-aliens.

This type of political arrangement was not at all unique to the Romans. However, because Roman imperialism has so thoroughly influenced subsequent Western civilization, it is useful for us to see how this type of triumphalist logic influenced Christian toleration of Jews in the Middle Ages, when Christendom was considered the legitimate continuation of the *pax romana*. And although Jews did not actually have political control over Christians, the same type of logic can be seen in those interpretations of the Noahide laws that regarded them as laws that Jews are to force all others to accept if and when they have the political power to do so.[5] These interpretations also entailed that the adjudication of these laws remain within Jewish control.[6] Furthermore, although it can be noted here only en passent, now that Jews do have actual political control over non-Jews (including many Christian Arabs) in the state of Israel, this type of imperialist tolerance is being advocated in some Jewish circles. Needless to say, the advocates of this approach are hardly those involved in our concern for Jewish–Christian dialogue. Finally, this relation of the singular over the general never offers the subjugated party any reasons for accepting the authority of the singular conquerer other than the fact of conquest itself. Neither the interests of dialogue nor even more general interests of world peace are at all served by this approach. On the contrary, it poses a great danger to both.

Even when actual political dominance of Christians by Jews was not being advocated, there were still those who saw Christian moral and religious legitimacy as derived from Judaism and therefore subordinate to it. The important eighteenth-century German halakhist Rabbi Jacob Emden (d. 1776) argued for the legitimacy of Christianity (for non-Jews, of course) by stating:

> The writers of the Gospels never meant to say that the Nazarene came to abolish Judaism, but only that he came to establish a new religion for the Gentiles from that time onward. Nor was it new, but actually ancient; they being the Seven Commandments of the sons of Noah, which were forgotten. The Apostles of the Nazarene established them anew.[7]

Emden's positive view of Christianity appeared in the context of a polemic against the followers of the false messiah Shabbtai Zevi (d. 1676), where he says, in effect, that *even* Christians are more law-abiding than they. He might be exaggerating somewhat.[8] Nevertheless, Emden does regard Christians' acceptance of the moral teaching of the Old Testament as revealed law as the basis for Jewish acceptance of their legitimacy. As we have seen, this was a point made much earlier by Maimonides.[9] But even so, Emden draws no further conclusions from this commonality between Judaism and Christianity. At best, he seems to be advocating that Jews and Christians have reason to admire each other's morality—from afar.[10]

Emden's whole theory is based on the dubious historical assumption that the doctrine of the seven Noahide laws was actually known and accepted in the days of Jesus and Paul. It is more probable, however, that this doctrine was formulated in reaction to the rise of Christianity, to distinguish clearly between Jewish normativeness and gentile normativeness, thus eliminating any quasi-Jews *(sebomenoi)* who were diverted from full integration into Judaism by Paul especially. Paul was not interested in founding a new religion but wanted to broaden the definition of Judaism itself in order to make those who had accepted the Messiahship of Jesus as "olive shoots grafted on to the tree" of Israel.[11] Finally, as for Jesus wanting to found a religion for the gentiles, the Gospels report that he was reluctant to deal with them at all, claiming that he was sent "only to the lost sheep of the house of Israel."[12] Therefore, Christians can hardly be expected to recognize themselves in Emden's characterization of them, even though it is a favorable one.

The second way to see the relation between the singular and the general is with the singular taken to be that which leads toward the general. The history of Stoicism provides a good example. Stoicism is the philosophical enunciation of what was taken to be the underlying significance of the world conquest of Alexander the Great. Unlike the world conquest of the Romans, in which the singular maintained its own political identity by dominating the more general sphere outside itself, Alexander's conquests were seen as the movement from a uniquely Hellenic civilization to the construction of a truly universal world civilization, the *oikoumenē*. Such a movement could be predicated only on the assumption of a cosmic order lying above and beyond the present historical singularities within the world.[13] These singularities are here regarded as particularities, as parts of an all-inclusive whole. This cosmic order was seen as the macrocosm of which the human soul was a microcosm. Thus for Stoicism, the task of the truly rational human person is to transcend the particularities of his or her own political situation in history by directly relating to the universal cosmic order within one's own soul. The transcendence of the historical can be seen in the thought of Stoics as politically diverse as the slave Epictetus and the Roman emperor Marcus Aurelius.[14] Unlike the dominance of the general by the singular, this movement of the particular into the general does not involve the degradation of conquest but can be accomplished only by rational persuasion: the general is the true home of the particular, to which its own reason leads it.

This type of Stoic universalistic reasoning about the relation between the particular and the general had a strong influence on a certain type of Jewish thinking about the relationship between Judaism and the non-Jewish world. Under direct Stoic influence, it can be seen in the ancient world in the first century C.E. in the theology of Philo of Alexandria especially. In the modern world, it arose indirectly in the theology of those Jewish thinkers who were heavily influenced by Kantian universalism, especially Hermann Cohen (d. 1918) and Leo Baeck (d. 1956). Both approaches are highly polemical and hence do not have an essential orientation toward dialogue. Nevertheless, they must be carefully examined, because so much of the Jewish–Christian relationship has been polemical. And although only the modern version of this type of reasoning deals specifically with Christianity, it is important to see its ancient version because that is where this kind of logic originated and was most clearly enunciated.

Stoicism offered a unique challenge to Judaism in late antiquity because it did not claim to confront it as one historical singularity facing another historical singularity. Rather, Stoicism claimed to represent a vision of universal humanity rooted in the rational principle (logos) of the cosmos itself. Judaism was seen as something particular and therefore peripheral in the true cosmic order of things. To have accepted this, where particularity is equated with the metaphysically dispensable, would have been tantamount to admitting that Judaism is essentially passé. If that were the case, then total Jewish assimilation into the more general culture would have been the only intelligent option for Jews.[15] In the intellectual environment of the Hellenistic age, at a time when Stoicism had engaged many of the best and most impressive philosophical minds, Philo, more than any other Jewish thinker at that time, attempted to show that Judaism, rather than anything the pagan world had to offer, constituted the most authentic universalism intended by human reason.

For Philo, Judaism—that is, the Mosaic Torah as properly interpreted by the philosophically constituted allegorical method— is truly in the vanguard of universalism. This is because of the persistent survival and continuance of Jewish law and Judaism's attraction for many non-Jews searching for an authentic universalistic faith, and because the God who is the subject of the Mosaic Torah uniquely transcends every worldly limit. Philo continually emphasizes how the laws of the Torah are "stamped, as it were, with the seals of nature herself."[16] By "nature" he means the fundamental intelligible structure of the cosmos. Thus Judaism alone is the general standard by which every particularity is to be judged regarding its degree of participation in the universal realm. Faced with the insufficiency of the Greek philosophers in this area, Philo could be rather explicit in his criticism. When dealing with the insufficiency of the Roman Empire, from whose political and military might he and his fellow subjugated Jews had much to fear, he was more circumspect in his criticism of the notion advanced by such Stoic thinkers as Plutarch, Strabo, and Polybius that this empire was itself the universal order intended by reason.[17] Nevertheless, when he wrote "that the whole world [oikoumenē] should be as one city, enjoying that best of constitutions, democracy,"[18] he was certainly thinking of the ideal, but as yet unrealized, Mosaic state. For he did not mean by "democracy" any existing political system, but the ideal system of true proportional equality in which everyone gets what he or she truly deserves. The insightful contemporary reader could make the inference that Philo was contrasting this ideal constitution with the inauthentic universalism of the Roman imperialism that was at hand.

When it came to the popular pagan religions of his time, religions that many non-Jews in the new cosmopolitan Hellenistic–Roman world already found hopelessly parochial, Philo did not have to make any direct comparisons. Clearly, by the philosophically constituted standards of universality, which he seems to assume are held by his non-Jewish readers especially, Judaism should be more convincing even at the prima facie level, and even more so when its underlying doctrines are properly explicated.[19]

Jewish singularity is to be maintained precisely because it emerges as the true universalism once every other particularism vanishes before its spiritual power. To abandon it prematurely would be to surrender this true universalism before it could be realized in human history. Philo, then, connects Judaism's universalism with his own vision of a messianically united humankind. He advocates this most emphatically in this forceful passage:

> Thus the laws are shown to be desirable [zēlotai] and precious in the eyes of all, ordinary citizens and rulers alike, that too though our nation has not prospered for many a year. . . . But if a fresh start [tis aphormē] should be made to brighter prospects, how great a change for the better might we expect to see! I believe that each nation would abandon its peculiar ways [ta idia] and, throwing overboard their ancestral customs, turn to our laws alone.[20]

Stoicism differed from the earlier elitism of both Plato and Aristotle in emphasizing that philosophical excellence was much closer at hand than the earlier philosophers had thought. For the Stoics, reason is much more intuition than the long, arduous process of ratiocination. It is considered to be far more accessible than either

Platonic or Aristotelian *nous*. In this emphasis, Stoicism is a close precedent for Kant's notion of practical reason, whether or not Kant himself was aware of it. For Kant thought that human universalism is to be found in the moral sense of even people who are quite ordinary intellectually. In fact, in contrast with the novel intellectual feats he performed in his limitation of "pure reason" in his first Critique, when dealing with practical reason, Kant emphasized that he was only formulating more clearly what ordinary decent people already knew and were practicing in their lives.[21] The categorical imperative in its two basic formulations stated that proposed acts were to be considered moral if they could be conceived as possible for all other rational subjects under the same circumstances, and that all autonomous moral subjects were to be treated as ends in themselves rather than as means to someone else's individual purposes. In both these formulations, the essential point is universalism. In the first formulation, the essential point is the universalizability of a moral maxim—namely, as what all other rational subjects would do. In the second formulation, the essential point is that no moral subject is part of anyone's universe but that all are equally universal—that is, equally irreducible as members of the ideal "kingdom of ends."[22] Indeed, only such a universe unto itself could possibly be seen as the basis for universalizable norms. Without the constitution of this basic universalism within the moral subject himself or herself, any general norm would always smack of the particular self-interest of a participant in a larger sensuous whole.

This Kantian universalism made a tremendous impression on a number of nineteenth- and early-twentieth-century Jewish thinkers, of whom the most prominent were Hermann Cohen and the man he saw as his spiritual and intellectual successor, Leo Baeck.[23] They saw it as the way to reconstitute Judaism in order to make it universally compelling. In so doing, they had to counter Christian charges, especially those of nineteenth-century German Protestantism *(Kulturprotestantismus)*, that only Christianity and not Judaism was so compelling.

Cohen's great theological project was to demonstrate that Judaism is in the vanguard—ahead of every other religion and philosophy—in striving for the Messianic age, which for him was the realization of a universal reign of justice and peace.[24] Although they were separated by nineteen centuries, and although Cohen did not have a high opinion of Philo, the logic of his emphasis on Jewish universalism against what he considered to be the lesser particularities of his time is surprisingly similar to Philo's.[25] Thus in emphasizing how, for him, Judaism teaches that ethics are not to be deduced from religious dogma (although, for Cohen, ethics are ultimately grounded in the metaphysical correlation between man and God), Cohen pointed to Judaism's universalism as superior to Christian particularisms.[26] Here Cohen is appealing to an assumption he posits in his "modern" readers—the historical advancement of the modern secular state over ecclesiastically dominated medieval nations. Cohen brings this point out by showing that non-Jewish citizenship in the ancient Jewish polity, according to the Talmud, did not entail any dogmatic affirmations of Judaism by such non-Jews:

> With the principle involved in the notion of the pious of the peoples of the world, the Talmud has achieved a fundamental distinction between Judaism, on the one hand, and Christianity in all its variations, on the other. Salvation for all of the latter means salvation through faith in Christ. . . . Thus, there is within this affiliation no true humanity. . . . Through the Talmudic sentence, however, bliss is granted to man as such [dem Menschen an sich] and the conditions of humanity are determined only within pure human morality.[27]

Cohen can be seen as confronting Christian pretensions to universalism in the same way as Philo, more circumspectly to be sure, confronted Roman pretensions to universalism. And Cohen's attempt to carry Kant's premises to conclusions beyond those to which Kant himself carried them (especially when dealing with the centrality of God) can be compared with what Philo did with the premises of Plato especially, and also with those of Aristotle and the Stoics. Finally, Cohen's justification of Jewish particularism in the pre-Messianic era is similar to Philo's—namely, that any capitulation to the inauthentically universalistic majority culture, which for Cohen was still too traditionally Christian, would be pseudo-Messianic and thus a fundamental betrayal of Judaism's historical mandate, a mandate not yet fulfilled.[28] As he writes:

> Monotheism is at stake; in the face of this how could the community of the world of culture be its legitimate tribunal? With monotheism, the world of culture is at stake . . . there is general consent that culture as a whole has no fixed center in God. However, here the

reason for this general consensus is disclosed: only the unique God of Jewish monotheism can form this firm center, which bestows on culture a steady balance for the plurality of its interest. Therefore, isolation is indispensable for its cultural work.[29]

Nevertheless, there is one point in the development of this universalism at which Cohen takes a step far beyond anything Philo ever did and at which, I think, Philo's conservatism is more admirable. Cohen sees a reconciliation between Judaism and Christianity, not on the infinite Messianic horizon, but on the horizon of the secular German state founded by Bismarck after 1871.[30] Cohen saw the liberal Protestantism of his time—best exemplified by his Marburg colleague, the Christian theologian Wilhelm Herrmann—and his type of liberal or "prophetic" Judaism coming together in an idealistic neo-Kantian socialist (as opposed to a materialist Marxist) constitution for the new German state, with its claims to universalism.[31] Despite all his philosophical opposition to Hegel's later attempt to merge the ideal and the historically real, Franz Rosenzweig was quite correct in seeing Cohen's own German pseudomessianism as essentially "Hegelian."[32] This point, which Cohen continued to emphasize until the end of his life in 1918, distorts both traditional Judaism and traditional Christianity in the service of a secular state that, in truth, required neither faith. Aside from the easy hindsight of those who have seen Hitler, this glorification of the German state as the authentic potential universalism at hand—or of any such state, for that matter—is a compromise of Cohen's own idealism, which in its purer expressions recognized a much deeper gap between present reality and future ideality.[33] Philo's more prudent view of the Roman Empire, which had better claim to universalism than Wilhelmine Germany, was far wiser and more consistent.

Leo Baeck, who was even more of a polemicist against Christianity than Cohen, also argued that Christianity is premature Messianism and therefore cannot claim to be truly realized universalism. Only Judaism can make that claim, because, as "contrasted with . . .Christianity . . . Judaism stresses the kingdom of God not as something accomplished but as something yet to be achieved, not as a religious possession of the elect but as the moral task of all."[34] Like Cohen, Baeck appealed to the modern secular assumption that the era is more progressively universalistic than the ecclesiastically dominated Middle Ages. Seeing Judaism's emphasis on the practical commandments as very similar to Kant's emphasis on morality (a highly dubious analogy, since Kantian autonomy is not the same as Jewish theonomy at all),[35] Baeck stresses how much better than Christianity Judaism looks based on these Kantian criteria.[36] This itself is an ironic tour de force in that it was well known to students of Kant's philosophy that he regarded Judaism as hopelessly parochial.[37] Despite this, Baeck offers the following criticism of Christianity:

> What is thus taken away from humanity is at the same time a loss for universalism. It had already been narrowed down considerably by the conception of the Church, which had done away with the unity of mankind and all but reduced the God of all men to a God of the Church.[38]

And following Philo and Cohen, Baeck argues for continued Jewish singularity on Messianic grounds.[39]

Despite such attempts to transcend Judaism's singularity without assimilation, this logic of the relation of the singular and the general is inadequate for our constitution of the relationship of Jews and Christians in the dialogue. Both Judaism and Christianity are themselves grounded originally and irrevocably in revelatory events. Jews and Christians cannot step out of them to assume a simple humanity and still be intimately related to God and their own faith communities. There is no cosmic order lying above them that can simply be rationally appropriated in a way that is sufficient to the human task appointed by God. Whatever such universal order there is to be will result from only a redemptive act of God in no wise under human control. Hence, the metaphysical priority assigned to the general over the singular is inconsistent with the theological primacy of the singular road from Sinai to the Messianic Jerusalem.[40] For Christians, the road from Calvary to the Parousia is just as singular.

The third view of the relation of the singular and the general is one in which the general is seen as an undifferentiated mass that develops into structured singularity at the completion of its process. This view was most cogently and most influentially worked out by Aristotle. For example, an acorn is the simple mass that develops into a more complex oak tree as its intended result.[41]

The oak tree itself is explained by reference to four interrelated points: (1) the acorn *from which* it grew (material cause); (2) the intended end, that is, the plan *by which* the acorn is to be fulfilled (formal cause), which has received powerful reconfirmation of late with the discoveries about the genetic code; (3) those additional forces *through which* an acorn is enabled to become an oak tree (efficient cause); and (4) the end result *for which* all is directed— the oak tree itself (final cause). It is evident that the defining poles in this interrelation are the acorn and the oak tree—the material cause and the final cause, the former being more general and the latter more singular. In Aristotelian terms, the fundamental, all-encompassing relation is between potency and act. The oak tree itself is the actualized acorn; the acorn is the potential oak tree.

In this framework, potency is understood only in relation to act.[42] The acorn has one and only one inherent function, and that is to be an oak tree. The oak tree is its raison d'être. If it does not become an oak tree because of some internal deficiency, then it must be considered to be an acorn only by morphological analogy. But if it fails to become an oak tree because of some external accident—let us say, it was eaten by an animal—then it ceases to be an acorn by being totally assimilated into something else, the animal's food.

Although Aristotle himself had a number of problems applying this potency–act logic in explaining the structure of the cosmos,[43] it lent itself very well to the type of theology of history with which a Jewish theologian would have to be concerned. A theologian as astute as Maimonides, who was so deeply influenced by Aristotelian teleology, found a very good application for this potency–act logic in his constitution of the relation of the Mosaic Torah and the Noahide law. Maimonides saw the more general Noahide law as the preparation for the full Torah revealed to Moses. In his words, the Noahide law was "completed" *(ve-nishlamah)* by the Mosaic Torah.[44] In his use of the Hebrew word for "completed," Maimonides may very well have had in mind the same sense in which the Talmud calls the Torah "the complete Torah" *(Torah shlaymah)*.[45] However, whereas the Talmud uses the term only to contrast the complete Torah with "useless conversation" *(seehah betelah)*, Maimonides uses the complete Torah to mean the actualization of the potential Torah of the Noahides. What Maimonides has done, then, is to take a traditional Jewish term and redefine it along the lines of Aristotelian potency–act logic. And what is important to remember here is that the Noahide law is far more general than the Mosaic Torah in all its singularity.[46] Thus the Noahide law is the general gentile mass out of which the full and complete Torah emerged as its actualization. The very purpose (telos) of Noahide law, then, is to become the complete Torah.

This logic receives further application in Maimonides's specific treatment of the relationship between Judaism and Christianity. It will be recalled that Maimonides argued that Jews may teach Scripture to Christians for two reasons. First, Christians (unlike Muslims) accept the full text of Scripture, which for them is the Old Testament; they already accept it as authentic, intact revelation. Second, the Christians' error in deviating from the original true Jewish meaning of Scripture was not because they rejected the authenticity of its revelation per se, but because they misinterpreted it. Therefore, the task of Jews is to teach them the correct interpretation of what both communities accept as the word of God. As the intended result of all this, those Christians who sincerely study Scripture with insightful Jewish teachers will be able "to return to what is best [ha-mutab]," namely, Judaism as the authentic, undiluted interpretation of this revelation.

One might say that these Christian students of Scripture are potential Jews whose religious actualization is being facilitated by their Jewish teachers, who see in advance the intended result of this whole process. Furthermore, this development moves from what is lower and less differentiated to what is higher and more differentiated. For the singular is only better when it is higher, that is, more intelligible. And because this is a progression of higher and higher intellectual insight, it can be achieved only by a process of rational persuasion. It cannot be the result of any sort of coercion, physical or political.

Despite the fact that at this point in the history of the Halakhah, someone working within its system could not advocate a totally overt type of proselytizing, Maimonides can be seen as advocating at least covert proselytizing of those Christian scholars interested in the true—which, for him, was the philosophically determined—interpretation of Scripture. Obviously, they had to be the ones to seek out Jewish teachers. We have no record of whether Maimonides himself ever actually had any Christian disciples, but that is not the key point for our purposes. Instead, it is important to see how Maimonides constitutes the relation between the general and the singular, first as regards the relation between Noahide law and the Mosaic Torah and second, more specifically, in the relationship between Christianity and Judaism.

For Maimonides, it seems that Christianity in its biblicism is potential Judaism. At first glance, this seems odd in that the emergence of Christianity is later than the emergence of Judaism in history. But it must be remembered that Maimonides sees this relationship in an essentially messianic perspective. Judaism's completion on earth will occur only when the Messiah reigns. This will entail the restoration of Jewish sovereignty in the land of Israel, including the full restoration of the Temple and its cult, and it will culminate in universal monotheism. As such, Christianity (and Islam) will contribute to this historical culmination. Hence, there are degrees of potential Messianic fulfillment. Judaism is at the highest level of potentiality because it has the full Mosaic Torah along with its most authentic traditional interpretation and application in Halakhah and Aggadah. Christianity, having the complete Torah but lacking the authentic tradition of interpretation, is at a lower level of potentiality.[47]

Within this process, we can see all four points of the Aristotelian potency–act developmental logic at work.

1. The Jews, and to a lesser extent the Christians, are the potential *from which* the messianic kingdom will emerge (material cause).
2. The full Mosaic Torah and its authentic traditional interpretation are the plan *by which* this potential is to be actualized (formal cause).
3. Jewish philosophical exegetes of the Torah will be the forces *through which* this human potential will properly be actualized (efficient cause).
4. The Messianic kingdom itself will be the end result *for which* all is intended (final cause).

Thus although in Maimonides's more specifically halakhic writings, such as the *Mishneh Torah* and his responsa, his Aristotelianism is often only implicit, explicating the Aristotelian logic lying just beneath the surface of these writings helps us understand his full scheme much better.

At any pre-Messianic point in history, only the most insightful Christians can be expected to see the true teleology inherent in their biblicism. And what is most important to bear in mind here is that this Christian study of Scripture *with* Jews is to take place in an atmosphere of philosophical discourse, in which a dialogue is to be enacted. The question for us, however, is whether this model of dialogue is adequate to constitute *the dialogue* between Jews and Christians in the present and for the future.

If dialogue is to be based on this Aristotelian constitution of the relation of the general and the singular, then its agenda must be largely covert. It is like those "Socratic" dialogues in which Plato has Socrates bring forth the truth latent in the student's soul. (The *Meno* is the best example.) The teacher, Socrates, must feign surprise when the student actually utters the truth he wants brought forth by the student himself. For if the teacher himself were to simply put it forth overtly in advance, the student would be a passive spectator rather than an active participant in the process that is discovery for him and rediscovery for the teacher. Here the dialogue is not between two independent persons, but between a teacher and a student whom he sees as a potential version of himself.[48] Now, although the agenda of this method—one used by good teachers where wisdom, not just information, is the issue— is covert, it is not necessarily sinister. The explicit precondition of this exalted type of learning is that the student recognize the superiority of the teacher and the teacher recognize the inferiority of the student. For the sake of eventually equalizing their situation, however, in the process of learning, the teacher must act as though he were more ignorant than he really is and act as though the student were more learned than he really is.[49] But in the end, they are to be united (optimally) in one truth that will then encompass them both. Nevertheless, the teacher *already* knows this truth.

In this way of dialogue, the teacher is clearly a missionary, but not the type of missionary who tells the prospective convert that he or she has nothing and the missionary has everything for the prospective convert. Rather, the teacher is the type of missionary who tells the prospective convert that he or she has the potential for true salvation within him- or herself. Jews will clearly recognize that this is how Christians have attempted to missionize them: the former approach being more blatant, and the latter more subtle. But this subtle approach is more sinister if it pretends to be an open-ended dialogue in which the participants are equal, coming from distinct backgrounds now and to remain so in the future. For the dialogue presupposes a true mutuality based on a duality that is not to be overcome in the process of the dialogue itself. In this sense, the dialogue is not "Platonic."

This is why the disavowal of proselytizing intent has been the indispensable precondition for Jewish–Christian dialogue.[50] This makes a greater demand on the Christian participants. Christianity is a missionizing religion. For this reason, a number of more traditional Christians have held, in all good faith and honesty, that the acceptance of this precondition is totally inconsistent with what the Gospel requires of them. While other types of relationship are not ruled out for them, the dialogue in its authenticity cannot be part of it. And although proselytizing has not been part of the practical Jewish agenda for many centuries, it is clear from what we have seen in Maimonides, especially, that its absence might be more a matter of external restraint (it has been dangerous for Jews to proselytize Christians in Christian societies) than internal Jewish prohibition. But the very integrity of the dialogue requires that Jews, despite all the reverence they should have for anything taught by Maimonides, not adopt his Aristotelian model for the relationship with Christians and Christianity. It is simply inappropriate for the task at hand.

## Another Model for the Relation of the Singular and the General

In dealing with the relation between the general and the singular in which Judaism is the singular realm for the one constituting this relation, one must recognize that Judaism is such a singularity because of revelation.[51] It is the Torah that makes Judaism stand out from anything else in the human background. "Our nation is only a nation by virtue of its laws," as was succinctly stated by the ninth-century Jewish theologian Saadyah Gaon.[52] If the Jewish–Christian dialogue is between Jewish singularity and Christianity, which lies within the more general human background, this relationship should be seen in the overall context of the relation of revelation to that general human background, which makes its appearance possible. One must begin the constitution of the dialogue from the point of view in which revelation is central.

For Jews, revelation is the singularity of God's election of Israel and his giving the Torah to them. Indeed, the inadequacy of the other three relations between the general and the singular just examined might be because revelation is not central enough for any of them. In the relation of the singular *over* the general, the central factor is the political power of the singular to enforce its rule over the general. In the relation of the singular as the particular *leading toward* the general, the central factor is the sense of the particular being subsumed as part of a greater whole. In the relation of the general *developing into* a higher singularity, the central factor is the intellectual insight into cosmic teleology. In other words, their inability to be used to adequately constitute the Jewish—Christian dialogue might well stem from their inability to adequately constitute the centrality of revelation in their theologies. If these two inadequacies are so closely connected, then the adequate constitution of the Jewish—Christian dialogue is not something lying on the apologetic periphery, but is something close to the heart of the whole enterprise of Jewish theology. Our question now is: How is revelation related to the general human background, and how is Christianity an aspect of that background?

The last way to understand the relation between the general and the singular from within Jewish tradition—and the one I shall develop here as my own preferred approach in constituting the Jewish—Christian dialogue—is to see the general as the background of possibility, part of which is realized in the singularity of Jewish revelation. The presentation of this approach requires that we look at a seminal rabbinic statement about revelation, its context in the Babylonian Talmud, its elaboration by Maimonides, its fuller philosophical implications, and, finally, its application to the task of theologically constituting the Jewish—Christian dialogue in the present and for the future. The issues raised here must be properly examined and appropriated lest our constitution of the dialogue be philosophically naive and theologically superficial.

The Talmud reports a statement of the third-century Palestinian sage Rabbi Yohanan bar Nappaha that "the Holy-One-blessed-be-He only makes His divine presence [*Shekhinato*] dwell upon one who is powerful [*gibbor*], wealthy, wise [*hakham*] and humble [*'anav*]; and all these characteristics are exemplified by Moses."[53]

There are a number of ways to interpret this rabbinic statement. First, it could be taken as a rabbinic continuation of the scriptural theme of Moses as the superlative prophet, compared with whom all other prophets are merely partial reflections.[54] Second, considering the fact that Rabbi Yohanan was very much involved in polemics against the new Christian community, it could be taken perhaps as an oblique critique of the centrality of Jesus for the new community; Moses is greater than Jesus. Jesus certainly does not qualify by the criteria of power and wealth. Nevertheless, the editors of the Babylonian Talmud seem to have seen this as a statement about the phenomenology of revelation, for they placed it in a larger literary unit *(sugya)* that deals with the distinction between Moses's human qualities and God's revelation through Moses to Israel. Hence, just before Moses's wisdom is mentioned, a statement of a later Palestinian sage, Rabbi Hama son of Rabbi Hanina, is interpreted to mean that one of Moses's human qualities was his analytic acumen *(pilpula b'alma)*.[55] The traditional commentators emphasize the difference between the communication of method and of revealed content: Moses had to deliver the former to Israel; he delivered the latter out of his own kindness, since it was given to him as his own possession.[56] However, the text itself seems to make a deeper distinction between revelation and reason.[57] Indeed, to emphasize Moses's finite human intelligence compared with the divinely given content of revelation, this literary unit concludes with another statement of Rabbi Yohanan along the same lines: "At first, Moses learned Torah and forgot it until it was given to him as a gift [from God] as it says in Scripture, 'And He gave it to Moses when He finished speaking with him' (Exodus 31:18)." Clearly, the gift here is the content of the Torah, not the method for understanding it.

In what was undoubtedly an elaboration of the statement of Rabbi Yohanan about the preconditions of revelation from the context in which it was primarily presented in the Talmud, Maimonides, in his initial discussion in his code of the centrality of prophecy for Judaism, states:

> It is one of the foundations of the faith to know that God made human beings prophesy *[menabe]*. And, prophecy only occurs *[halah]* with a sage great in his wisdom, with one who is mighty in his moral qualities . . . one whose intellect is always open to what is above it. . . . Those who desire to be prophets are called the disciples of the prophets *[benay he-nebi'im]*. Nevertheless, even though they so di-

rect [she-mekhavnim] their intellect, it is possible ['efshar] that the divine presence [Shekhinah] will dwell upon them and it is possible that it will not.[58]

Here Maimonides emphasizes the fact that although proper preparation, both intellectual and moral, is a prerequisite for prophecy, prophecy is not simply the actualization of moral and intellectual potential. Rather, these prerequisites are only the conditio sine qua non of prophetic revelation. They are not its conditio per quam; that is, they are no guarantee of its realization. By introducing the concept of possibility, Maimonides has made revelation ultimately, but not completely, a matter of grace. In other words, it is possible after all this preparation that God will elect one to be a prophet, and it is equally possible that God will not. However, for Maimonides, it is impossible for one to become a prophet without these prerequisites. Revelation, then, has a wider general background and a narrower singular foreground. It is necessary for a prophet to have already reached the apex of intellectual and moral excellence, but it is not necessary that one who has reached this apex become a prophet. Finally, most importantly for our purposes here, Maimonides speaks of prophecy as a human possibility, and states that its prerequisites are not uniquely Jewish.[59]

In his more specifically philosophical-theological work, *The Guide of the Perplexed*, Maimonides presents three opinions about the conditions necessary for prophecy.[60] In his delineation of each, the relation between the general background and the singular foreground is the distinguishing characteristic. The first opinion, which is the most popular one among both Jews and non-Jews, states that the only prerequisite for prophecy is that the person who becomes a prophet be of sound morality. Everything else is the result of divine election. The second opinion, which is that of the philosophers, states that if one has fully developed his or her human potential both morally and intellectually, and also has a perfected imagination (what we today would call political creativity), then prophetic actualization will be automatic. Only some external impediment could prevent this automatic actualization. Here God is the ultimate object of perfected human conduct and insight, but God does not act here as an external cause. The external impediment, which is always a possibility, is an accident.

The last opinion, which Maimonides designates as the basic view of the Torah, states that even if one has all the philosophical pre-requisites for prophecy, it can always be God's will that he not become a prophet. Maimonides states that this point alone distinguishes the Jewish opinion about prophecy from the philosophical one. The question is, however, just how God's will is to be distinguished from the external impediment that can also prevent a philosopher from becoming a prophet. The answer, which has great significance for the relationship between Judaism and Christianity, is to be found in Maimonides's differentiation of possibility from potentiality.

In discussing the passage from potentiality to actuality, along the lines of Aristotelian metaphysics, Maimonides sees the function of the efficient cause as the removal of any obstacle that might prevent the internal process of development from reaching its completion (final cause). It would seem that any such obstacle is something external that entered the developing entity and does not fit into its developmental plan (formal cause). The efficient cause, then, is the entity's capacity for self-correction. In a biological organism, one might see such an efficient cause in the body's immune system, which is able to ward off infections coming from foreign organisms that have entered the body as intruders.[61] The important thing to remember here is that the role of the efficient cause is negative; that is, it rectifies accidents from external sources. The essential process of development, however, is internal. And it will be recalled that, for Maimonides, the function of the Jewish teachers of Christians is to help them overcome the incorrect interpretations of Scripture so that they may "return" to what is, in effect, their primordial Judaism: the highest level of truth before the coming of the Messiah. However, let me make it clear right here that if one adopts Maimonides's possibility–realization logic rather than his Aristotelian potency–act logic and applies it to constituting the Jewish–Christian relationship, one will conclude differently from Maimonides himself on this question. That is what I shall attempt to do.

In discussing the passage from possibility to realization—and possibility is the key factor in the phenomenology of prophecy—Maimonides makes this point: "Everything that has a cause for its existence is only possible with regard to existence in respect to its own essence. For it exists if its causes are present. If, however, they are not present . . . that thing does not exist."[62] What Maimonides is saying here is that even when one can see an entity's indispensable structure (its essence) as a possibility, that possibility can be realized (existent) only if its cause is present. Clearly, that "presence" is from a transcendent source; that is, it is external and can never be seen as an internal factor within the realized entity itself. Thus for this view of causality, the entity's realization is the result of the relation between the realm of possibility, with its own structure, and that which transcends it. For Maimonides, that key transcendent factor is God's will. The necessary natural transition from potency to act, then, has been superseded.[63]

Scholars have long pointed out that Maimonides's view is heavily influenced by the view of the Islamic philosopher Ibn Sina (Avicenna).[64] That is highly significant because I contend that only a philosophy coming out of a theology in which divine creativity and divine revelation are key factors could make this decisive distinction between possibility and potentiality. It is no accident that Ibn Sina (a Muslim), Maimonides (a Jew), and Thomas Aquinas (a Christian) make this clear distinction, using different terms for possibility and for potentiality in Arabic, Hebrew, and Latin, respectively.[65] Moreover, in dealing with prophecy, Maimonides emphasizes that this difference between the Torah and the philosophers is essentially connected with their differences over creation and miracles, namely, that aspect of reality asserted by Judaism (and Christianity and Islam) in which God's role is too direct and free for it to be adequately explained by potency–act logic.[66] The compatibility of Aristotelian potency–act logic and theologically based possibility–realization logic in Maimonides's overall system might be compared with the compatibility of Einsteinian relativity theory and traditional Newtonian mechanics in contemporary physics. The latter still better explains the usual questions of locomotion and so on; the former is used to explain larger cosmic issues. So, for Maimonides, Aristotelian potency–act logic better explains more ordinary issues, whereas possibility–realization logic is used to explain more metaphysically significant issues. Maimonides himself used potency–act logic to explain the relationship of Judaism and Christianity. I am trying here to see this relationship as more theologically significant and therefore wish to use the logic Maimonides himself used for such significant questions. Our difference, then, is one of contextuality, possibly because of the different phenomenology of Christianity in our time. The issue for us has become more important.

The factor of divine will becomes central only when there is no automatic process of becoming. And possibility, unlike potentiality, entails more than one outcome. That is the point we shall be following, because, as we shall soon see, this enables one faith community (faith being the response to revelation, community being the historically sustained context for faith) to recognize that revelation is possible for another faith community without having to constitute what that revelation is in that other community. In other words, it can apprehend it *(an sit)*, but it cannot judge it *(quid est)*, for any such judgment would require the constitution of a genus including both faith communities as species. The faith claims of both communities, however, would be lost in any such move.

For Aristotle, though, there are only higher and lower levels of potentiality. For example, Aristotle says that both earth and semen have the potential to become a human being, but only semen can be considered a proper potency *(dynamis)* because it is the potential factor most proximate to the actualization—the conception and birth of a human being.[67] The most proximate potentiality is the most proper potentiality in that it necessarily leads (barring any accidents) to only one outcome. Efficient causality's role here at the final nexus is quite minor. In fact, at the level of the causal relations among the heavenly bodies, which for Aristotle is the level of being that all intelligence (including human intelligence) strives to imitate, efficient causality collapses completely into final causality.[68] Thus when a phenomenon is seen in terms of possibility–realization logic as opposed to potency–act logic, there is a greater role for God's direct and free action and a greater number of imaginable outcomes. The divine freedom that theology asserts and the pluralism manifested in dialogue at its best are now correlated.

We need not jump over modern philosophy is making this correlation in our own thesis here. Kant, the most influential of all the modern philosophers, also correlates freedom and pluralism in his theoretical philosophy, although for very different reasons, to be sure, and using different terms. If we can appropriate Kant's insights as we have appropriated Maimonides's insights, we can make an even better case for our constitution of the Jewish–

Christian dialogue because Kant's philosophical influence is more proximate than Maimonides's.

In constituting the relation between the general conditions of a finite experience and the singular objects it encounters—which closely approximates our understanding of the relation between singular revelation and its general background—Kant writes:

> Our mode of intuition is dependent upon the existence *[Dasein]* of the object, and is therefore possible *[moeglich]* only if the subject's faculty of representation is affected by that object. . . . But however universal this mode of sensibility may be . . . It is derivative *[abgeleitet]* . . . not original . . . that intuition determines its existence to given *[gegebene]* objects.[69]

An object's appearance, its phenomenality, can be understood only through the conditions of experience, but these conditions do not cause the object to appear. It could just as properly not appear. Rather, the object must be a datum; it must be "given."[70] It comes from a source that forever transcends the one who experiences it. These conditions, conversely, make the appearance of the object possible from the side of the perceiving subject. This is how the perceiving subject relates himself to the object given before it.[71] Moreover, unlike Aristotle and the medievals, Kant understands the essence of the object—that is, its universalizable conditions—as not in the object per se, but in the subject who perceives it. The subject is now more and more of an active participant and less and less of a passive spectator in the relation of knowing *(noēsis)* and that which is known *(noēma)*. Nevertheless, for the medievals and for Kant, as opposed to Aristotle, the object's presence *(da-sein)* is always only possible, that is, contingent.

The object *(Gegenstand)* in its very objectivity—its being-there-for-us—is not to be reduced to finite experience or finite intelligence. Kant, therefore, posits something behind it as its ultimate source. This thing-in-itself *(Ding an sich selbst)* is assumed to be intelligent (a *noumenon*) but so beyond the conditions of experience and the categories of understanding that one can only posit its existence; one can in no way comprehend it. For Kant, it is "an unknown something which functions as a limit *[Grenzbegriff]* on the pretensions of finite intelligence."[72] Thus that which appears is contingent on a transcendent source and cannot be made to appear by finite intelligence. Furthermore, Kant speaks about "objects" in the plural.[73] Thus although the prior conditions of possibility (a priori) compose one unified and universalizable standard, the experienced objects themselves that presuppose them are varied and not covered by one unified and universalizable standard. Each of them in its subsequent singularity (a posteriori) has its own unique and nonuniversalizable standards.[74] Thus both the source of the object and the object's singularity are not universalizable precisely because they are not constituted by finite intelligence. The object's contingency and its singularity, then, go hand in hand.

Kant himself, of course, would not apply his own experiential scheme to religious experience of revelation. His theory of experience—in which external transcendence is affirmed—is confined to the experience of the objects of sense. And his interest was not in the empirical variety of those objects but in their a priori universal conditions, not in the thing *(Ding)* but in what made it experienceable *(Bedingung)* by a perceiving subject. Moreover, in the realms of morality and religion (the latter, at best, dependent on the former for its justification)—where the experiential origins are in the presence of persons, not things—only the transcendence of the subject is affirmed. Persons are only analogues of the moral self already aware of itself as such.[75] However, just as Maimonides appropriated the categories of Aristotelian teleology and applied them to history, whereas Aristotle confined them to nature, so I am here appropriating categories of Kantian epistemology and applying them to revelation as a real event, which Kant himself was most unwilling to do.[76]

We now have enough philosophical development behind us to properly constitute the relation between the singular and the general, in the case of the relation between revelation and its human background, for the sake of the Jewish–Christian dialogue in the present and for the future. One can see Judaism and Christianity (and perhaps Islam as well) as acknowledging a realm of possibility that is taken to be the human precondition for God's revelation to singular faith communities. And this realm of possibility can be constituted as the border they share. Revelation is, then, the object given to finite human experience and its structures. These structures make its presence, its being-there-for-us, possible and at least immediately understandable to its recipients. However, because this realm of possibility is not a proximate potentiality that automatically develops by its own internal dymanism, one cannot posit only one exclusive outcome from that realm of possibility. Revelation is univocal only if one posits that God spoke to only one people, or that if God did speak to other peoples, what they received can be ultimately understood only within the context of the one, true, actual revelation, of which their revelation is at best the potential. The first assumption, however, can be ruled out by the fact that there is enough Jewish tradition that affirms that God did communicate with gentile prophets.[77] The second assumption is an option that the theory of possibility explicated here overcomes.

It would seem, then, that from its singularity Judaism relates to the general world as a realm of possibility; namely, with what it sees out there as its own preconditions it can converse. The question for us now is: How does Christianity function for Judaism within that general background? Does Christianity play a special role there for Judaism? And how can that role be constituted without collapsing into relativism? Finally, how can that role be constituted so that each community can be viewed in its phenomenological integrity even in the midst of the dialogue itself?

## Morality, Human Nature, and God

In constituting the difference between looking at the other faith community as one's own potentiality and looking at it as lying within the realm of possibility for the emergence of one's own faith community, I appropriated, to a large extent, Maimonides's distinction between the pinnacle of philosophical insight and prophetic revelation. The former is understood in terms of the logic of potency–act, the latter, in terms of the logic of possibility–realization. In presenting Maimonides's distinction, I mentioned his rejection of what he considered the "vulgar" view of prophecy—namely, that the only precondition for God's election of one as a prophet is that the one so elected be of sound moral character. Interestingly, then, all three views accept some sort of moral prerequisite for revelation. None of them asserts that all morality is subsequent to revelation and therefore totally derivative from it. Revelation's most evident precondition is morality.[78]

Even when prophecy is seen as the realization of a possibility rather than the actualization of one's own potential, however, sound morality must be coupled with intellectual excellence as the necessary (but not sufficient) prerequisites for it. Why does Maimonides insist on this dual prerequisite? How are moral and intellectual excellence correlated?

For Maimonides, ethics has theological significance only when it is more than simply a theory for the management of human conduct in society.[79] Thus in a famous passage, about which much has been written and argued, he indicates that if a non-Jew practices the seven Noahide laws out of a sense of what we might call pragmatic prudence, such a person might be considered intelligently decent ("a sage," in his words), but he or she cannot be considered a participant in the realm of the transcendent world-to-come (*'olam ha-ba*).[80] Only a person whose moral conduct is oriented in the context of a relationship with God can be considered such a participant. The reason for this distinction is that the whole orientation of the human person is to be related with God; that relationship is the telos for which human nature is ordered at creation.[81]

In Chapter 3, where we critically examined Maimonides's view of the relationship betwen Judaism and Christianity, issue was taken with his specifically Aristotelian constitution of intellectual excellence. After Galileo and Newton, one cannot assume that concern with the objects of the heavens (astrophysics for us) and their theory of teleology (metaphysics for the Aristotelians) can be constituted as a realm intrinsically higher than the ethical concern with one's fellow humans and therefore a normative model for that earthly concern.[82] Nevertheless, even here concern with one's fellow humans must be seen as more than just the observance of rules. Rather, it must be constituted by a broader theory of human nature, one that recognizes a basis for concern with one's fellows. This realm of concern is what Kant called a "metaphysics of morals" and Buber called "philosophical anthropology."[83] It helps explain the rules that structure the relationship between humans in society and even the supreme relationship with God.

Without this constitution of human nature, moral rules quickly develop a life of their own (legalism), and the relationship with God gets lost altogether. Maimonides recognizes this in principle when he admits that we can be intelligently decent without being oriented to the realm of the transcendent, the realm wherein one is directly related with God. And it is important to remember that Maimonides does not constitute the relationship between Judaism and Christianity in this totally mundane context. No society of which he was aware was founded on the premise that the prudent management of human conduct needs no broader context and no deeper root. What was only a theoretical option in his time, however, has become a live practical option—the most ready option at hand in our own time. For secularism, as we have already seen, regards a broader context for human conduct as at best superfluous and at worst counterproductive. This means that if either Judaism or Christianity is to constitute its relationship with the other in the area of the management of human conduct, purposely bracketing each faith community's attempt to recognize a common human nature and a fundamental human orientation toward a relationship with God, then the only agenda will be a secular one. This agenda, at best, relegates both Judaism's Torah and Christianity's Gospel to a corner of historical obscurity where they pose no threat or challenge to the status quo in the world.

There are, to be sure, areas of the religious life of each faith community that lie in the interior where there is no common border between the communities. These areas, although capable of being viewed on the surface, cannot be the content of authentic dialogue with an outsider simply because their true presence can be directly understood only within the total context of singular faith. And it should be emphasized that these interior areas are the most important for each faith community.[84] They comprise singular revelation proper. Indeed, only when this is acknowledged ab initio is the dialogue protected from collapsing into relativism. For when relativism declares the equality of truth in the respective religious communities and their traditions on *all* levels, it affirms a higher universally evident truth that encompasses and transcends the *partial* truth of each community. Singularity, then, collapses into particularity: a part of a larger whole. And this higher truth is alone capable of being a source of rational action because it alone can be the criterion for distinguishing between better and worse. In our world today, such a higher criterion invariably turns out to be secularist.

In those areas of religious life that do lie on the common border, especially issues of morality, conversations (let alone *the dia-*

*logue*) between Jews and Christians will quickly be absorbed into the secular environment of our time if the Jewish and Christian participants are not allowed to discuss the philosophical and theological grounds of their specific moral positions. (In Chapter 1, I argued against the opinion of Rabbi Joseph B. Soloveitchik, which does not allow just that.) By philosophical grounds, I mean theories about human nature and its capacity for concern with fellow humans, its sociality. By theological grounds, I mean theories about the human capacity for a relationship with God.

## Theonomous Morality

The dialogue, then, is to be constituted on the common anthropological border between Judaism and Christianity. It is to be ever cognizant of what is common and what is uncommon. In other words, I propose that there is, indeed, a "Judeo-Christian ethic," however misunderstood that term has become. There is no "Judeo-Christian faith," however.

The Judeo-Christian ethic as the common anthropological border between Judaism and Christianity seems to be based on four theological affirmations. And it is because of their mutual acceptance of the Hebrew Bible as authentic revelation that Judaism and Christianity can sustain the sharing of this border. These theological affirmations are as follows.

1. The human person is created by God for the primary purpose of being related to God.
2. This relationship with God is primarily practical, its content being response to commandments from God.
3. The human person is created as a social being. This sociality is the human precondition for covenant with God; that is, singular divine revelation is to a historically extant community of persons, not to isolated individuals. Human response to such singular revelation is, then, within the context of such a covenantal community. Thus the covenant presupposes a general morality of socially pertinent standards as well as entailing specific intercovenantal norms.
4. The ultimate fulfillment of human personhood, both individ-

ually and collectively, lies in a future and universal redemptive act by God, one as yet on the unattainable historical horizon.

If one calls the morality grounded in these affirmations *theonomous*, then it should be contrasted with the two noncovenantal moral options available in history: *autonomy* and *heteronomy*.[85] In making this essential contrast, Judaism and Christianity can discover together the present force of the anthropological border they share. This discovery involves a close look at the scriptural foundations of this common border, that is, what lies behind the commandments—especially those governing interhuman relationships—that both Judaism and Christianity affirm. And it must look at what these commandments ultimately intend, namely, what is beyond the realm of the merely interhuman.

## Theonomous Morality and Scripture

Theonomous morality, as I understand the term, emphasizes the primacy of God's commandments for human action. The possibility for the relationship-with-God-in-commandment is seen in the account of creation in Scripture. Both Judaism and Christianity affirm creation as the necessary background for their respective revelations.

Along these lines, Rashi, the most important of the medieval Jewish Bible commentators, the one who best explicated rabbinic interpretations of Scripture, presents the opening verses in Genesis as follows: "At the onset of creation *[be-re'sheet bero]* of heaven and earth, when the earth was dark and chaotic, the divine spirit was moving over the surface of the waters, and God said, 'let there be light,' and there was light." According to this paraphrase, all the verbs prior to the commandment "let there be light" *(yehi 'or)* function as participles. Creation itself is in essence a commandment, a speech-act establishing a reality that is to be.[86] It is revelation in the most general sense, for it is what makes the singular revelations possible. For this reason, the "light" of Genesis 1:3 is taken by rabbinic and Kabbalistic exegetes to be the spiritual criterion for the rest of the creative process; it is the light seen only by the righteous; it is not physical incandescence.[87] The end of the verse ("and there was light"), then, describes the commandment's fulfillment.[88] Unlike Plato, as we shall see, Scripture presents order as subsequent, nor prior, to creation.[89]

One should carefully note how this fulfillment is presented: "God said, 'let there be light,' and there was light. And God saw it was good" (Genesis 1:3–4). The sequence emphasizes God's speech before God's vision. Language is initially and essentially prescriptive and only subsequently descriptive and evaluative. Thus light, with all the rest of creation, subsists and is valuable because God created it and invested it with an integral order. Nevertheless, the prescriptive speech-act is both logically and choronologically prior to both the subsistence and the value of any created entity. Creation ex nihilo presupposes nothing: "But our God transcends the world [ba-shamayim]; He does whatever He wants" (Psalms 115:3). In this way, the prescriptive and descriptive aspects of creation are correlated. Only God's will is always prior; all evaluation is subsequent. Thus the scriptural ethic is deontological qua act and teleological qua consequences. Existence is prior to essence.[90]

Speech precedes sight in the divine order of creation. The human person is created "according to the image and likeness of God," the God who speaks and who sees. This special created status does not mean that woman and man are miniature gods, somehow equal to and therefore independent of God the creator. Indeed, this very suggestion—"and you shall be like gods" (Genesis 3:5)—is regarded by Scripture as the origin of the sinful rebellion against God, which is the ultimate distortion of human creaturehood. Therefore, the human person does not speak creatively and then judge his or her own creation like God. Rather, the human person is uniquely endowed with the ability to freely hear God's commands, which the rest of creation does not seem to have.[91] Hence, for the human person, hearing the commanding voice of God is to be followed by doing what that voice has commanded. Thereafter, one attempts to discover the meaning and value of what has been commanded. Indeed, this is even necessary for the subsequent task of relating one commandment to another and determining priorities when conflicts arise among them, as they inevitably do.[92] However, one's doing of the commandment is because one heard it spoken by God, not because one saw its specific value and then ordered one's own doing in accordance with that vision. Vision of what is good is justifiable only if it is for the sake of what is heard and what is to be done. In fact, even the descriptive "God-talk" of the scriptural and rabbinic authors should be taken as the liturgical responses to the commandment, "to love the Lord your God with all your heart" (Deuteronomy 11:13), which the rabbis take to be the basic obligation to engage in communal worship.[93] And one can understand why the rabbis limited liturgical representation to the descriptions the community finds appropriate for its experience of the presence of God.[94] Like the rest of the commandments, the descriptive praise of God requires the living covenantal community for its proper context.

Along these lines, morality, as that which regulates human doing in the world, is essentially a question of to whose voice one is to hearken. Human life fulfills its created promise when it hearkens primarily to the voice of God and subsequently to those other voices (parents, teachers, leaders) who are given authority by God and who subordinate their secondary authority to God's commanding voice as the *Grundnorm*.[95] To make any other voice that *Grundnorm* is an idolatrous rejection of God the creator. And, as we shall see, both autonomy (listening primarily to one's own voice) and heteronomy (listening primarily to some other creature's voice) essentially entail this idolatrous attitude even when they do not necessarily entail specifically idolatrous acts (*'adodah zarah*).[96] Thus although Jews and Christians can certainly find that the content of some of the norms they theonomously affirm is also affirmed by secularist advocates of either autonomy or heteronomy, they must ever bear in mind that the ultimate meaning of this normative content is something very different for them. For them, the ultimate meaning of all true norms is that they are God's will.

The choice, then, is not between hearkening to God's voice and not hearkening to God's voice. The choice is, rather, hearkening to God's voice or hearkening to the voice of that which is not God. Hearkening is coequal with human existence itself.[97] Human existence is, then, an inescapable *vocatio*.[98] Eve and Adam chose to listen to the voice of the serpent and thereby rejected the voice of God. They evaluated their world based on a heteronomous *Grundnorm* (which the serpent represents to them as their autonomy), and their evaluation led them to reject the specific commandment they heard God address to them.[99] "And the woman saw the tree is good for food and it is craved by the eyes and that the tree is desirable to make one intelligent" (Genesis 3:6).

### The Primacy of Hearing in Scriptural Morality

In order to continue this reflection, two philosophical questions must be raised: Why must morality be conceived of as the hearkening to a voice? Why must one hearken to the voice of God rather than to other voices in the world?

In approaching the first question about hearkening to a voice itself, some of the findings concerning the psychology of children might help us to better understand the primacy of hearkening in human moral development.

Children are not born speaking, but only hearing. As their auditory powers develop, they become more and more cognizant of the human environment, whose members beckon them to enter their adult world. The child is called into this world and becomes more of a participant by being able to hear commands and to verbally respond to them and practice them. ("Yes, Mama, I hear you calling; I am coming!") However, in order for this incorporation into the world to be fulfilling to the developing child, he or she must hear behind the commanding voices an acceptance and a promise of future acceptance. The commanding voices must be beckoning if crossing over the linguistic threshold is to be a fulfillment of the human desire to be present with other persons and to abide with them in the world. This is why the child's name is so important. Being called by his or her name, the child experiences a personal address, a presence to be extended into the future. In fact, some studies of autistic children, who do not cross over that linguistic threshold for emotional reasons, explain this as their refusal to hearken to voices that come from a rejecting, manipulative world, a world that commands the child to behave, to keep distance, rather than to act and be included.[100] The developing child thus responds to the voice that accepts him or her and promises acceptance into a mutual future. A still small voice beckons; a shout repells.

Returning to Scripture, one learns that even the beckoning voices of the adult world are not to prevent the child from listening to the higher voice and thereby confuse it:

> The Lord called to Samuel . . . and he ran to Eli and he said, "I am here because you called me," and he said, "I did not call" . . . and Eli understood that the Lord called the boy. And Eli said to Samuel,

"go and lie down and when He calls to you, say, 'speak Lord for
your servant is listening.' " (1 Samuel 3:4–9)

Samuel hears the voice "even before the word of the Lord was
revealed to him" (1 Samuel 3:7). In other words, the openness to
the voice precedes the knowledge of the Lord and what the voice
is actually saying. That is also why the Halakhah emphasizes that
listening to the voice of one's parents cannot assume priority over
listening to the voice of God.[101]

In Scripture, the moral primacy of hearing a voice is emphasized
by the fact that a commandment is addressed to a person who is
called by his or her own name. A name is that by which one is
most immediately addressed. Only by being directly addressed in
this way is one able to have a unique place in the world. Otherwise, one is only an individual part in a larger mass (*das Man*) but
not a person.[102] One can only hear his or her own name; it is not
a description to be seen first of all as a common noun: "And
the messenger of the Lord called to him from beyond [*min ha-
shamayim*] saying, 'Abraham, Abraham!' And he said, 'here I am!' "
(Genesis 22:11). A nameless entity, however, is less than personal.
"And Jacob asked and said, 'what is your name?' And he said,
'why do you ask my name?' " (Genesis 32:30).

Morality is hearkening primarily to a voice if it is taken as the
extension of a future out of a present response. A voice calls one
from the present and promises a future if one will act toward it.
The object of vision, conversely, is something already there, an
appropriation of the present into the past. Thus a morality arising
out of the experience of sight is basically an understanding of a
prior order and an attempt to include human existence in it. Such
an inclusion of human existence in what-is-already-there means
that the essential task is the subsumption of presence into order.
This is the case with any kind of heteronomy, either sociological
(that is, the subsumption of the human person into a larger social
whole) or natural law (that is, the subsumption of the human person into the order of the cosmos itself, nature). Ecclesiastes, using
visual metaphors, rejects the idea of a future: "What was will be;
what was done will be done; there is nothing new under the sun.
If one would say about something, 'see this new thing,' it has already been in the ages which were before us" (Ecclesiastes 1:9–
10).[103]

For this reason, it seems, Scripture is concerned with removing the thought that God can be seen, but encourages the thought that God can be heard: "And they said to Moses, 'you speak with us and we shall listen, but let not God speak with us lest we die' " (Exodus 20:16). Moses attempts to assure the people that God's voice is heard in order to prevent sin, not life. And then God says to Moses, "You have seen that I have spoken from beyond *[min ha-shamayim]*. Do not make with Me gods of silver and gold" (Exodus 20:19). Here it is clear that the verb *see* is used metaphorically for the overall experience of revelation. For if the people had actually seen the source of the revelation, they could surely depict what they had seen.[104] Yet, "a voice uttering words you heard, but an image you did not see—only a voice" (Deuteronomy 4:12). Only seeing God, not hearing God, is deadly, "for no one sees Me and lives" (Exodus 33:20).[105] Moreover, God reveals to Moses the names whereby Moses might directly call upon God.[106]

It should be obvious by now that this has nothing to do with the medieval philosophical problem of anthropomorphism. If it did, then one would have to eliminate the voice of God just as much as the form of God. Indeed, voice is more uniquely personal than visual form, which is more easily compared with other forms in the realm of experience.[107] However, it seems that a voice is far less susceptible to idolatrous appropriation than a form precisely because the voice of God is understood in Scripture as that which calls the human subject toward a novel future, whereas a form comes out of a past already there. A form comes out of a limited past having no further possibility, whereas a voice calls one toward that which is as yet unlimited possibility.[108] This is not to say that God is the future, for that would make God pure possibility and, as such, devoid of actual presence and actual present authority.[109] One is commanded toward the future; the future itself does not command. Nevertheless, it does say that God's creative thrust is present, leading into a mutual future all those who hearken to God's commandments and do them as best as they can here and now: "There is hope for your future *[tiqvah l'ahareetekh]*, says the Lord" (Jeremiah 31:16). Only the finite can be seen and depicted as a form; what is still possible and therefore unlimited cannot be so depicted. It can only be addressed to a free person called by his or her own name. Idolatry is the attempt to substitute the certainty of depiction for the uncertainty of presenting the human person with a free opening into the future. Thus the prophets warned that cult becomes akin to idolatry when it becomes a form rather than obedient hearkening to the commanding voice of God that beckons: "To hearken is better than to sacrifice" (1 Samuel 15:22). Lot's wife violated the commandment "do not look behind you" (Genesis 19:17). She was destroyed because she chose to see what was behind her rather than listen to the voice calling her to what was ahead of her. Thus both Jewish and Christian assertions of morality—even morality whose immediate content they share with some secularists—must ever bear in mind the eschatological horizon, the respective hope of each faith community for final redemption. Eschatology has moral import for Jews and Christians because the final redemption—contrary to the view of the gnostics within both communities—is redemption *of* the world, not redemption *from* it.

## The Challenge to Theonomous Morality from Kantian Morality

Whereas the ancient Greek philosophers, beginning with Plato, were moving away from the earlier Greek experience of authentic human action as the response to a divine call (it will be recalled that Socrates's philosophical career begins with the voice of the Oracle,[110] certain modern philosophers seem to have attempted to return to a position in which the task of the human person and human society is to listen to a voice. For them, however, that voice is not the voice of God. Thus for Kant, for whom the source of all moral obligation is autonomy—the rule of the self over itself—the voice to be listened to is that of one's own reason. The self legislates a world for itself and for all other comparable rational selves with itself. That is why the form of such moral legislation is the categorical imperative. Out of this self-legislation, conducted by autonomous wills qua ends in themselves, emerges the collective future they have willed: the Kingdom of Ends.

Here we seem to have all the benefits of the scriptural ethic: the primacy of personality over the impersonal, external form and the future as a limitless horizon into which one is called.[111] And it seems that we have overcome the one big drawback of the scriptural ethic, that the voice of God is too often silent. The voice of autonomous reason, conversely, is always at hand.[112] This voice is without mystery, something fully known. It has total knowledge and control of itself. Thus for Kant, the divine is an adjective to describe autonomous self-legislation *(goettliche Gebote)* rather than the source of commandments to fallible human creatures *(Gebote Gottes).*[113] Moral autonomy, especially in its most cogent philosophical formulation by Kant, poses the greatest modern challenge to the theonomous morality affirmed by Judaism and Christianity.

Nevertheless, it can be shown that if morality is the person's hearkening to a voice—which is the only way to maintain the centrality of personhood and future—then it is preferable to hearken to the voice of God than to the voice of any other creature, even one's own self. For what autonomy gains in terms of its independent will, it loses in terms of its connection with a world already there; and what heteronomy (the voice of some other creature) gains in terms of this connection, it loses in terms of the significance of personal action per se. Only theonomy (hearkening to the voice of God) can overcome this antinomy by a prior transcendence of its two disjuncts. The human response to God's voice can be only from freedom, which mediates between a heteronomy that would eliminate personal response and an autonomy that would reduce each person to an individual, unconnected to either history or nature. Autonomy is silent; heteronomy is deafening.

It has been noted that the self-legislating person is in total control of himself or herself. But if hearkening to a voice, even to one's own, is being called toward a future, then the self that answers its own call must be answering its own projection into the future. And, as Plato pointed out, to talk of self-control is to talk about one part of the soul controlling another part.[114] Thus "self-control" cannot be the act of one self, but only the act of a self essentially divided into two or more parts. Self-control as self-legislation is therefore the present self projecting a future identity out of itself and then subordinating its present action to that ideal. But how can the self have any certainty about its projected future when it is finite and mortal? Why should the future of such a self be any less finite and fallible than the present in which it finds itself here and now? Is not this present characterized as controlled by external phenomena that are totally indifferent to this self-legislating intelligence *(noumenon)* and that will eventually reclaim it altogether into its total past?

Kant's solution to this problem was to postulate the immortality of the soul and the existence of God. The immortal human soul is believed to transcend the phenomenal world's claim of death by merging with its infinite projected future. And God redeems the phenomenal world by ultimately subordinating it to the moral causality of the noumenal world. Virtue will finally have tangible consequences there.[115] If one is going to reconstitute faith's objects as ontological requirements of morality, then one can certainly take the historic faiths rooted in Scripture as competitors with this new philosophical faith. And, indeed, one can see the scripturally based faiths as having strengths for morality lacking in Kant's full constitution of the autonomous self. But that morality cannot be autonomous.

First, if autonomy is apprehended in the present, but its full intentionality of the future can be postulated only by faith, then the autonomous self is at present divided. For its future is now a projection-away-from-its-present rather than an extension-from-its-present-into-its-future. As such, as we see in Plato's critique by anticipation of Kantian autonomy, autonomy breaks down into a new heteronomy: the future projected self *(causa noumenon)* commanding the present phenomenal self. If, then, all obedience is one entity listening to the voice of another, is it not "better to trust in the Lord than in man" (Psalms 118:8)?[116] Furthermore, if God is postulated as only the guarantor of future success in this autonomous projection, is not God's voice totally silent in the present? Is this God "that which nothing greater than can be conceived"?[117] Is this "god" really *God* at all?

The scripturally based faiths, however, understand the human person here and now as the full subject of the commandments uttered by God. Because this voice is that of God the creator, human hearkening to it is not a projection-away-from-its-present, and human existence is not something totally separate from the rest of creation.[118] The difference is in the mode of hearkening to the creator's voice: the human person answers freely; nonhuman creatures answer instinctively.[119] But none of them is autonomous; only God the creator has that power and that wisdom. And only God the creator owns the future. "The secret things belong to the Lord our God; and the revealed things are for us and our children throughout the time of this world [*ad 'olam*]: to do all the words of this Torah" (Deuteronomy 29:28). "I am the first and I am the last—says the Lord" (Isaiah 44:6). Finally, immortality is not an aspect of such faith.[120] Even life after death is from God's grace, not from human nature. Indeed, the moral act is apprehended as of immediate urgency only when human mortality is affirmed and not denied. As Franz Rosenzweig astutely and movingly noted:

> God gives man the freedom to make the most significant decision, he gives freedom for just that—only for that. But giving it, he yet retains the powers of recognition in his own treasure trove. . . . He grants man the fief of today, and so makes himself the Lord of tomorrow. That is why man must tremble for his today so long as there can be a tomorrow. . . . There is the driving force of the fear roused by God, the fear that perhaps this day will not be followed by a tomorrow. And through this fear the deed is born at last, the deed that transports today across into the eternal tomorrow.[121]

To make autonomous response to one's own voice the content of human action, however, cuts the human self off from the rest of finite, fragile creation (something brought home at this point in history by the ecological-technological crisis for civilization). And to assume that the future can be fully projected here and now as our own creation, rather than being seen as the mostly mysterious night we enter at our own peril, is to fly in the face of the continual experience of our own finitude. Only the voice of God enables the human person to act as a whole, to be fully responsive, tending toward a future before God and together with the nonhuman realm with which it shares creaturely dependence.[122] That is why that-which-one-is-to-hearken-to is the voice of God rather than the voice of anyone else. For to make any other voice the *Grundnorm,* be it a voice from within (autonomy) or from without (heteronomy), is to hearken to that which is less, not more, than fully human. "Their idols are silver and gold, the works of human hands . . . like them will all who trust in them become" (Psalms 115:4, 8). Or, as the rabbis put it, " 'Other gods' (Exodus 20:3) are gods who make those who serve them other [*'aherim*]," that is, other than their created nature and destiny.[123]

## The Objections from Plato and Nietzsche to Theonomous Morality

The position that morality is hearkening to a voice and that the only voice to be hearkened to unconditionally is the voice of God must defend itself against at least two objections raised by philosophers. (1) The objection of Plato: Must not God's voice be subordinate to God's vision of the Good if it is to be normative for a rational being? In other words, is not goodness an a priori standard for rational moral action, not just an a posteriori consequence of it? (2) The objection of Nietzsche: Assuming that God did indeed speak in earlier times, what does one do when one is no longer able to hear the voice of God, when for that person (and the culture in which he or she lives) "God is dead"?[124]

In dealing with Plato's question, the so-called *Euthyphro* problem, many philosophers have assumed that a problem raised in the context of ancient Hellenic religion can be automatically raised again in the context of Hebraic religion. However, this is quite typical of the historical naiveté of too many philosophers today, especially Anglo-American analytical philosophers, with regard to the philosophical questions bequeathed by tradition. (And what philosophical question is not bequeathed by tradition?)

The gods with whom Plato was concerned in the *Euthyphro* and elsewhere are first of all part of a polytheistic system. To speak of their commanding voice as one consistent will is to speak of a standard of agreement among them.[125] This standard of agreement must be either a priori or a posteriori. If a posteriori, it is essentially a compromise among various individual points of view— a divine social contract, if you will. But such a contract, like any contract, is normative only for those who are equal parties in the original agreement. Thus inasmuch as humans are not equals of the gods, and they are not participants in the primordial time of the gods, this compromise cannot be normative for them. Hence, the only standard of agreement that would be normative for those who are not gods is a priori. It is a transcendence of individual positions based on that which eternally subsists intelligibly and is therefore universally binding. For Plato, the gods are conscious persons—"souls" *(psychai)*—for whom these eternal Forms are the ultimate criteria for action. They, in turn, show lesser human souls how to live by them.[126] These gods are certainly not "that which nothing greater than can be conceived." Indeed, these gods are not presented as either creators of the Forms or creators of the material substratum that is the *terminus ad quem* of all creativity.[127] Their finite power is bound by an intelligible limit above them and a sensible limit below them.

The God of Scripture is the creator of the world, of everything that exists. He is thus bound by nothing a priori. Everything, both substance and structure, is a posteriori in relation to God. The *Grundnorm* is God's commanding/creative will. This will is revealed in the context of the covenant with his people, and in this covenantal context all subsequent commandments find their system. "Thus says the Lord, 'if my covenant not be by day and by night, then I have not appointed the laws of heaven and earth' " (Jeremiah 33:25). Each succeeding commandment presupposes that which went before it and that which comes after it in the covenant. The covenant, like creation, generates its own order. Its own future is promised in it. "And here and now *[heneni]* I uphold My covenant with you and with your children after you" (Genesis 9:9).

Because of this covenantal continuity, God's commandments are not capricious and do display an intelligibility to their intelligent subjects. Each one is part of a covenantal whole, which itself functions as a subsistent system dependent on God, and each one is related to every other part. Thus each one can be the basis of an analogy with any other at any point in time or space. The entire process of midrashic exegesis in rabbinic literature attests to that. This is because the covenant begun at Sinai is with the whole people of Israel, both vertically and horizontally. "Not only with you do I specify *[koret]* this covenant and its consequences *[ha'alah ha-z'ot]*, but with whoever is standing here with us today before the Lord our God and with whoever is not here with us today" (Deuteronomy 29:13–14).[128] This historical people of Israel is coeval with revelation and its tradition. Furthermore, limiting primary normative revelation to the written Torah and a few undoubtedly ancient traditions *(halakhot)* firmly establishes the demarcation between prior revelation and subsequent reason. Each is thus allowed to function without being subsumed by the other.[129]

The direct commandments of the one God, presented within an ongoing covenantal system, have so little in common with the indirect and unsystematic commands of the subordinate deities with whom Plato was concerned in the context of ancient Greek culture that I fail to see how objections raised against unconditionally obeying these deities can apply to the Torah of the Lord God. However, these objections have been so persistently raised that they must be addressed.

Socrates's question to Euthyphro is this: "Is the holy loved by the gods because it is holy, or is it holy because the gods love it?"[130] His answer is that the holy *(to hosion)* as a subset of cosmic justice *(to dikaion)* is prior to the will of the gods inasmuch as the gods themselves are part of the cosmic order (nature), which is identical with this cosmic justice.[131] However, in Scripture, the Lord God is the creator of this cosmic order, and as creator he transcends its limits. Holiness *(qedushah)* is not part of the cosmic order. Being God's own relational capacity with man, it, too, transcends that order. Those addressed by God's covenant also transcend therein the limits of that order: "You shall be holy because I the Lord your God am holy" (Leviticus 19:2). This relationship, on the human side, only presupposes the cosmic order for its formal structure, but it transcends it in its substantial being-with-God. Creation's very finite limitation is both its own immanent order *in itself* and its leaving room *for* the transcendence/holiness of the covenant. Thus the holy is holy because God ordains it as the substance of his personal relationship with his covenanted people. This is indicated by the holiness of the Sabbath as creation's culmination and telos.[132] The commandments are initiated as instantiations of this prior holiness. God designates the specific commandments to be holy because all conform to what is originally holy as *Grundnorm*. But what is originally holy follows after and does not precede God's creation of the world.[133] The covenant itself presupposes the creation of its possibility. "Remember the Sabbath day to hallow it . . . for in six days the Lord made heaven and earth . . . thereafter *['al ken]* the Lord blessed the Sabbath day and hallowed it" (Exodus 20:8, 11).[134] Hallowing the Sabbath, then, is *imitatio Dei,* and the Sabbath is the paradigm for all the other commandments.[135] Hence, covenantal holiness is a priori in relation to the specific commandments, but it is a posteriori in relation to the fundamental act of divine creation.[136] For this reason also, the more general covenant that God made with Noah and his descendants becomes an a priori standard for interpreting the subsequent and more specific covenant with Israel at Sinai.[137]

Nietzsche's objection is the hardest to answer. For only the human person himself or herself can hear the voice of God. No one can prove its presence, and no one can fill its absence. "Seek the Lord where He is to be found; call upon Him when He is near" (Isaiah 55:6).[138] But for some—nowadays for many—God has not been found, and God has never been near. What does one who has heard God's voice—however dimly—say to one who has never heard that voice? Those who have heard the voice do have something to say to one another; they have much to say to one another. "Then the fearers of the Lord speak, each man to his neighbor, and the Lord gives ear and hears" (Malachi 3:16). Jews and Christians today can be such communicating neighbors. Indeed, it is precisely because they have faith that the Lord hears and speaks that they can speak and hear the words of one another. These words alone penetrate the heart. But, again, what does one say to one who does not have such faith because that person has heard neither the voice nor its echo?

It seems that such a person must choose either to listen to other voices or to wait. If he or she chooses to listen to other voices—and they are always there—there is nothing we can say to him or her. But if that person chooses to wait, then he or she must be silent, for silence precedes the speaking of the voice. "And the Lord is in His holy abode, be silent before Him all the earth" (Habbukuk 2:20). And we who have heard it must be silent with them, for we need to hear it once again. No one taught the truth of waiting in our age better than Franz Rosenzweig:

> In Judaism, man is always somehow a remnant. He is somehow a survivor *[ein Uebriggebliebener]* . . . what is left of him remains standing on the shore. . . . Something within him is waiting. . . . What he is waiting for and what he has he may call by different names; often enough he may barely be able to name it. But he has a feeling that both the waiting and the having are most intimately connected with each other. And this is just that feeling of the "remnant" which has revelation and awaits salvation.[139]

## The Final Redemption

The final redemption will be such that "No eye but Yours O Lord will see what will be done for those who wait for You."[140] Until that time, we are all travelers passing through a vale of tears until we appear before God in Zion.[141] Jews and Christians begin at the same starting point, and both are convinced that we will meet at the all-mysterious end. Yet we cannot deny that our appointed tasks in this world are very different and must remain so because the covenant is not the same for both of us. It is God alone who will bring us to our unknown destination in a time pleasing to him.[142]

That time has not yet come. In the meantime, the constitution of the Jewish–Christian dialogue might have a message for the larger body of humankind for whose peace we must all be concerned. Our dialogue might be able to show the world that the hope it needs for its very survival can only be the hope for its final redemption. Neither nature nor history nor the self can supply hope in these days. Beginning with creation and nurtured by our respective revelations, Jews and Christians can and do hope for the future. From creation and revelation comes our faith that God has not and will not abandon us or the world, that the promised redemption is surely yet to come.

# Notes

ABBREVIATIONS

B.  Babylonian Talmud
M.  Mishnah
R.  Rabbi (used only for rabbis of Talmudic period)
T.  Tosefta
Y.  Talmud Yerushalmi (Palestinian Talmud)

## Introduction

1. An example of this can be found in Howard Singer, "The Rise and Fall of Interfaith Dialogue." *Commentary* 83, no. 5 (May 1987): 50–55. See the response of D. Novak, *Commentary* 84, no. 3 (September 1987): 9.

2. The most articulate spokesperson for this point of view has been the Orthodox theologian Rabbi Eliezer Berkovits, who insists on the guilt of every Christian eo ipso because of what he sees as Christian complicity in, indeed responsibility for having caused, the Nazi murder of 6 million European Jews. See his "Facing the Truth," *Judaism* 27, no. 3 (Summer 1978): 324–26.

3. See Paul van Buren, *Discerning the Way: A Theology of the Jewish–Christian Reality* (New York, 1980), esp. pp. 47–48.

4. See Will Herberg, "The Social Philosophy of Karl Barth," in intro. to Karl Barth, *Community, Church, and State* (Garden City, N.Y., 1960), pp. 38ff.; Jacques Maritain, "The Christian Teaching of the Story of the Crucifixion," in *The Range of Reason* (New York, 1952), pp. 129–33.

5. See Milton Himmelfarb, "No Hitler—No Holocaust," *Commentary* 77, no. 3 (March 1984): 37–43.

6. Joseph B. Soloveitchik, "Confrontation," *Tradition* 6, no. 2 (Spring–Summer 1964): 26. For the most critical yet sympathetic treatment of Soloveitchik's thought to date, see D. Singer and M. Sokol, "Joseph Soloveitchik: Lonely Man of Faith," *Modern Judaism* 2, no. 3 (October 1982): 227–72.

7. Soloveitchik, "Confrontation," p. 18.

8. Ibid., p. 19.

9. This point was argued by my colleague and friend Michael Wyschogrod in an unpublished lecture he delivered to the Mid-Winter Conference of the Rabbinical Council of America on January 28, 1986. There he writes, "It is simply not possible to split a Jew into two, demanding of him to keep what is most important about his very identity out of the dialogue. All Jewish values are ultimately rooted in revelation and to pretend otherwise is to play a charade which will convince no one" (p. 10).

10. Soloveitchik does refer to "the *logos,* the word, in which the multifarious religious experience is expressed [which] does not lend itself to standardization or universalization" ("Confrontation," p. 23). However, *logos* precisely denotes that aspect of reality that is communicable to others. See Plato, *Crito* 46B–D.

11. Soloveitchik, "Confrontation," p. 24. Tthe term *secular orders* comes out of Lutheran theology, with its emphasis on the "two kingdoms": God's and Caesar's. See Helmut Thielecke, *Theological Ethics: Foundations,* trans. G. Bromiley (Grand Rapids, Mich., 1979), vol. 1, pp. 359ff.

12. Soloveitchik, "Confrontation," p. 24, n. 8.

13. Ibid., p. 21.

14. Ibid., p. 28.

15. See D. Berger, "Jewish–Christian Relations—A Jewish Perspective," *Journal of Ecumenical Studies* 20, no. 1 (Winter 1983): 32.

16. Jakob J. Petuchowski, "A Jewish Response to 'Israel as a Theological Problem for the Christian Church,' " *Journal of Ecumenical Studies* 6, no. 3 (Summer 1969): 349.

17. See Leo Strauss, *Natural Right and History* (Chicago, 1953), pp. 165ff.

18. See Richard John Neuhaus, *The Naked Public Square* (Grand Rapids, Mich., 1984).

19. Thus the most influential work of political philosophy in the past twenty-five years is John Rawls's *A Theory of Justice* (Cambridge, Mass., 1971). See especially pp. 255–56, 396, 447, 516, and 587. For the classical Jewish recognition of social contract in a secondary sense, see D. Novak, *The Image of the Non-Jew in Judaism: An Historical and Constructive Study of the Noahide Laws* (New York and Toronto, 1983), pp. 66ff.

20. See D. Novak, "American Jews and America: The Mission of Israel Revisited," *This World* 17 (Spring 1987): 95ff.

21. See Neuhaus, *The Naked Public Square,* pp. 20ff.

22. Note Maimonides, *The Guide of the Perplexed* 2.40, trans. S. Pines (Chicago, 1963), p. 382: "Therefore I say that the Law, although it is not natural, enters into what is natural." For rabbinic precedent, see M. Sanhedrin 10.1; M. 'Abot 2.12; B. Kiddushin 54a and parallels; B. Baba Metzia 59b.

23. "Dialogical" philosophy has a number of expressions. My preference for it is clearly not its Buberian expression, in that I regard it as far more structured than Buber did. See D. Novak, *Law and Theology in Judaism* (New York, 1976), vol. 2, pp. 10ff. It is more closely influenced by the dialogical philosophy of Emmanuel Levinas (primarily because of the influence of Husserl's emphasis of structure). See Emmanuel Levinas, "Moi," *Revue de metaphysique et de morale* 59 (1954): 353–73; S. G. Smith, *The Argument to the Other* (Chico, Calif., 1983), pp. 53ff.

24. The term *constitution* is regularly used in this work. I use it in the fundamental sense that Husserl did—a reconstruction of a datum from within consciousness, as opposed to representation in the empirical sense in which a datum is posited as being viewed as it immediately appears. See Edmund Husserl, *Ideas: A General Introduction to Pure Phenomenology,* trans. W. R. B. Gibson (New York, 1962), sec. 86; see also M. Farber, *The Foundations of Phenomenology,* 3d ed. (Albany, N.Y., 1968), pp. 265ff., 556ff. I differ from Husserl in that the basis of this constitution is not the ego qua cogito, but a standpoint from within Judaism as a living religious tradition to which I am primarily bound.

25. See H. A. Wolfson, *Spinoza* (Cambridge, Mass., 1934), p. 10.

26. See D. Berger, "Jewish Christian Polemics," *Encyclopedia of Religion* (New York, 1986), vol. 11, pp. 389ff.

27. See, for example, Augustine, *De civitate Dei* 4.34, 18.46.

28. Note, for example, R. Judah Ha-Levi, *Kuzari* 1.116, trans. H. Hirschfeld (New York, 1964), p. 81, where the pagan king of the Khazars converts to Judaism, rather than to Christianity or Islam, because "there has been nothing new since your religion." See also 1.4–1.25, pp. 40–47.

29. See B. Blumenkranz, "Juedische und Christliche Konvertiten im Juedisch–Christlichen Religionsgespraech des Mittelalters" in *Judentum im Mittelalters,* ed. P. Wilpert (Berlin, 1966), pp. 264–82.

30. See especially the statement on the Jews ("Nostre Aetate") of Vatican Council II in *The Documents of Vatican II,* ed. W. M. Abbot, S.J. (London and Dublin, 1966), pp. 664–65.

31. See, for example, J. D. Bleich, "Teaching Torah to Gentiles," *Tradition* 18, no. 2 (Summer 1980): 192–211.

32. The late Dr. Jacob B. Agus wrote: "The way is infinite, and it consists of many twisted paths . . . a peculiar truth is found in nearly every faith" ("Revelation as Quest," *Journal of Ecumenical Studies* 9, no. 3 [Summer 1972]: 537–38). See also his "The Covenant Concept—Particularistic, Pluralistic, or Futuristic," *Journal of Ecumenical Studies* 18, no. 2 (Spring 1981): 217ff.

33. See Isaiah 29:13–14; Proverbs 21:30.

34. B. Berakhot 12b.

35. See Maimonides, *The Guide of the Perplexed* 1.26.

36. Jewish law requires martyrdom rather than conversion to *any* other

religion (see B. Sanhedrin 74a), even to another monotheistic religion. See
R. Abraham Gumbiner, *Magen 'Abraham on Shulhan Arukh: 'Orah
Hayyim* 128.37.

37. Thus the demand to be ready for martyrdom seen in "You shall
love the Lord your God with all your life *[be-khol nafshekha]*—even if
He takes your life" (Sifre: Debarim, no. 32, re Deuteronomy 6:5, ed.
Finkelstein, p. 55 and note; M. Berakhot 9.5; T. Berakhot 6.7; B. Berakhot 61b) is to be recited at least twice daily by every Jew as the most
important liturgical utterance. See Sifre: Debarim, no. 34, p. 62; B. Berakhot 2a.

38. B. Kiddushin 66a.

39. Spinoza, *A Political Treatise* 3.10, trans. R. H. M. Elwes (New
York, 1951), pp. 305–6 [*Tractatus Politicus*, ed. S. Zac (Paris, 1968), pp.
64–66]. See Leo Strauss, *Spinoza's Critique of Religion*, trans. E. M. Sin-
clair (New York, 1965), pp. 246ff., and John Locke, *First Letter on Toleration*, in *The Works of John Locke* (Aalen, 1963), vol. 6, pp. 5ff.

40. See Moses Mendelssohn, *Jerusalem*, trans. A. Arkush (Hanover,
N.H., 1983), pp. 89ff., and Alexander Altmann, *Moses Mendelssohn*
(University, Ala., 1973), pp. 514ff.

41. See Novak, *The Image of the Non-Jew in Judaism*, pp. 369ff.

42. See D. Novak, review of *The Jew: Essays from Martin Buber's
Journal "Der Jude," 1916–1928*, edited by Arthur A. Cohen, *Modern
Judaism* 2, no. 1 (February 1982): 105. See also Alice Eckhardt and Roy
Eckhardt, "The Achievements and Trials of Interfaith," *Judaism* 27, no.
3 (Summer 1978): 319.

43. See Will Herberg, *Prostestant, Catholic, Jew*, rev. ed. (Garden City,
N.Y., 1960), esp. pp. 263ff.

44. The attempt to distill truths from religion without acknowledgment of historical revelation in this century found its most influential
spokesperson in John Dewey. See his *A Common Faith* (New Haven,
Conn., 1934), pp. 1ff. Dewey, of course, went far beyond the God of the
deists. They, however, by constituting the value of religion solely on the
basis of its secular consequences, laid the groundwork for Dewey's type
of humanism.

45. See *Ecumenical Bulletin* 44 (November–December 1980): 36–40.

46. B. Berakhot 4b.

47. 1 Samuel 16:7.

48. See Shalom Spiegel, *Amos versus Amaziah*, Essays in Judaism, no.
33, Jewish Theological Seminary of America (New York, n.d.).

49. See Maimonides, *Hilkhot Melakhim* 10.9.

50. See, for example, Ignatius, *To the Magnesians*, chap. 10.

51. See D. Novak, *Law and Theology*, vol. 1, pp. 1ff.

52. See D. Novak, "The Role of Dogma in Judaism," *Theology Today*
45, no. 1 (April 1988): 49ff.

## 1. The Doctrine of the Noahide Laws

1. T. 'Abodah Zarah 8.4 following Ms. Vienna, ed. Zuckermandl, p. 473. For the dual denotation of the term *ben Noah*, see T. Hullin 7.8; Hullin 100b; cf. M. Nedarim 3.11 and B. Nedarim 31a. This chapter is based on D. Novak, *The Image of the Non-Jew in Judaism: An Historical and Constructive Study of the Noahide Laws* (New York and Toronto, 1983), intro. and chaps. 1–4, 9. Fuller discussion and documentation are found there.

2. B. 'Abodah Zarah 64b. See Y. Tebamot 8.1/8d, and S. Lieberman, *Greek in Jewish Palestine* (New York, 1942), pp. 81–82.

3. See M. Guttmann, *Das Judenthum und seine Umwelt* (Berlin, 1927), p. 110.

4. Maimonides, *Hilkhot 'Abodah Zarah* 10.6 and *Hilkhot Melakhim* 8.7.

5. 'Arakhin 29a. See Maimonides, *Hilkhot Shemittah ve-Yobel* 10.8–9.

6. Sifra: Behar, ed. Weiss, 107a; Y. Shebi'it 10.2/39c; 'Arakhin 32b.

7. See Maimonides, *Hilkhot 'Abodah Zarah* 10.5–6; *Hilkhot Isuray Bi'ah* 14.8. Cf. *Hilkhot Millah* 1.6; *Hilkhot Shabbat* 20. 14.

8. Concerning (1) adjudication, see Genesis 2:16 (with which the Talmud, Sanhedrin 56b, attempts to associate all the Noahide laws; see R. Judah Ha-Levi, *Kuzari* 3.73). Concerning (2) blasphemy, see Genesis 2:16, 11:4; Exodus 5:2. Concerning (3) idolatry, see Genesis 2:16, 3:5. Concerning (4) bloodshed, see Genesis 4:10–11, 9:6; Exodus 1:17, 2:11–12. Concerning (5) sexual immorality, see Genesis 6:2, 6:13, 26:9, 34:7; Leviticus 18:27. Concerning (6) robbery, see Genesis 2:16, 21:25, 26:20, 27:35–36, 30:33, 31:30, 37:26–27; Exodus 12:36. Concerning (7) eating a limb torn from a living animal, which is the most explicitly scriptural of these seven laws, see Genesis 9:4.

9. See also Exodus 20:10; Leviticus 16:29, 17:8–13, 18:26; Numbers 9:14, 15:15–29, 19:10; Deuteronomy 5:14.

10. See also Genesis 15:13, 23:4; Exodus 2:22, 18:3, 22:20; Leviticus 19:34, 25:35, 25:47; Deuteronomy 10:19, 16:11, 16:14, 23:8.

11. See B. Bamberger, *Proselytism in the Talmudic Period* (New York, 1968), pp. 38ff.

12. See Sifra: Behar 110a and Targumim on Leviticus 25:47.

13. See Numbers 33:50–54.

14. See Numbers 18:1–24.

15. See Leviticus 25:13–18; T. Nega'im 6.2; B. Gittin 47a.

16. See Sifre: Bamidbar, ed. Horovitz 78.

17. See A. Bertholet, *Die Stellung der Israeliten und der Juden zu Fremden* (Freiburg, 1896), pp. 27–36.

18. See C. Tchernowitz, *Toldot Ha-Halakhah* (New York, 1934), vol.

1, pp. 296–98; Y. Kaufmann, *Toldot Ha'Emunah Ha-Yisra'elit* (Jerusalem, 1953), vol. 5, p. 459, n. 5; vol. 3, p. 636.

19. See E. Bickerman, *From Ezra to the Last of the Maccabees* (New York, 1962), pp. 82–83.

20. See LXX on Psalms 118:2–4; Josephus, *Antiquities* 14.110 and *Bellum Judaicum* 2.463.

21. See, for example, Mekhilta: Mishpatim, ed. Horovitz-Rabin, 312; Y. Megillah 3.2/74a and parallels; B. Shabbat 31a.

22. Juvenal, *Satires* 14.96, trans. G. C. Ramsey (Cambridge, Mass., 1940), pp. 271–273. See Tacitus, *History* 5.5.

23. See J. Juster, *Les Juifs dans l'empire romain* (Paris, 1914), vol. 1, pp. 275–76; Lieberman, *Greek in Jewish Palestine*, pp. 85–86.

24. See S. Belkin, *Philo and the Oral Law* (Cambridge, Mass., 1940), pp. 47–48; H. A. Wolfson, *Philo* (Cambridge, Mass., 1947), vol. 2, pp. 373–74; J. B. Agus, *The Evolution of Jewish Thought* (New York, 1959), p. 68.

25. Y. 'Abodah Zarah 2.1/40c; Hullin 92a–b.

26. B. Sanhedrin 58b/bot.; 74b/bot.; Y. Berakhot, end re Psalms 12:1.

27. See Acts 10:2, 13:16, 18:4; J. Klausner, *From Jesus to Paul*, trans. W. F. Stinespring (Boston, 1961), p. 42; S. W. Baron, *A Social and Religious History of the Jews*, rev. ed. (New York, 1952), vol. 1, p. 375, n. 15; Bamberger, *Proselytism*, pp. 135–38.

28. T. Sanhedrin 13.2, ed. Zuckermandl, p. 434; B. Sanhedrin 105a. See T. Nedarim 2.4 re Judges 14:3.

29. B. Sanhedrin 58b/bott.; S. Atlas, *Netivim Be-Mishpat Ha'Ibri* (New York, 1978), p. 39.

30. B. Sanhedrin 58b–59a. See B. Hagigah 13a re Psalms 147:20; S. Lieberman, *Hellenism in Jewish Palestine*, 2d imp. ed. (New York, 1962), pp. 18–19, n. 111.

31. See B. 'Abodah Zarah 3a and Tos., s.v. "she'afilu."

32. B. Sanhedrin 74a; Y. Sanhedrin 3.6/21b; also Sifra: 'Aharay-Mot 86a re Liviticus 18:5.

33. See Baron, *A Social and Religious History of the Jews*, vol. 2, pp. 102ff.

34. *Nimuqay Yosef* on 'Alfasi: B. Sanhedrin 74a–b, ed. Vilna, 17b. See Maimonides, *Hilkhot Yesoday Ha-Torah* 5.7.

35. See B. Sanhedrin 74a–b; Maimonides, *Hilkhot Melakhim* 10.2.

36. See T. Sotah 6.6 and S. Lieberman, *Tosefta Kifshuta: Nashim* (New York, 1973), pp. 670–71; Pesiqta Rabbati, ed. Friedmann, 47b.

37. See L. Ginzberg, *The Legends of the Jews* (Philadelphia, 1925), vol. 5, pp. 278, n. 51, 223, n. 82.

38. B. Sanhedrin 57a/top.

39. See ibid., 45b–46a re Deuteronomy 21:23; Y. Sanhedrin 6.6/23c, 7.9/25b; Keritot 7b.

40. See Mekhilta: Yitro 188 and Zebahim 116a.

41. Maimonides, *Hilkhot Melakhim* 9.14.

42. Ibid., 8.10. See ibid., 10.11; ct. note of Radbaz thereon.

43. See Genesis 34:30, 49:5–7.

44. See Nahmanides's comment on Genesis 26:5.

45. See *Responsa Ramo*, ed. Ziv (Jerusalem, 1970), no. 10, pp. 45–46; *Encyclopedia Talmudit*, vol. 3,.p. 355.

46. This point was already made by the medieval commentators R. Solomon ibn Adret (Rashba), in *Response Rashba* 4, no. 334, and Rabbenu Bahya ben Asher, in his commentary on the Torah: Deuteronomy 31:15 re Deuteronomy 4:19–20.

47. See Psalms 96:5; M. 'Abodah Zarah 4.7; T. 'Abodah Zarah 6.7; B. 'Abodah Zarah 54b; Mekhilta: Yitro 226.

48. See Exodus 12:38.

49. See Shemot Rabbah 42.6, 43.8.

50. See Genesis 26:34–35; Numbers 25:1–3; Bekhorot 5b; Beresheet Rabbah 20.23.

51. See M. Sanhedrin 2.4; B. Kiddushin 68b re Deuteronomy 7:4; Philo, *De Specialis Legibus* 3.29.

52. See T. 'Abodah Zarah 4.6; B. 'Abodah Zarah 8a, 36b.

53. See Isaiah 13:11, 16:6, 24:1–5; Ezekiel 25.

54. See Sifre: Debarim, ed. Finkelstein, no. 354 re Deuteronomy 33:19.

55. See Exodus 7:5, 14:4, 18; 1 Kings 89:41–43; Isaiah 24:14–15, 25:1–8, 45:3–8, 45:18–24, 55:4–5, 60:1ff; Ezekiel 29:6, 29:9, 30:8, 30:25–26; Psalms 47:2–5, 47:10, 98:2–3, 105:1ff, 117:1–2. See also Y. 'Abodah Zarah 4.7/44a.

56. See Rashbam's comment on Genesis 37:2.

57. B. Megillah 9a–b.

58. LXX on Exodus 22:27.

59. Hullin 13b. See B. Cohen, *Jewish and Roman Law* (New York, 1966), vol. 2, p. 386.

60. José Faur, *Iyunim Be-Mishneh Torah Le-Ha-Rambam* (Jerusalem, 1978), pp. 227–29.

61. B. Shabbat 156a. Cf. B. Sanhedrin 67b.

62. See B. Sukkah 29a.

63. See Josephus, *Antiquities* 4.207, *Contra Apionem* 2.144; Philo, *De Vita Mosis* 2.205–6, and *De Specialus Legibus* 1.51, 1.53, 2.164–67.

64. See Maimonides, *The Guide of the Perplexed* 2.5.

65. Menahot 110a and E. E. Urbach, *Hazal: 'Emunot ve-De'ot* (Jerusalem, 1971), pp. 118–19.

66. Solomon ibn Gabirol, *Selected Religious Poetry of Solomon ibn Gabirol*, trans. I. Zangwill, ed. I Davidson (Philadelphia, 1923), pp. 86–87.

## 2. The Status of Christianity in Medieval European Halakhah

1. See S. W. Baron, *The Jewish Community* (Philadelphia, 1945), vol. 1, pp. 208ff.

2. B. Baba Batra 54b and parallels.

3. On this whole topic, the most comprehensive study is S. Shilo, *Dina de-Malkhuta Dina* (Jerusalem, 1974); see also L. Landman, *Jewish Law in the Diaspora: Confrontation and Accommodation* (Philadelphia, 1968); D. Novak, *The Image of the Non-Jew in Judaism: An Historical and Constructive Study of the Noahide Laws* (New York and Toronto, 1983), pp. 66ff.

4. Rashbam on B. Baba Batra 54b, s.v. "mi."

5. M. ʿAbodah Zarah 1.1.

6. Rashi on B. ʿAbodah Zarah 2a, s.v. "lifnay."

7. B. ʿAbodah Zarah 2a, Tos., s.v. "asur." See Novak, *The Image of the Non-Jew in Judaism*, pp. 130ff.

8. Concerning Sunday, see Rashi on B. Sanhedrin 58b, s.v. "ʾamar Rabina."

9. Hullin 13b.

10. B. ʿAbodah Zarah 7b.

11. See Menahem Meiri, *Bet Ha-Behirah* on B. ʿAbodah Zarah 6b, ed. Sofer (Jerusalem, 1964), p. 9.

12. See B. ʿAbodah Zarah 6b.

13. See ibid., 65a.

14. See, for example, B. Bekhorot 2b, Tos., s.v. "shema"; E. E. Urbach, *Baʿalay Ha-Tosafot*, 4th rev. ed. (Tel Aviv, 1980), vol. 1, pp. 60ff.

15. See B. Sanhedrin 60b; B. ʿAbodah Zarah 29b; also D. Novak, *Law and Theology in Judaism* (New York, 1976), vol. 2, pp. 174ff.

16. See B. ʿAbodah Zarah 36b and parallels.

17. See B. Kiddushin 68b re Deuteronomy 7:4; R. Abraham Gumbiner, *Magen ʾAbraham* on *Shulhan ʿArukh: ʾOrah Hayyim* 128.37.

18. B. ʿAbodah Zarah 57b, Tos., s.v. "lʾafooqay."

19. See *Responsa Rashi*, ed. Elfenbein (New York, 1943), nos. 59, 155, 327.

20. B. ʿAbodah Zarah 57b, Tos., s.v. "lʾafooqay."

21. See *Responsa Tashbatz* (Amsterdam, 1739), vol. 2, no. 48.

22. See B. Baba Batra 60b and parallels; *Responsa Ramo*, ed. Ziv (New York, 1970), no. 124.

23. See B. ʿAbodah Zarah 57b, Tos., s.v. "lʾafooqay," end; *Rosh: ʿAbodah Zarah* 3.7; R. Moses Iisserles (Ramo) on *Shulhan ʿArukh: Yoreh Deʿah* 123.1.

24. For this reason, the tractates in the Mishnah, the Tosefta, and the two Talmuds that deal with this subject (Nedarim and Shebuʿot) have many discussions about intention and how it can be determined.

25. B. Sanhedrin 63b.

26. Ibid.

27. Ibid., Rashi, s.v. "lo yigrom."

28. See Mekhilta: Mishpatim, ed. Horovitz-Rabin, 332. See Genesis 31:43ff.

29. B. Sanhedrin 63b, Tos., s.v. "asur." Cf. *Responsa Rashi,* no. 180; Maimonides, *Hilkhot Shebu'ot* 11.2 re B. Sukkah 45b and parallels.

30. See R. Samuel Ha-Levi Kellin, *Mahatzit Ha-Sheqel* on *Shulhan 'Arukh: 'Orah Hayyim* 156; José Faur, *'Iyunim Be-Mishneh Torah Le-Ha-Rambam* (Jerusalem, 1978), p. 231, no. 10.

31. See Jacob Katz, *Exclusiveness and Tolerance* (New York, 1961), pp. 163–64.

32. See ibid., p. 163, n. 2.

33. See Novak, *The Image of the Non-Jew in Judaism,* pp. 132–33.

34. B'er Ha-Golah on *Shulhan 'Arukh: Hoshen Mishpat* 425.5. For an attempt to see Christians as idolators by an Ashkenazic authority after Rabbenu Tam, following Maimonides *(Hilkhot Ma'akhalot 'Asurot* 11.7 in the Amsterdam and Venice editions), see R. Moses Schreiber, *Responsa Hatam Sofer: Yoreh De'ah* (Vienna, 1855), no. 131.

35. See Nahmanides's comment on Exodus 20:2 and, earlier, R. Judah Ha-Levi, *Kuzari* 1.25.

36. See Gershom Scholem, *Major Trends in Jewish Mysticism,* 3d rev. ed. (New York, 1961); *On the Kabbalah and Its Symbolism,* trans. R. Manheim (New York, 1969), pp. 32ff. Cf. Maimonides, *The Guide of the Perplexed* 1.52, 1.58. For the general philosophical problem faced by both Judaism and Christianity—indeed, by any revealed religion—see Paul Tillich, *Systematic Theology* (Chicago, 1951), vol. 1, p. 228.

37. *Responsa Ribash* (Constantinople, 1547), no. 157. See also Zohar: Beresheet 1:22b and I. Tishby, *Mishnat Ha-Zohar* (Jerusalem, 1961), vol. 2, pp. 279–80.

38. See, for example, R. Meir ibn Gabbai, *'Abodat Ha-Qodesh* 2.13 (Venice, 1566); Scholem, *Major Trends in Jewish Mysticism,* p. 129.

39. See, for example, Hermann Cohen, *Religion of Reason out of the Sources of Judaism,* trans. S. Kaplan (New York, 1972), pp. 61ff., 414.

40. 1 Corinthians 3:12–14. Interestingly enough, Rashi, in his comment on Exodus 34:33, states that the veil over Moses's face was removed when he spoke with God (v. 35) and with Israel, when he communicated the word of God to them. It is uncertain whether Rashi was aware of Paul's interpretation of this verse. However, it reflects a Jewish attitude that there is no barrier or intermediary between God and Israel. See B. Sotah 38b and Tos., s.v. "mehitzah" (39a re B. Berakhot 32b; see Maharsha thereon).

41. See D. Novak, *Halakhah in a Theological Dimension* (Chico, Calif., 1985), pp. 120ff.

42. Meiri, *Bet Ha-Behirah* on Sanhedrin 57a, ed. Sofer (Jerusalem, 1965), p. 226. Cf. Maimonides, *Hilkhot Melakhim* 8, end. See Katz, *Exclusiveness and Tolerance*, pp. 114ff., and his more detailed Hebrew study, "Soblanut Datit Be-Shitato shel Rabbi Menahem Ha-Meiri," *Zion*, 18 (1953): 15–30; Novak, *The Image of the Non-Jew in Judaism*, pp. 351ff.

43. For his critique of the Tosafists for their overly specific method of reinterpretation in this area, see *Bet Ha-Behirah* on B. ʿAbodah Zarah 13a, p. 28, and chap. 2, beg., p. 53.

44. *Bet Ha-Behirah* on B. ʿAbodah Zarah 20a, p. 46.

45. See ibid., 15b, p. 39.

46. Ibid., 26a, p. 59, and *Bet Ha-Behirah* on Kiddushin 17b, ed. Sofer (Jerusalem, 1963), p. 108.

47. *Bet Ha-Behirah* on ʾAbot, intro., ed. Prag (Jerusalem, 1964), p. 16. Cf. Maimonides, *The Guide of the Perplexed* 2.40; Novak, *The Image of the Non-Jew in Judaism*, pp. 285ff.

48. See *Bet Ha-Behirah* on Ketubot 15b, ed. Sofer (Jerusalem, 1968), pp. 67–68; R. Bezalel Ashkenazi, *Sheetah Mequbetzet* on Baba Kama 38a; Novak, *The Image of the Non-Jew in Judaism*, pp. 63–64.

49. T. Sotah 8.6; Y. Sotah 7.5/21d. See Novak, *The Image of the Non-Jew in Judaism*, pp. 59–60.

50. Sifre: Debarim, no. 343, ed. Finkelstein, p. 343; B. ʿAbodah Zarah 2b–3a. See Novak, 254ff.

51. B. Kiddushin 31a and parallels.

52. B. Kiddushin 31a, Tos., s.v. "dela." See Novak, *Law and Theology in Judaism*, vol. 1, pp. 15ff.

53. *Bet Ha-Behirah* on Kiddushin 31a, p. 181.

54. See *Encyclopedia Judaica*, vol. 13, pp. 1260–61.

55. See, for example, M. Niddah 4.1; Hullin 4a.

56. See B. Yoma 69a; Hullin 6a; also S. W. Baron, *A Social and Religious History of the Jews*, 2d rev. ed. (New York, 1952), vol. 2, pp. 26–35.

57. See R. R. Ruether, *Faith and Fratricide: The Theological Roots of Anti-Semitism* (New York, 1979), pp. 117ff.

## 3. Maimonides's View of Christianity

1. See D. Novak, "The Treatment of Islam and Muslims in the Legal Writings of Maimonides," in *Studies in Islamic and Judaic Traditions*, ed. W. M. Brinner and S. D. Ricks (Atlanta, 1986), pp. 233–50. A number of the points in this chapter were originally made in this essay.

2. Maimonides, *Commentary on the Mishnah*: ʿAbodah Zarah 1.3, Hebrew trans. Y. Kafih (Jerusalem, 1965), vol. 2, p. 225.

3. Ibid., 1.4, vol. 2, p. 226. Targum Onqelos on Deuteronomy 4:28

seems to be the basis for Maimonides's exegesis of this verse here. See also B. 'Abodah Zarah 8a and parallels re Exodus 34:15.

4. Maimonides, *Hilkhot 'Abodah Zarah*, 9.4. See also *Epistle to Yemen*, ed. A. S. Halkin, trans. B. Cohen (New York, 1952), p. iv.

5. Maimonides, *Hilkhot Ma'akhalot 'Asurot* 11.7.

6. B. Sanhedrin 60b; B. 'Abodah Zarah 29b and Maimonides, *Hilkhot Ma'akhalot 'Asurot* 11.4; also B. Gittin 52b–53a and Y. Gittin 5.5/47a.

7. B. 'Abodah Zarah 36b. See B. Shabbat 17b.

8. Maimonides, *The Guide of the Perplexed* 1.50, trans. S. Pines (Chicago, 1963), p. 111.

9. See Maimonides, *Hilkhot Melakhim* 12.3

10. See Maimonides, *Hilkhot Yesoday Ha-Torah* 1.7.

11. See Maimonides, *Hilkhot Teshubah* 3.7; *Guide* 1.35.

12. Maimonides, *Hilkhot Yesoday Ha-Torah* 8.3.

13. Maimonides, *The Guide of the Perplexed*, 2.40, p. 384.

14. See Pines's introduction to ibid., p. 1xxxviff.

15. Maimonides, *Hilkhot Melakhim* 11, end, uncensored ed. Rabinowitz (Jerusalem, 1962), p. 416. Maimonides's use of Zephaniah 3:9 as his proof text is significant because this verse was also the proof text for a rabbinic view that advocated growing gentile observance of the Torah as potential Judaism. See Y. 'Abodah Zarah 2.1/40c; B. 'Abodah Zarah 24a; Hullin 92a–b; D. Novak, *The Image of the Non-Jew in Judaism: An Historical and Constructive Study of the Noahide Laws* (New York and Toronto, 1983), pp. 24ff.

16. *Kuzari* 1.4, 1.9–11.

17. Ibid., 4.23, trans. H. Hirschfeld (New York, 1964), p. 227.

18. Maimonides, *Hilkhot Melakhim* 11, end, p. 416. See his *Commentary on the Mishnah*: Sanhedrin, chap. 10, prin. 9; I. Twersky, *Introduction to the Code of Maimonides (Mishneh Torah)* (New Haven, Conn., 1980), pp. 452–53, n. 235. For a similar logic in explaining the role non-Christian religions play in the Christian economy of history, see the most influential Roman Catholic theologian of the second half of the twentieth century, Karl Rahner, S.J., *Theological Investigations*, trans. D. Bourke (New York, 1977), vol. 10, pp. 38ff.

19. Maimonides, *Hilkhot Melakhim* 12.1ff. See D. Novak, "Maimonides' Concept of the Messiah," *Journal of Religious Studies* 9, no. 2 (Summer 1982): 42ff., and "Does Maimonides Have a Philosophy of History?" *Proceedings of the Academy for Jewish Philosophy* 4 (1983): 53ff.

20. Maimonides, *Teshubot Ha-Rambam*, no. 149, ed. Blau (Jerusalem, 1960), vol. 1, pp. 284–85. For the Talmudic ban of teaching Torah to gentiles, see B. Sanhedrin 59a; B. 'Abodah Zarah 3a.

21. Maimonides, *Hilkhot Melakhim* 8.10.

22. Ibid.

23. Maimonides, *Sefer Ha-Mitzvot*, pos. no. 9, ed. Heller (Jerusalem

and New York, 1946), pp. 37–38. For another example of Maimonides's Jewish missionary zeal, see *Hilkhot Isuray Bi'ah* 14.3–4. Cf. B. Yebamot 47a–b and note of R. Zvi Hirsch Chajes thereon; *Hilkhot 'Edut* 11.10; and *Hilkhot Melakhim* 8.11. See also Y. Yebamot 8.6/9c/ concerning 2 Samuel 17:25 and 1 Chronicles 2:17.

24. B. Sanhedrin 74a.

25. See Maimonides, *Teshubot Ha-Rambam,* no. 148, vol. 2, p. 726, and no. 293; vol. 2, pp. 548–50.

26. See notes 10 and 11.

27. See Maimonides, *Hilkhot Shemittah ve-Yobel,* end, and *Qobetz Teshubot Ha-Rambam ve'Igrotav,* ed. Lichtenberg (Leipzig, 1859), vol. 2, pp. 23b–24a; S. Atlas, *Netibim Be-Mishpat Ha'Ibri* (New York, 1978), pp. 13–14; Novak, *The Image of the Non-Jew in Judaism,* pp. 302–4. The distinction between *ratio per se* and *ratio quoad nos* is from Thomas Aquinas, *Summa Theologiae* 1, q.2, a.1.

28. See Maimonides's comment on 'Abot 1.14; also B. Sanhedrin 38b.

29. See T. S. Kuhn, *The Structure of Scientific Revolutions* (Chicago, 1962), pp. 43ff.

30. See, for example, Maimonides, *Hilkhot Yesoday Ha-Torah* 4.13; Aristotle, *Nicomachean Ethics* 1103a5ff. and 1145a15.

31. Cf. John Finnis, *Natural Law and Natural Rights* (Oxford, 1980), pp. 52–53.

32. Aristotle, *Physics* 215a1.

33. Aristotle, *Nicomachean Ethics* 1177a10–15.

34. Maimonides, *The Guide of the Perplexed* 2.4.

35. Ibid., 2.5.

36. For *telos* as being inherently a limit *(peras),* see Aristotle, *Metaphysics* 1022a10 and 1065a30ff.; also *Nichomachean Ethics* 1100a10ff.

37. See Immanuel Kant, *Critique of Pure Reason* Bxiii; also Martin Heidegger, "Modern Science, Metaphysics and Mathematics," trans. W. B. Barton, Jr., and V. Deutsch, in *Heidegger: Basic Writings,* ed. D. F. Krell (New York, 1977), pp. 265ff.

38. See especially Kant, *Critique of Pure Reason* B805ff.

39. For the ethical implications of this fundamental paradigm shift, see Leo Strauss, *Natural Right and History* (Chicago, 1953), pp. 8–9; Juergen Habermas, *Communication and the Evolution of Society* (Boston, 1979), p. 201; Alasdair MacIntyre, *After Virtue* (Notre Dame, Ind., 1981), p. 52.

40. Maimonides, *The Guide of the Perplexed* 1.54, p. 637, based on Beresheet Rabbah 35, end. Cf. Y. Peah 1.1/15d.

41. Ibid.

42. See Julius Gutmann, *Philosophies of Judaism,* trans. D. W. Silverman (New York, 1964), p. 357; Novak, *The Image of the Non-Jew in Judaism,* p. 311, n. 64.

43. See Hermann Cohen, *Juedische Schriften* (Berlin, 1924), vol. 3, pp. 238–59, and *Religion of Reason out of the Sources of Judaism*, trans. S. Kaplan (New York, 1972), pp. 94–95; Zvi Diesendruck, "Die Teleologie bei Maimonides," *Hebrew Union College Annual* 4 (1928): 499ff.; S. Schwarzschild, "Moral Radicalness and 'Middlingness' in the Ethics of Maimonides," *Studies in Medieval Culture* 1 (1977): 89ff. For a different interpretation—one decidedly non-Kantian—of Maimonides's new emphasis of practical excellence, see Abraham Joshua Heschel, *Maimonides: A Biography*, trans. J. Neugroschel (New York, 1982), pp. 243ff.

44. Thus even the rabbinic emphasis of study of the Torah over the practice of the commandments (see Sifre: Debarim, no. 41; B. Kiddushin 40b and parallels) refers to the study of Jewish practical reason. See B. Kiddushin 40b, Tos., s.v. "talmud"; B. Baba Kama 17a, Tos., s.v. "veha'amar"; M. 'Abot 1, end. Cf., however, Maimonides, *Commentary on the Mishnah: Introduction*, ed. Kappah (Jerusalem, 1971), vol. 1, p. 23, re B. Kiddushin 40b and parallels.

45. See Maimonides, *Shemonah Peraqim*, beg.

# 4. The Quest for the Jewish Jesus

1. See Romans 10:4. Cf. Matthew 5:17 and *The Anchor Bible: Matthew*, notes by W. F. Albright and C. S. Mann (Garden City, N.Y., 1971), pp. 57–58.

2. See B. Shabbat 104a re Leviticus 27:34 and parallels; Maimonides, *Hilkhot Yesoday Ha-Torah* 9.1–2 and *Hilkhot Melakhim*, chap. 11 (uncensored ed.); Nahmanides, *Vikuah* in *Kitbay Ramban*, ed. C. B. Chavel (Jerusalem, 1963), vol. 1, p. 311.

3. Albert Schweitzer, *The Quest of the Historical Jesus*, trans. W. Montgomery (New York and London, 1922), p. 399; see pp. 200, 400.

4. For liberal Christian efforts to reconstruct "the Jewish Jesus," see ibid., pp. 321ff. Also, it is important to recall that the earliest efforts to present a Jewish Jesus in England were by a Unitarian minister, R. Travers Herford. See his *The Pharisees* (New York, 1962).

5. See D. F. Strauss, *The Life of Jesus: Critically Examined*, trans. M. Evans (New York, 1860), vol. 2, pp. 887ff. For a critique of this whole anthropocentric theological project, see Karl Barth, *Protestant Theology in the Nineteenth Century: Its Background and History*, trans. B. Cozens and J. Bowden (London, 1972), pp. 305ff., 655ff.

6. Adolf von Harnack, *What Is Christianity?* 2d rev. ed., trans. T. B. Saunders (New York and London, 1901), pp. 122–23.

7. See Hermann Cohen, *Religion of Reason out of the Sources of Judaism*, trans. S. Kaplan (New York, 1972), pp. 338–39.

8. See Kaufmann Kohler, *Jewish Theology: Systematically and Historically Considered* (Cincinnati, 1918), p. 43, n. 1, re II Maccabees 15:9.

9. Ibid., p. 45.

10. See Abraham Joshua Heschel, *God in Search of Man* (New York, 1955), pp. 320ff.; D. Novak, *Law and Theology in Judaism* (New York, 1974), vol. 1, pp. 1ff.

11. Kohler, *Jewish Theology*, p. 47.

12. Sanford Seltzer, "Reactions to Jesus in the Reform Rabbinate" (M.A. thesis, Hebrew Union College–Jewish Institute of Religion, 1959), p. ii. The data for much of this section are taken from Seltzer's thorough study.

13. *Jewish Daily Bulletin*, December 23, 1925, p. 1, quoted in ibid., p. 1. The book that Wise was reviewing and promoting was Joseph Klausner, *Jesus of Nazareth: His Life, Times and Teachings*, trans. H. Danby (New York, 1925).

14. See Seltzer, "Reactions to Jesus," pp. 2ff.

15. *Christian Century* 43 (February 1926): 203, quoted in ibid., p. 2.

16. Cf., however, Aimé Pallière, *The Unknown Sanctuary*, trans. L. W. Wise, pref. by D. Novak (New York, 1985), pp. 163–64.

17. *North American Review* 191 (January 1910): 130, quoted in Seltzer, "Reactions to Jesus," p. 21.

18. See Seltzer, "Reactions to Jesus," pp. 4–5.

19. This was even extended to Paul by Rabbi Emil G. Hirsch (d. 1923). See ibid., p. 86.

20. Joseph Krauskopf, *A Rabbi's Impression of the Oberammergau Passion Play* (Philadelphia, 1901), p. 216, quoted in ibid., p. 19.

21. Quoted in Ginzberg's biography by his son, Eli Ginzberg, *Keeper of the Law: Louis Ginzberg* (Philadelphia, 1966), p. 69.

22. Martin Buber, *Two Types of Faith*, trans. N. P. Goldhawk (New York, 1961), pp. 12–13.

23. Martin Buber, "Two Foci of the Jewish Soul," trans. G. Hort, in *Israel and the World* (New York, 1963), p. 28.

24. Ibid., p. 40. For Buber's dialogue with the Protestant theologian K. L. Schmidt, see H. J. Schoeps, *Juedisch–Christliches Religionsgespraech in 19 Jahrhunderten* (Berlin, 1937), pp. 134ff.

25. See Martin Buber, *I and Thou*, trans W. Kaufmann (New York, 1970), pp. 100–101.

26. See ibid., p. 164; Martin Buber, *Eclipse of God*, trans. E. Kaminka and M. S. Friedman (New York, 1957), p. 95.

27. See B. Berakhot 31a.

28. See Alfasi, Berakhot, ed. Vilna, 22a and Rabbeu Jonah Gerondi thereon; also B. Berakhot 31a, Tos., s.v. "Rabbanan" and "Rab Ashi"; Tur: 'Orah Hayyim 93. Cf. M. Berakhot 5.1 and Maimonides, *Hilkhot Tefillah* 4.15–16.

29. See Buber, *Israel and the World*, p. 87.

30. See Buber's letter to Franz Rosenzweig in *Franz Rosenzweig: On Jewish Learning,* trans. N. N. Glatzer (New York, 1955), pp. 115, 117–18.

31. Buber, *I and Thou,* pp. 157–58 [= *Ich und Du,* (Heidelberg, 1962), pp. 110–11, 113]. Interestingly enough, the greatest modern scholar of Kabbalah, Gershom Scholem, who was the severest critic of Buber's view of Hasidism, shared Buber's proclivity for recognizing nonhalakhic options within the history of Judaism. See Scholem's "Redemption Through Sin," trans. H. Halkin, in *The Messianic Idea in Judaism* (New York, 1971), pp. 84ff.; Scholem, *Major Trends in Jewish Mysticism,* 3d rev. ed. (New York, 1961), p. 211.

32. Buber, *I and Thou,* pp. 157–58 [= *Ich und Du,* pp. 69–70].

33. Buber, *Two Types of Faith,* p. 55. In an earlier essay, Buber categorizes rabbinic Judaism and "present-day Western Orthodoxy" as "neo-Sadducean" in their "crystalization-like transition" and as "untrue to the Pharisaic form of life" which is "continuous discussion" ("Pharisaism," in *The Jew: Essays from Martin Buber's Journal "Der Jude,"* 1916–1928, ed. Arthur Cohen, trans. J. Neugroschel (University, Ala., 1980), p. 229.

34. Buber, *Two Types of Faith,* p. 46; emphasis added.

35. Ibid., p. 63.

36. Ibid., p. 132.

37. See note 24.

38. Quoted in Maurice S. Friedman, *Martin Buber: The Life of Dialogue* (New York, 1960), p. 279.

39. Immanuel Kant, *Religion Within the Limits of Reason Alone,* trans. T. M. Greene and H. H. Hudson (New York, 1960), p. 57.

40. See Buber, *I and Thou,* pp. 62–63.

41. See ibid., p. 129.

42. See Nicolai Berdyaev, *The Destiny of Man,* trans. N. Duddington (New York, 1960), p. 57; Austin Farrer, *Reflective Faith* (Grand Rapids, Mich., 1974), pp. 180, 190–91.

43. See, for example, Thomas Aquinas, *Summa Theologiae* 1–2, q.108, a.1–3.

44. Karl Barth, *The Knowledge of God and the Service of God According to the Teaching of the Reformation,* trans. J. L. M. Haire and I. Henderson (New York, 1939), pp. 125.

45. Ibid., p. 126.

46. See B. Berakhot 7a re Exodus 33:19; B. Pesahim 118b re Psalms 116:1; B. Sanhedrin 108a re Genesis 6:8; Sifre: Bamidbar, ed. Horovitz, no. 41 re Numbers 6:25.

47. See M. Abot 1.3; B. ʿAbodah Zarah 19a re Psalms 112:1; B. Sotah 22b; Y. Berakhot 9.5/14b; Maimonides, *Hilkhot Teshubah* 10.1–2. For the notion that God's grace is best appreciated through human active effort, see M. Makkot, end; also B. Pesahim 118a re Genesis 3:18–19.

48. See M. ʾAbot 2.1; B. Kiddushin 40a–b; B. ʿAbodah Zarah 10b.

49. See Buber, *I and Thou*, pp. 156ff. For a critique of this view, see Novak, *Law and Theology in Judaism*, vol. 2, pp. 10–15.

50. See *Franz Rosenzweig: On Jewish Learning*, p. 118; Franz Rosenzweig, *The Star of Redemption*, trans. W. W. Hallo (New York, 1970), pp. 176–77; *Franz Rosenzweig: His Life and Thought*, 2d rev. ed., presented by N. N. Glatzer (New York, 1961), pp. 242–47.

51. See Martin Buber, *Between Man and Man*, trans. R. G. Smith (Boston, 1955), pp. 40ff.

52. See T. Rosh Hashanah 1.18; B. Rosh Hashanah 25a–b; M. 'Eduyot 1.5 and comment of Rabad thereon a là T. 'Eduyot 1.4.

53. See M. 'Abot 2.4; Sifre: Debarim, ed. Finkelstein, no. 154 re Deuteronomy 17:9; B. Shabbat 23a re Deuteronomy 17:11 and 32:7; B. Yebamot 20a and parallels.

54. See Maimonides, *Sefer Ha-Mitzvot*, intro., no. 3; Novak, *Law and Theology in Judaism*, vol. 1, p. 81.

55. See B. Nedarim 22b. However, the prophets were seen as coming to inspire the people to keep the Torah and were, therefore, at all times secondary to its authority. See note 2; Sifre: Debarim, no. 175; B. Yebamot 90b re Deuteronomy 18:15; B. Baba Kama 2b and parallels; Shemot Rabbah 42.7. Cf. Matthew 12:6–8.

56. See B. Shabbat 88a re Exodus 19:17; B. Baba Kama 28b; also D. Novak, "Natural Law, Halakhah and the Covenant," *The Jewish Law Annual* 7(1988):51–54.

57. See B. Rosh Hashanah 28a–b; *Shulhan Arukh: 'Orah Hayyim* 60.4; also Heschel, *God in Search of Man*, pp. 314–19.

58. See Heschel, *God in Search of Man*, p. 320.

## 5. Franz Rosenzweig's Theology of the Jewish–Christian Relationship

1. See especially Rosenzweig's essay, "Das Formgeheimnis der biblischen Erzaelungen" originally a letter of February 8, 1928, to Martin Buber), in *Franz Rosenzweig: Die Schrift*, ed. K. Thieme (Koenigstein, 1984), pp. 13ff., also pp. 81ff.

2. See, for example, Alexander Altmann, "Franz Rosenzweig and Eugen Rosenstock-Huessy: An Introduction to Their 'Letters on Judaism and Christianity,'" in *Judaism Despite Christianity*, ed. Eugen Rosenstock-Huessy (New York, 1971), p. 27 (quoted from an article in *Journal of Religion*, October 1944); Fritz Kaufmann, "Karl Jaspers and a Philosophy of Communication," in *The Philosophy of Karl Jaspers*, ed. P. A. Schilpp (New York, 1957), p. 214; Thieme, *Franz Rosenzweig*, p. 253.

3. See Franz Rosenzweig, *The Star of Redemption*, trans. W. W. Hallo (New York, 1970), pp. 6–7.

4. Thus the section on religion in Hegel's most important work, *Phaenomenologie des Geistes,* is the penultimate section, the ultimate one dealing with "Absolute Knowing." See Emil L. Fackenheim, *The Religious Dimension in Hegel's Thought* (Bloomington, Ind., 1967), pp. 160ff.

5. See Rosenzweig, *The Star of Redemption,* pp. 138ff.

6. See G. W. F. Hegel, *The Phenomenology of Spirit,* trans. A. V. Miller (Oxford, 1977), pp. 11–12.

7. For the influence of Rosenzweig's teacher, Friedrich Meinecke, on his reading of Hegel, see Ya'akov (Eugène) Fleischmann, *Bay'at Ha-Notzrut Be-Mahshavah Ha-Yehudit Me-Mendelssohn 'Ad Rosenzweig* (Jerusalem, 1964), pp. 148–50.

8. Rosenzweig, *The Star of Redemption,* p. 3.

9. See Franz Rosenzweig, *Kleinere Schriften* (Berlin, 1937), pp. 355–56; Karl Loewith, "M. Heidegger and F. Rosenzweig or Temporality and Eternity," *Philosophy and Phenomenological Research* 3 (1942): 53ff.

10. Rosenzweig, *The Star of Redemption,* p. 7.

11. Ibid.

12. Ibid., p. 9 [= *Der Stern der Erloesung* (Frankfurt am-Main, 1921), pp. 14–15]. See also *Franz Rosenzweig: His Life and Thought,* 2d rev. ed., presented by N. N. Glatzer (New York, 1961), p. 5.

13. See Hegel, *The Phenomenology of Spirit,* pp. 8–9. Cf. Fleischmann, *Bay'at Ha-Notzrut,* p. 166, n. 5, for the great influence of the early Schelling on Rosenzweig; also Julius Gutmann, *Philosophies of Judaism,* trans. D. W. Silverman (New York, 1964), pp. 373ff.

14. Rosenstock-Huessy, *Judaism Despite Christianity,* p. 71.

15. For Rosenstock's criticism of Rosenzweig's too easy dismissal of Islam, see ibid., p. 156. Rosenzweig insisted that all religions other than Judaism and Christianity are "founded" (*gestiftet;* Rosenzweig, *Kleinere Schriften,* p. 390); that is, they are humanly devised and established.

16. See his November 6, 1909, letter to his parents in Glatzer, *Franz Rosenzweig,* p. 19.

17. Ibid., p. 25.

18. For the locale of this experience, which only became known long after Rosenzweig's death, see R. Horowitz, "Judaism Despite Christianity," *Judaism* 24, no. 3 (Summer 1975): 316–17.

19. See "Divine and Human," in Glatzer, *Franz Rosenzweig,* pp. 242–47.

20. *Briefe,* ed. E. Simon and E. Rosenzweig (Berlin, 1935), p. 71. Fleischmann shows, convincingly, I think, that Rosenzweig's "Ich bleibe also Jude" may well be his paraphrase of Goethe's "Ost–West Divan": "Jedes Leben sei zu fuehren, wenn man sich nicht selbst vermisst; Alles koenne man verlieren, wenn man bleibt was man ist" (quoted in Fleischmann, *Bay'at Ha-Notzrut,* p. 162).

21. Glatzer, *Franz Rosenzweig,* p. 19.

22. Rosenzweig, in a play on the usual German word for "remember" *(erinnern)* stresses that "Und eben indem Jude so allein um seines Hoechsten, um Gottes willen, sich in sein Inneres hinein er-innert" *(Der Stern der Erloesung,* p. 511).

23. An example of Rosenzweig's unfairness to Islam is when he quotes Maimonides's famous treatment of the Messianic role of both Christianity and Islam *(Mishneh Torah: Hilkhot Melakhim,* chap. 11, uncensored ed.) as though it applied only to Christianity. See Rosenzweig, *The Star of Redemption,* p. 336. Even if he did not actually know the text firsthand—perhaps having only heard about it from Hermann Cohen, for whose universalism it would have been a good precedent—his use of it indicates his prejudice.

24. Rosenzweig, *The Star of Redemption,* pp. 415–16 [= *Der Stern der Erloesung,* pp. 520–21].

25. Ibid.

26. For Hegel, of course, "Das Wahre ist das Ganze" *(Phaenomenologie des Geistes,* ed. J. Hoffmeister [Hamburg, 1952], p. 21).

27. Rosenzweig, *The Star of Redemption,* p. 298.

28. Ibid., p. 341.

29. Rosenzweig, *Der Stern der Erloesung,* p. 375 [= *The Star of Redemption,* pp. 288–89].

30. See, for example, Rosenzweig, *The Star of Redemption,* p. 326.

31. Ibid., p. 305.

32. Ibid., p. 329 [= *Der Stern der Erloesung,* p. 413]. Note the much later expression of Leo Baeck along the same lines: "Es soll so nicht nur ein Volk einer Geschichte, sondern Volk der Geschichte sein. Und damit, es das sein will, wird es zugleich zum Volke der Menschheit. Wie es sich ohne Gott nie denken darf noch kann, so auch ohne die ganze Menschheit. Auch Gesamtgeschichte und eigene Geschichte wachsen hier zusammen" *(Dieses Volk: Juedische Existenz* [Frankfurt-am-Main, 1955], p. 17).

33. In his understanding of the meaning of *Einzigkeit* as opposed to *Einheit* in the usual metaphysical sense, Rosenzweig was clearly influenced by Hermann Cohen. See Cohen, "Einheit oder Einzigkeit Gottes," in *Juedische Schriften* (Berlin, 1924), vol. 1, pp. 87ff.

34. B. Berakhot 6a.

35. Rosenzweig, *The Star of Redemption,* p. 398 [= *Der Stern der Erloesung,* p. 499]: "der auseinanderstrahlende Weg der Christenheit."

36. See, for example, ibid., pp. 331, 346.

37. Glatzer, *Franz Rosenzweig,* pp. 341–42. Cf. John 14:6.

38. Note: "Im Gottesvolk ist das Ewige schon da, mitten in der Zeit" (Rosenzweig, *Der Stern der Erloesung,* p. 417).

39. In Rosenstock-Huessy, *Judaism Despite Christianity,* p. 113.

40. Rosenzweig, *The Star of Redemption,* p. 350.

41. In his letter of October 31, 1913, in which he announced to Rudolf Ehrenberg, "Ich bleibe also Jude." Rosenzweig explicitly stated, "chosen by its Father, the people of Israel gazes fixedly across the world and history, over that last, most distant, time when the Father the One and Only, will be 'all in all.' Then, when Christ ceases to be the Lord, Israel will cease to be the chosen people. On this day, God will lose the name by which Israel calls him; God will then no longer be 'its' God" (Glatzer, *Franz Rosenzweig*, p. 342). Even in *Der Stern der Erloesung* (p. 382), when Rosenzweig says about the Law, "nicht aber es andern kann," he still seems to mean only that this is so while history is still in process. The Law's reign is coeval with history but not subsumed by it, "aus aller Zeit-und-Geschichtlichkeit des Lebens heraushebt" (ibid). But at redemption, it seems as though the inner reign of the Law and the outer reign of history will be jointly overcome. Conversely, when classical Jewish texts do speak of the revocation of many of the Torah's precepts at the time of the Messiah (see, e.g., T. Berakhot 1.10–11; Vayiqra Rabbah 13.3; cf. Niddah 61b; Maimonides, *Hilkhot Melakhim* chaps. 11–12), none of them ever suggests that Israel would then cease to be God's chosen people or that the Torah itself would be abrogated. For the subsequent influence of this notion of Rosenzweig's, see Hans-Joachim Schoeps, *Juedisch–Christliches Religionsgespraech in 19 Jahrhunderten* (Berlin, 1937), pp. 156–59.

42. See Rosenzweig, *The Star of Redemption*, p. 404.

43. Glatzer, *Franz Rosenzweig*, p. 343. The influence of Hegel's "master–slave dialectic" is evident here: the master's dependence on the slave makes the slave the ultimate master. See Hegel, *The Phenomenology of Spirit*, pp. 111–19; Louis Dupré, *The Philosophical Foundations of Marxism* (New York, 1966), pp. 31–32. Note also B. Kiddushin 20a: "Whoever acquires a Hebrew slave acquires a master for himself."

44. Rosenzweig, *The Star of Redemption*, p. 402 [= *Der Stern der Erloesung*, p. 504].

45. Ibid., p. 414.

46. See Glatzer, *Franz Rosenzweig*, p. 274.

47. Rosenzweig, *The Star of Redemption*, p. 415.

48. Perhaps Rosenzweig had read these words of Heinrich Heine written almost 100 years earlier: "Christianity—and this is its noblest merit—mitigated in a measure that brutal Germanic lust for war; it could not destroy it, however. Should the taming talisman, the cross, shatter some day, there will burst forth the ferocity of the old warriors, the insane beserk-rage of which the Nordic poets sing and speak so much" (*Judaic Lore in Heine*, trans. I. Tabak [Baltimore, 1948], p. 128). In this passage, Heine showed how thin is the line between poetry and prophecy. In having greater pessimism than Rosenzweig, he was more prescient on this point.

49. Rosenzweig, *The Star of Redemption*, p. 329 [= *Der Stern der Erloesung*, p. 413]. See also *The Star*, p. 347 [= *Der Stern*, p. 436].

50. Ibid., p. 413.

51. See ibid., p. 352.

52. See ibid., p. 305 [= *Der Stern*, p. 384].

53. Ibid.

54. Ibid., p. 313.

55. Ibid.

56. Ibid., p. 305 [= *Der Stern*, p. 384].

57. Rosenzweig's first theological essay, "Atheistische Theologie" (1914), was the beginning of this polemic. See *Kleinere Schriften*, pp. 278ff.; also his polemic against Max Brod and Leo Baeck in "Apologetisches Denken" (1923), ibid., pp. 31ff. And if Jewish universalism is based on a return to Kant, then note Rosenzweig's thanks to Buber for liberating contemporary Judaism from dependence on Kantianism, ibid., pp. 109–10.

58. Note, for example, *The Star of Redemption*, p. 404 [= *Der Stern der Erloesung*, p. 507]: "All secular *[weltliche]* history deals with expansion. Power *[Macht]* is the basic concept of history because in Christianity revelation began to spread over the world, and thus every expansionist urge, even that which was purely secular *[nur rein weltlich]*, became the servant of this expansionist movement."

59. Even T. S. Eliot, who advocated a "Christian society," admitted that "it can neither be medieval in form, nor be modelled on the seventeenth century or any previous age" (*The Idea of a Christian Society*, 2d ed. [London, 1982], p. 55). Thus even for Eliot, this Christian society is not what Rosenzweig seemed to mean by *Christenheit*.

60. Rosenstock-Huessy, *Judaism Despite Christianity*, p. 66.

61. Ibid., pp. 139–40.

62. Ibid., p. 121.

63. See Stanley Hauerwas, *A Community of Character: Toward a Constructive Christian Social Ethic* (Notre Dame, Ind., 1981), esp. pp. 89ff.

64. Rosenstock-Huessy, *Judaism Despite Christianity*, pp. 122–23.

65. Ibid., pp. 88, 140.

66. Ibid., p. 159.

67. See, for example, Glatzer, *Franz Rosenzweig*, esp. pp. 113, 354–56.

68. See Rosenzweig, *The Star of Redemption*, p. 414. Concerning classic German Orthodox anti-Zionism, see Isaak Breuer, *The Jewish National Home*, trans. M. Aumann (Frankfurt-am-Main, 1926). For Rosenzweig's differences with Breuer's type of Orthodoxy, see Glatzer, *Franz Rosenzweig*, pp. 158, 211.

69. See Arthur A. Cohen, "Zionism and Theology," *Sh'ma* 17, no. 324

(December 26, 1986): 25–27; D. Novak, "Land, State and God—Differing Loves," *Sh'ma* 17, no. 324 (December 26, 1986): 28–29.

70. Martin Buber, *Israel und Palaestina* (Zurich, 1950), p. 7.

71. Rosenzweig, *The Star of Redemption*, p. 415 [= *Der Stern der Erloesung*, p. 520].

72. For example, "Dieses Verhaeltnis, diese Notwendigkeit des Daseins—nichts weiter als Dasein—des Judentums fuer eigenes Werden ist auch der Christenheit selber wohl bewusst." (Rosenzweig, *Der Stern der Erloesung*, p. 518). For the distinction between *Verhaeltnis* and *Beziehung*, which Buber so well understood, see Martin Buber, *Ich und Du* (Heidelberg, 1962), p. 10; also D. Novak, "Buber's Critique of Heidegger," *Modern Judaism* 5, no. 2 (May 1985): 132–33.

73. Rosenstock-Huessy, *Judaism Despite Christianity*, p. 136.

74. Rosenzweig, *Der Stern der Erloesung*, p. 375 [= *The Star of Redemption*, pp. 288–289].

75. Simon and Rosenzweig, *Briefe*, pp. 638–39.

76. Rosenstock-Huessy, *Judaism Despite Christianity*, pp. 71–72.

77. For an impressive attempt to build a Christian theology largely on the basis of Rosenzweig's scheme, see Paul van Buren, *A Theology of the Jewish–Christian Reality* (New York, 1980), vol. 1; D. Novak, "A Jewish Response to a New Christian Theology," *Judaism* 31, no. 1 (Winter 1982): 112–20.

## 6. A New Theology of Jewish–Christian Dialogue

1. Note the warning of Professor Abraham Joshua Heschel (d. 1972), a pioneer in Jewish–Christian dialogue: "The first and most important *prerequisite of interfaith is faith. . . .* Interfaith must come out of depth, not out of a void absence of faith. It is not an enterprise for those who are half learned and spiritually immature" ("No Religion Is an Island," *Union Seminary Quarterly Review* 21, no. 2/1 [January 1966]: 123).

2. Concerning the Sabbath as epitomizing covenantal intimacy between God and Israel, see B. Betsah 16a re Exodus 31:17 and Nahmanides's comment on Deuteronomy 5:15.

3. See, for example, Maimonides, *Hilkhot Melakhim* 10.9, and Ignatius, *To the Magnesians*, chap. 10.

4. See H. F. Jolowicz, *Historical Introduction to Roman Law* (Cambridge, 1932), pp. 100ff. Cf. Ernst Bloch, *Naturrecht und Menschliche Wuerde* (Frankfurt-am-Main, 1972), p. 35.

5. Maimonides, *Hilkhot Melakhim* 8.10.

6. See ibid., 10.11; D. Novak, *The Image of the Non-Jew in Judaism: An Historical and Constructive Study of the Noahide Laws* (New York and Toronto, 1983), pp. 53ff. The little-known nineteenth-century Jewish

theologian Rabbi Elijah Benamozegh (d. 1900) argued for a gentile religious subordination to Judaism. (His analogy was that the gentiles are to the Jews as laypeople are to the Aaronide priests.) However, Benamozegh did not conceive of Christianity in this subordinate role, knowing full well that Christianity could not accept such a role in a Jewish triumphalist scheme. See his *Israel et l'humanité* (Paris, 1914), pp. 461ff., and the Hebrew paraphrase of his 1867 work *Morale juive et morale chrétienne, Be-Shebilay Ha-Musar,* trans. S. Marcus (Jerusalem, 1966), pp. 118ff. For the ambivalent Christianity of his one gentile disciple, Aimé Pallière (d. 1949), see Pallière, *The Unknown Sanctuary,* new ed., trans L. W. Wise; preface D. Novak (New York, 1985).

7. *Seder 'Olam Rabba ve-Zuta,* Appendix, trans. H. Falk, in *Journal of Ecumenical Studies* 19, no. 1 (Winter 1982): 108–9. Falk himself develops this thesis in *Jesus the Pharisee: A New Look at the Jewishness of Jesus* (Mahwah, N.J., 1985).

8. See Blu Greenberg, "Rabbi Jacob Emden: The Views of an Enlightened Traditionalist on Christianity," *Judaism* 27, no. 3 (Summer 1978): 351ff.

9. See Moses Mendelssohn, *Schriften,* jubilee ed. (Berlin, 1929–32), vol. 16, pp. 178–80.

10. See Falk's translation of *Seder 'Olam Rabba ve-Zuta,* p. 111.

11. See Romans 11:7ff.

12. See Matthew 15:21 and parallels.

13. See G. Reale, *A History of Ancient Philosophy: The Systems of the Hellenistic Age,* trans. J. R. Catan (Albany, N.Y., 1985), vol. 3, pp. 5ff.

14. See *Arrian's Discourses of Epictetus* 1.9; Marcus Aurelius, *Meditations* 3.12, 12.36.

15. See H. A. Wolfson, *Philo* (Cambridge, Mass., 1947), vol. 2, pp. 374ff.

16. Philo, *De Vita Mosis* 2.14, trans. F. H. Colson, *Philo* (Cambridge, Mass., 1935), vol. 6, pp. 456–57.

17. See Wolfson, *Philo,* vol. 2, pp. 423–24.

18. Philo, *Quod Deus Immut.* 176, trans. Colson, *Philo,* vol. 3, pp. 96–97. See *De Vita Mosis* 2.51; *De Spec. Leg.* 4.237.

19. See Wolfson, *Philo,* vol. 1, pp. 27ff., 175ff.

20. Philo, *De Vita Mosis* 2.43–44 (pp. 468–71).

21. See Immanuel Kant, *Critique of Practical Reason,* trans. L. W. Beck (Indianapolis, 1956), p. 8, n. 5.

22. See D. Novak, *Suicide and Morality: The Theories of Plato, Aquinas and Kant and Their Relevance for Suicidology* (New York, 1975), pp. 83ff.

23. See L. Baker, *Days of Sorrow and Pain: Leo Baeck and the Berlin Jews* (New York, 1978), pp. 24–25.

24. See Novak, *The Image of the Non-Jew in Judaism,* pp. 385ff.

25. See Hermann Cohen, *Religion of Reason out of the Sources of Judaism*, trans. S. Kaplan (New York, 1972), pp. 48–49, 107, 239.

26. See, for example, Hermann Cohen, *Ethik des reinen Willens*, 2d ed. (Berlin, 1907), p. 304, *Begriff der Religion im System der Philosophie* (Giessen, 1915), pp. 66–67, and *Juedische Schriften* (Berlin, 1924), vol. 1, pp. 42ff., and vol. 3, pp. 135ff.

27. Cohen, *Religion of Reason*, p. 330 [= *Religion der Vernunft aus den Quellen des Judenthems*, 2d ed. (Darmstadt, 1966), p. 384].

28. See ibid., p. 391.

29. Ibid., p. 366; see ibid., p. 240.

30. See Cohen, *Ethik des reinen Willens*, pp. 300–301, and *Juedische Schriften*, vol. 2, p. 300, and vol. 3, pp. 114–15, 168. For the most insightful discussion of this, see Ya'akov (Eugene) Fleischmann, *B'ayat Ha-Notzrut Be-Mahshavah Ha-Yehudit Me-Mendelssohn 'Ad Rosenzweig* (Jerusalem, 1964), pp. 139ff.

31. See William Kluback, *The Idea of Humanity: Hermann Cohen's Legacy to Philosophy and Theology* (Lanham, Md., 1987), pp. 26, 163ff.

32. See *Briefe*, ed. E. Simon and E. Rosenzweig (Berlin, 1935), p. 299.

33. See, for example, Cohen, *Religion of Reason*, p. 249.

34. Leo Baeck, *The Essence of Judaism*, trans. V. Grubenwieser and L. Pearl (New York, 1948), p. 252.

35. See D. Novak, "Natural Law, Halakhah and the Covenant," *Jewish Law Annual* 7(1988): 62–67.

36. See Leo Baeck, "Romantic Religion," in *Judaism and Christianity: Essays by Leo Baeck*, ed. and trans. W. Kaufmann (Philadelphia, 1958), pp. 193, 254. Later in his theological career, Baeck deemphasized Judaism's Kantian affinities. See his "Mystery and Commandment," in *Judaism and Christianity*, p. 178; *Dieses Volk: Juedisch Existenz* (Frankfurt-am-Main, 1957), vol. 2, p. 324.

37. See Immanuel Kant, *Religion Within the Limits of Reason Alone*, trans. T. M. Greene and H. H. Hudson (New York, 1960), pp. 116ff; N. Rotenstreich, *Jews and German Philosophy* (New York, 1984), pp. 3–4, 60ff.

38. Baeck, "Romantic Religion," p. 270.

39. See Baeck, *The Essence of Judaism*, pp. 260ff.

40. The most recent important advocate of this type of Jewish universalism was Dr. Jacob B. Agus (d. 1986): "the Jews have to see Israel as a *part* of the universalistic messianic vision" ("Jewish–Christian Dialogue," *Journal of Ecumenical Studies* 6, no. 1 [Winter 1969]: 31).

41. See Aristotle, *Physics* 194b16ff., and *Metaphysics* 1044b1ff.

42. See Aristotle, *Physics* 201a1, 204a8ff.

43. See W. D. Ross, *Aristotle* (New York, 1959), pp. 126–27.

44. Maimonides, *Hilkhot Melakhim* 9.1. See Novak, *The Image of the Non-Jew in Judaism*, pp. 275ff.

45. B. Baba Batra 116a.

46. See Novak, *The Image of the Non-Jew in Judaism*, pp. 341–42.

47. See Aristotle, *Physics* 255a30ff.

48. For a Jewish example of this pedagogical assumption, see B. Ta'anit 7a re Proverbs 3:18 and Rashi and Maharsha thereon; M. 'Abot 4.12.

49. Not only is that why a Jewish teacher is permitted to waive the full reverence due him, but some suggest that it is necessary for the sake of the education of the students, an equalization by anticipation. See D. Novak, *Law and Theology in Judaism* (New York, 1976), vol. 2, p. 196, n. 5.

50. See, for example, "Declaration on Religious Freedom," in *Documents of Vatican Council II*, ed. W. M. Abbott, S.J. (London and Dublin, 1966), pp. 682–83.

51. See B. Berakhot 6a re Deuteronomy 6:4 and 1 Chronicles 17:21.

52. Saadyah Gaon, *Book of Beliefs and Opinions* 3.7, trans. S. Rosenblatt (New Haven, Conn., 1948), p. 158.

53. B. Nedarim 38a.

54. See Louis Ginzberg, *The Legends of the Jews* (Philadelphia, 1928), vol. 6, p. 44, n. 242; Maimonides, *Hilkhot Yesoday Ha-Torah* 7.6.

55. See B. Nedarim 38a, Rashi, s.v. "pilpula b'alma"; B. Shabbat 31a and Maimonides, *Hilkhot Talmud Torah* 1.11.

56. See Rashi, Tosafot, Rosh, Maharsha, and 'Etz Yosef thereon. See Maharsha on B. Shabbat 31a quoting Rashi on Exodus 31:3.

57. See D. Novak, *Halakhah in a Theological Dimension* (Chico, Calif., 1985), pp. 4–5, 133, n. 24.

58. Maimonides, *Hilkhot Yesoday Ha-Torah* 7.5. His conflation of physical and moral strength in this passage is based on M. 'Abot 4.1 re Proverbs 16:32. In his earlier discussion in his commentary on the Mishnah (intro., ed. Kafih, pp. 4–5; *Shemonah Peraqim*, chap. 7, ed. Kafih, pp. 259–60), he does not mention the factor of prophecy's prerequisites only making its realization possible. Rather, he seems to mention these prerequisites as only potential. The strong implication there is that they will necessarily lead one to the prophetic vision. Plato also regards the human intellect's vision of the truth to be dependent on some action of the gods (*Republic* 492A, 499B), but this action is that of chance *(tychē)*. As such, it can hardly be the true cause *(archē/aitos)* of this state of the intellect's discovery of its proper and sufficient object.

59. See Rabbi Judah Ha-Levi, *Kuzari* 1.15, for the more ethnocentric Jewish view of prophecy; also Vayiqra Rabbah 1.12–13.

60. Maimonides, *The Guide of the Perplexed* 2.32, trans. S. Pines (Chicago, 1963), pp. 360–62.

61. Ibid., 2, intro., no. 18. It functions much like rectifying justice. See Aristotle, *Nicomachean Ethics* 1130a15ff.

62. Maimonides, *The Guide of the Perplexed* 2, intro., no. 19, p. 238.

63. See H. A. Wolfson, *Crescas' Critique of Aristotle* (Cambridge, Mass., 1929), p. 680.

64. See ibid., pp. 692–93; also *Metaphysica of Avicenna (ibn Sina)*, trans. P. Morewedge (New York, 1973), pp. 45–48; Thomas Aquinas, *De Potentia Dei*, q. 1, a. 3ff. Concerning Aquinas's view of prophetic revelation being possible—that is, ultimately a matter of grace—see *Summa Theologiae* 1, q. 12, a. 4, 5, 13; 2–2, q. 171, a. 1.

65. The concept of possibility enunciated by ibn Sina and then by Maimonides, which is here contrasted with the Aristotelian concept of potentiality, is not the same as Plato's concept of the receptacle *(hypodochē)* in *Timaeus* 48Aff. For Plato, the receptacle is totally empty and can be anything. It itself is a surd. Everything it does become is because of the persuasion of reason *(nous)*. Yet Plato admits that he cannot constitute what commonality there is between *nous* and necessity *(anagkaion)*/receptacle to enable them to be so related in the process of becoming. Furthermore, he cannot explain why the receptacle is not totally persuaded by *nous* rather than being resistant and never wholly malleable. That is why, it seems, Aristotle eliminates the gap between *nous* and *anagkaion* by making *nous* necessary (see *Metaphysics* 1015b1–5). But possibility, which is a created background for subsequent realizations, is not a surd. It is thus less necessary than Aristotelian *dynamis* but more structured than Platonic *anagkaion*. A. N. Whitehead's concept of pure potentiality closely corresponds to this concept of possibility, especially considering his insistence on cosmic freedom *(Process and Reality* [New York, 1929], p. 173).

66. Maimonides, *The Guide of the Perplexed* 2.25.

67. Aristotle, *Metaphysics* 1049a1–15.

68. Thus at the level of astrophysics, the paradigm of all causality, the efficient cause collapses into the final cause. See Aristotle, *Physics* 195a5 and *Metaphysics* 1072a25. This had important ramifications for Jewish, Christian, and Muslim Aristotelian philosophers, who had to acknowledge in their theological speculation a more transitively active God than the God of Aristotle. Aristotle's God is a God without external relations.

69. Immanuel Kant, *Critique of Pure Reason* B72, trans. N. Kemp Smith (New York, 1929), p. 90 [= *Kritik der reinen Vernunft*, ed. R. Schmidt (Hamburg, 1956), p. 92].

70. Ibid., B33. See ibid., B100, B266. Note Martin Buber: "Of x we know what Kant points out to us of the thing in-itself, namely, that it is. Kant would say: 'And nothing more,' but we who live today must add: 'And that the existent meets us.' This is, if we take it seriously enough, a powerful knowing . . . there is not trait that does not stem from meetings, that does not originate in the co-working of the x in the meeting" *(The Knowledge of Man: A Philosophy of the Interhuman,* trans. M. Friedman [New York and Evanston, Ill., 1965], p. 157).

71. See Martin Heidegger, *Kant and the Problem of Metaphysics,* trans. J. S. Churchill (Bloomington, Ind. 1962), pp. 30–31. The reading of Kant presented here is a reaction against the idealistic and Husserlian readings of Kant, in which the only transcendence is the transcendence of reason or consciousness. Cf. J. Hyppolite, *Genesis and Structure of Hegel's Phenomenology of Spirit,* trans. S. Cherniak and J. Heckman (Evanston, Ill., 1974), pp. 102, 144; Hermann Cohen, *Kritik der reinen Erkenntnis,* 4th ed. (Hildesheim, 1977), pp. 376–77.

72. Kant, *Critique of Pure Reason* B311–312 [= *Kritik der reinen Vernunft,* 304–5]. Yet Kant had the same basic problem as Plato (see n. 64) in being unable to constitute a commonality between the more singular *Ding an sich* and the more general conditions that make its appearance possible. Like Plato's receptacle, the *Ding an sich* is a surd. Conversely, the scholastic formula *veritas est adaequatio rei ad intellectum* (or *intellectus ad rem*) presupposes both the Judeo-Christian doctrine of *ens creatum* and *intellectus humanus* being grounded in *intellectus divinus.* See Martin Heidegger, "On the Essence of Truth," trans. J. Sallis, in *Martin Heidegger: Basic Writings,* ed. D. F. Krell (New York, 1977), pp. 120–21. Theologically, that means that both creation and revelation reflect God's intentionality.

73. See Kant, *Critique of Pure Reason* A239. For a reading of pluralism in Kant, see Karl Jaspers, *Kant,* trans. R. Manheim (New York, 1962), p. 132.

74. See Kant, *Critique of Pure Reason* B60, B140.

75. See Immanuel Kant, *Groundwork of the Metaphysic of Morals,* trans. H. J. Paton (New York, 1964), pp. 100–101.

76. See Kant, *Critique of Pure Reason* B146–47.

77. See Ginzberg, *The Legends of the Jews,* vol. 5, pp. 381–82, n. 3; vol. 6, pp. 124–25, nn. 725–27.

78. Maimonides, *The Guide of the Perplexed* 2.32.

79. See ibid., 2.40, 3.27.

80. Maimonides, *Hilkhot Melakhim* 8.11. See Novak, *The Image of the Non-Jew in Judaism,* pp. 276ff.

81. See, for example, Maimonides, *Shemonah Peraqim,* chap. 5, and *Hilkhot Shemittah ve-Yobel,* end.

82. For the problems with natural teleology in ethics today, however, see Leo Strauss, *Natural Right and History* (Chicago, 1953), pp. 8–9; A. MacIntyre, *After Virtue* (Notre Dame, Ind., 1981), p. 152.

83. See Martin Buber, *Between Man and Man,* trans. R. G. Smith (Boston, 1955), pp. 118ff.

84. See M. 'Abot 4, end; Rabbi Joseph Karo, *Kesef Mishneh* commenting on Maimonides, *Hilkhot Yesoday Ha-Torah* 4, end.

85. I have borrowed this trichotomy from the work of Paul Tillich, although I constitute it somewhat differently. See D. Novak, "Theono-

mous Ethics: A Defense and a Critique of Tillich," *Soundings* 69, no. 4 (Winter 1986): 436ff.

86. See A. Marmorstein, *The Old Rabbinic Doctrine of God* (New York, 1968), vol. 1, p. 89.

87. See B. Hagigah 12a; Beresheet Rabbah 3.1ff.; Ginzberg, *The Legends of the Jews*, vol. 5, pp. 8–9, nn. 18–19; *Zohar:* Beresheet 1:31b. For the Kabbalistic development of the idea of creation as revelation, see Gershom Scholem, *On the Kabbalah and Its Symbolism*, trans. R. Manheim (New York, 1969), pp. 35ff.

88. See Abraham Joshua Heschel, *Who Is Man?* (Stanford, Calif., 1965), pp. 69–71, 97.

89. See *Timaeus* 29Aff.; Novak, *Suicide and Morality*, pp. 32ff. For the distinction between natural order à la Plato and created order à la Scripture, see Jacques Ellul, *The Theological Foundation of Law*, trans. M. Wieser (Garden City, N.Y., 1960), pp. 11, 65.

90. See Jacques Maritain, *Existence and the Existent*, trans. L. Galantiere and G. B. Phelan (Garden City, N.Y., 1956), pp. 32ff.

91. See Novak, *Halakhah in a Theological Dimension*, pp. 96ff.

92. See I. Heinemann, *Ta'amay Ha-Mitzvot be-Sifrut Yisrael* (Jerusalem, 1959), vol. 1, pp. 29–30.

93. Sifre: Debarim, no. 41; B. Ta'anit 2a; Y. Berakhot 4.1/7a.

94. See B. Berakhot 33b; B. Megillah 18a; Y. Berakhot 7.3/11c, 9.1/12d; Midrash Tehillim 19.2.

95. The term, but not the concept, is borrowed from Hans Kelsen, *The Pure Theory of Law*, trans. M. Knight (Berkeley, Calif., 1970), esp. pp. 193–94.

96. See B. Kiddushin 40a re Ezekiel 14:5; Maimonides, *Hilkhot Teshubah* 3.7 and note of Rabad thereon.

97. That is why, according to Halakhah, deafness is a greater religious disability than blindness. See *Encyclopedia Talmudit* 14:495ff., s.v. "heresh." Cf. B. Baba-Kama 86b–87a and Tos., s.v. "ve-khen" (2).

98. See Julian Jaynes, *The Origin of Consciousness in the Breakdown of the Bicameral Mind* (Boston, 1976), pp. 96–97. Jaynes's thesis in this widely discussed book is that the voices the ancients heard were actually one part of the brain communicating with the other (see p. 100 et passim). Once the brain is united at a higher level of evolution, the voices are only memories (pp. 320ff.). Only schizophrenics, who are relics from an earlier level of evolution, now hear voices. Jaynes's whole reconstruction is based on a generalization from schizophrenia. However, even schizophrenics can hear voices within themselves only because these "voices" ultimately intend real voices outside of them—that is, from past experience. Carried to its logical conclusion, his thesis is an argument for solipsism. For a critique of this type of thesis by anticipation, see Abraham Joshua Heschel, *The Prophets* (Philadelphia, 1962), chap. 23.

99. See Beresheet Rabbah 19.5. See also Ludwig Wittgenstein, *Philosophical Investigations*, trans. G. E. M. Anscombe (New York, 1967), 5e, 99e; Martin Heidegger, *Sein und Zeit*, 15th ed. (Tuebingen, 1979), pp. 163–64.

100. See Bruno Bettelheim, *The Empty Fortress: Infantile Autism and the Birth of the Self* (New York, 1967), pp. 45–47, 427ff. It is emphasized that God "called" Moses before speaking content to him. See Sifra, ed. Weiss, 3c re Leviticus 1:1.

101. See B. Yebamot 5b; D. Novak, *Law and Theology in Judaism* (New York, 1976), vol. 2, pp. 47ff.

102. See Heidegger, *Sein und Zeit*, pp. 128–30.

103. This very verse was used in the most famous rabbinic statement denying authentic human innovation re the Torah. See Y. Megillah 4.1/74d. However, cf. B. Hagigah 3a; Menahot 29b.

104. See Mekhilta: Yitro, ed. Horovitz-Rabin, 238 re Deuteronomy 4:36 (the opinion of Rabbi Ishmael).

105. See B. Yebamot 49b re Isaiah 6:1 and Tos., s.v. "ashviyayh," re Exodus 24:10 (cf. Rashi's Torah commentary thereon).

106. See Ibn Ezra's comment on Exodus 34:5, ed. Weiser (Jerusalem, 1977), vol. 2, p. 220, n. 11 following Ms. Paris.

107. See B. Gittin 23a and Hullin 96a and Nahmanides's comment on Genesis 27:15; also B. Sanhedrin 38a.

108. See 'Abot de-Rabbi Nathan A, chap. 12 re Ecclesiastes 9:4.

109. Cf. G. W. F. Hegel, *Phenomenology of Spirit*, trans. A. V. Miller (Oxford, 1977), sec. 800, p. 486.

110. See Plato, *Apology* 31D. It is worth noting that when Plato himself mentions Socrates's *daimonion,* he plays down its manifestation as a voice. See Plato, *Republic* 496C. See also George Bernard Shaw, *Saint Joan* (Baltimore, 1951), pp. 16–20.

111. See Kant, *Critique of Pure Reason* B839; also A. Kojève, *Introduction to the Reading of Hegel,* trans. J. H. Nichols, Jr. (Ithaca, N.Y., 1980), p. 135.

112. Thus Hermann Cohen, attempting to understand the Jewish doctrine of revelation in Kantian terms, interprets the assertion of Deuteronomy 30:12—"It is not in heaven"—as meaning that "its origin is made wholly subjective . . . in the rational speech of man. . . . Revelation has its foundation *[begruendet]* in the heart and in the most proper power of man" (*Religion of Reason,* p. 81 [= *Religion der Vernunft,* p. 94]). See also *Juedische Schriften* 1:16. However, in the rabbinic understanding of this verse, the Torah is interpreted by human reason (B. Baba Metzia 59b), but the Torah's origin, in rabbinic doctrine, is from God (M. Sanhedrin 10.1). It is neither grounded in nor exhausted by human reason. See Y. Pe'ah 1.1/15b re Deuteronomy 32:47.

113. Kant, *Critique of Pure Reason* B819.

114. Plato, *Republic* 431A, 436C. See *Laws* 923A and *Protagoras* 343B; Hannah Arendt, *The Human Condition* (Garden City, N.Y., 1959), p. 12.

115. See Kant, *Critique of Practical Reason* 126ff.

116. See Emmanuel Levinas, *De Dieu qui vient a l'idee* (Paris, 1982), p. 229.

117. See Karl Barth, *Fides Quarens Intellectum*, trans. I. W. Robertson (London, 1960), pp. 74–75; D. Novak, "Are Philosophical Proofs of the Existence of God Theologically Meaningful?" in *God in the Teachings of Conservative Judaism*, ed. S. Siegel and E. B. Gertel (New York, 1985), pp. 191–94.

118. See B. Sanhedrin 38a.

119. See B. Yebamot 65b and Tos., s.v. "ve-lo"; Rashi and Nahmanides on Genesis 9:7; B. Sanhedrin 59b re Deuteronomy 5:27; also Ellul, *The Theological Foundation of Law*, pp. 53–55, 102.

120. See Shir Ha-Shirim Rabbah 8.13 re Numbers 19:14.

121. Franz Rosenzweig, *Jehuda Halevi* (Berlin, 1927), p. 257, trans. N. N. Glatzer, in *Franz Rosenzweig: His Life and Thought*, 2d rev. ed. (New York, 1961), p. 291; also Heidegger, *Kant and the Problem of Metaphysics*, p. 223.

122. See Karl Rahner, *Hearers of the Word*, trans. M. Richards (New York, 1969), pp. 94ff.

123. Mekhilta: Yitro 223. See also E. LaB. Cherbonnier, "The Logic of Biblical Anthropomorphism," *Harvard Theological Review* 54, no. 3 (July 1962): 187.

124. It is important to note that Nietzsche did not deny God's existence altogether; he put it in the past. Man is to transcend *(ueberwinden)* God as he is to transcend himself. See F. Nietzsche, *Also Sprach Zarathustra*, in *werke* (Munich, 1967), vol. 1, p. 549. For Nietzsche, transcendence comes from within man and no longer approaches him from without. In this essential point, he is in the tradition of autonomy extending from Kant to Hegel to Feuerbach, although without their confidence in man. For the earlier, more qualified use of "Gott ist tot" by Hegel, see *Phenomenology of Spirit*, sec. 752.

125. Plato, *Euthyphro* 8Aff.

126. See Novak, *Suicide and Morality*, p. 32.

127. See Plato, *Timaeus* 50Cff.

128. See B. Shebu'ot 39a and Tanhuma: Nitzabim, end, ed. Buber, 25b.

129. See Novak, *Halakhah in a Theological Dimension*, pp. 4ff.

130. Plato, *Euthyphro* 10A.

131. Ibid., 11E.

132. See Beresheet Rabbah 10.9.

133. See David Weiss Halivni, *Midrash, Mishnah, and Gemara: The Jewish Predilection for Justified Law* (Cambridge, Mass., 1986), pp. 9ff.

134. See Nahmanides's comment on Exodus 20:2.

135. See Shemot Rabbah 25.16.

136. See Hugo Meynell, "The Euthyphro Dilemma," *Proceedings of the Aristotelian Society,* supp. vol. (1973): 223–34.

137. See B. Sanhedrin 59a and Maimonides, *Hilkhot Melakhim* 9.1.

138. See Martin Buber, *Moses* (New York, 1958), p. 190.

139. Franz Rosenzweig, *The Star of Redemption,* trans. W. W. Hallo (New York, 1970), p. 405. See also p. 347.

140. See B. Berakhot 34b re Isaiah 64:3; also 1 Corinthians 2:9.

141. See Psalms 84:7–8.

142. For a classical Jewish statement of the unredeemed status of the world, note: "May His kingdom be revealed and shown to be over us speedily and at a near time" (Sofrim 14.12), viz. "Thy kingdom come" (Matthew 6:10 and parallels). For a powerful contemporary Christian expression of this antitriumphalism, see Paul van Buren, *A Theology of the Jewish–Christian Reality* (New York, 1980), vol. 1, p. 69.

# Index

187